REBELS AND REDCOATS

HUGH BICHENO is the editor of *Gettysburg, Midway* and *Crescent and Cross*, a study of the historical themes that came together at the battle of Lepanto in 1571. A former intelligence officer and anti-terrorism consultant, after many years in the Americas he now lives in Cambridge.

RICHARD HOLMES is a celebrated military historian and television presenter. In addition to his bestselling books *Redcoat* and *Wellington: The Iron Duke* he has written and presented nine series for the BBC including *Battlefields, War Walks* and *The Western Front*. His dozen books include *Firing Line*, and he is general editor of the definitive *Oxford Companion to Military History*.

REBELS & REDCOATS

The American Revolutionary War

HUGH BICHENO

With a Foreword by

RICHARD HOLMES

HarperCollins*Publishers*

HarperCollins*Publishers*
77–85 Fulham Palace Road,
Hammersmith, London w6 8jb

www.harpercollins.co.uk

This paperback edition 2004
1 3 5 7 9 8 6 4 2

First published in Great Britain by
HarperCollins*Publishers* 2003

A catalogue record for this book is
available from the British Library

ISBN 0 00 715626 X

Set in PostScript Linotype Minion with
Bulmer and Gresham display by
Rowland Phototypesetting Ltd,
Bury St Edmunds, Suffolk

Printed and bound in Great Britain by
Clays Ltd, St Ives plc

To Graham Keene
and the hip-op team at Addenbrooke's

CONTENTS

LIST OF ILLUSTRATIONS

Nathanael Greene, oil on canvas by Charles Willson Peale, from life 1783 (Independence National Historical Park, Philadelphia)

Daniel Morgan, oil on canvas by Charles Willson Peale, from life *c*.1794 (Independence National Historical Park, Philadelphia)

François-Joseph-Paul, Comte de Grasse, oil on canvas by Jean Baptiste Mauzaisse, 1842 (Châteaux de Versailles et de Trianon/Giraudon/ Bridgeman Art Library)

Surrender of the Ville de Paris, Battle of the Saintes, oil on canvas by Thomas Whitcombe, 1782 (National Maritime Museum, Greenwich)

The Surrender of Cornwallis at Yorktown, oil sketch on canvas by John Trumbull, 1787 (Detroit Institute of Arts/Bridgeman Art Library)

Lord George Brydges Rodney, oil on canvas by an unknown artist (National Maritime Museum, Greenwich)

LIST OF MAPS

CHRONOLOGY

1688	Glorious Revolution in England.
1689	Locke's *Two Treatises of Civil Government*.
1696	Navigation Acts declare virtual monopoly of direct trade with the colonies, create Board of Trade and Admiralty Courts with jurisdiction to enforce.
1703	New Secretariat of State, Southern Department, takes over appointment of colonial governors from Board of Trade. Colonial population 275,000.
1707	Act of Union joins England and Scotland.
1721–42	First Minister Walpole lets sleeping dogs lie, especially in the colonies.
1752–6	Undeclared French and Indian War in North America.
1755	Defeat and death of Braddock at Monongahela.
1756–63	Seven Years' War (War for Empire).
1758	British capture Louisbourg, Fort Duquesne/Pitt and Fort Ticonderoga.
1759	British victories at Lagos, Quiberon Bay, Minden and Québec.
1760	French surrender Montréal. Accession of George III.
1762	Spain ceded Louisiana and Minorca by France, declares war on Britain.
1763	Peace of Paris recognizes British possession of Québec and lands east of the Mississippi. Proclamation Line defines frontier between colonies and Native American hinterland, fifteen-regiment garrison established.
1763–4	Pontiac's Rebellion.
1764	Sugar Act and Currency Acts – 'non-importation' protest.
1765	Mutiny/Quartering Act obliges colonists to house and feed soldiers.
1765–6	Stamp Act – 'Sons of Liberty' organized, Stamp Act Congress issues 'A Declaration of Rights and Grievances'. Act repealed but Declaratory Act weakly affirms Parliament's authority to tax the colonies.

1767	Townshend [Excise] Acts, to be enforced by Boston Customs Board, renewal of non-importation protest.
1768	Customs officials driven out of Boston (June), troops arrive (October).
1770	Riot against soldiers in New York (January), Boston Massacre (March). Repeal of Townshend duties except on tea (April).
1771	Regulator uprising crushed in North Carolina.
1772	Rhode Island smugglers burn HM schooner *Gaspée*.
1773	Tea Act (May), Boston Tea Party (December).

1775

March-June	Coercive/Intolerable Acts passed against Massachusetts. Québec Act.
May	Gage appointed military governor of Massachusetts.
September	Troops seize powder and cannon in Cambridge and Charles Town. First Continental Congress meets in Philadelphia, adopts principle of 'no taxation without representation', promises solidarity if Massachusetts refrains from further provocation and is attacked. Massachusetts radicals organize Committee of Security to conduct further provocation.
January	House of Lords rejects Earl of Chatham (Pitt) conciliation bill.
February	Parliament declares Massachusetts in rebellion, approves North's proposal to end all internal taxes on colonies that tax themselves.
March	Parliament rejects Burke's conciliation bill, Franklin returns to Philadelphia.
19 April	Battle of Lexington and Concord.
May	Second Continental Congress declares 'state of defence', begins to print paper money, as do Massachusetts and South Carolina. Allen and Arnold capture Ticonderoga. Howe, Clinton and Burgoyne arrive in Boston.
June	Gage declares martial law, offers amnesty for all except Samuel Adams and John Hancock. Battle of Breed's Hill.
July	Congress sends 'Olive Branch Petition' to George III, rejects North's plan but also Franklin's proposal to establish diplomatic relations with France.
August	George III rejects petition, declares the colonies are in 'open and avowed rebellion [and] must either submit or triumph'.
September	French government sets up front company under Beaumarchais

to funnel aid to the Rebels. Invasion of Canada by Montgomery and Arnold.

October — Howe replaces Gage.

November — Dunmore proclaims martial law and emancipation of slaves in Virginia, defeated at Great Bridge and driven out (December). Germain becomes Colonial Secretary. Congressional committee meets French envoy Bonvouloir, sends Deane to France to purchase war supplies.

December — Allen captured. Montgomery killed, Arnold wounded at Québec. French envoy Bonvouloir received by Congress, Deane to Paris as purchasing agent.

1776

January — Paine's *Common Sense*. Britain contracts for German troops.

February — Highlanders defeated at Moore's Creek (NC).

March — Rebels install guns on Dorchester Heights, British evacuate Boston.

May — Louis XVI authorizes first cash loan to the Rebels.

June — British fail to take Charleston (SC), abandon the South for two years. Rebel coup d'état in Pennsylvania.

July — Declaration of Independence. Howe brothers arrive New York as both military commanders and peace commissioners.

August — Battles for Long Island/Brooklyn Heights.

September — Staten Island peace conference founders on the issue of formal independence. Kip's Bay landings drive Rebels from southern Manhattan, Harlem Heights skirmish. Franklin and Arthur Lee sent to join/supervise Deane in Paris.

October — Battles of Valcour Island, Lake Champlain and White Plains.

November — Fall of Fort Washington, Fort Lee abandoned.

December — Washington divides his army, retreats across New Jersey to the Delaware. Capture of Charles Lee. Victory at Trenton.

1777

January — Victory over British rearguard at Princeton, Vermont secedes from New York.

April — Destruction of huge Rebel arsenal at Danbury (Ct).

June — Congress chooses 'stars and stripes' flag design.

July — Advance towards Albany by St Leger from Lake Ontario and Burgoyne from Montréal, Rebels abandon Ticonderoga and defeated at Hubbardton, Gates replaces Schuyler i/c Northern

Department. Howe invades Pennsylvania by sea.

Congress admits paper money has devalued by two-thirds.

August   St Leger stopped at Fort Schuyler, Brant defeats Rebel Militia relief column at Oriskany. Baum/Breymann columns defeated by Stark at Bennington.

September   Washington defeated at Brandywine and Paoli, fall of Philadelphia. Generals Conway, Gates and others correspond about the need for a new C-in-C. Arnold and Morgan check Burgoyne at Freeman's Farm.

October 4   Washington's attack fails at Germantown.

October 6   Clinton takes Forts Clinton and Montgomery on the Hudson.

October 7   Burgoyne defeated at Bemis Heights.

October 17   Convention of Saratoga agreed by Burgoyne with Gates includes repatriation of British troops, later repudiated by Congress at Washington's urging.

November   Howe takes Forts Mifflin and Mercer, clears the Delaware.

December   Washington's army to winter quarters at Valley Forge. So-called 'Conway Cabal' used by Washington to discredit Gates.

1778

February   France concludes formal alliances with the United States. Congress replaces Deane with John Adams. Franklin and Jay recognized as Ministers to France and Spain. Carlisle peace commission to New York.

April   Congress rejects negotiations with Carlisle.

May   Clinton replaces Howe.

June   Clinton retreats from Philadelphia to New York, fights successful rearguard action at Monmouth (NJ). Charles Lee cashiered.

July   French fleet under Estaing off New York. Naval battle of Ushant off coast of Brittany. Massacre of Connecticut settlers in Wyoming Valley. George Rogers Clark's Virginian expedition down the Ohio captures Kaskasia.

August   Franco-American attack on Newport abandoned when British fleet under Howe appears, some fighting until storm disperses both fleets, Estaing to Boston.

September   Rioting against the French navy in Boston and Charleston (SC).

November   Massacre of New York settlers in Cherry Valley.

December   British launch southern offensive by capturing Savannah (SC).

1779

January	British advance to Augusta (Ga).
February	Loyalists defeated at Kettle Creek (Ga), Moultrie defends Port Royal (SC). Clark captures Hamilton at Vincennes (Indian Territory).
March	Campbell defeats Ashe and Pickens at Briar Creek (Ga).
April	France obtains Spanish declaration of war against Britain by promising to help recover Gibraltar and Minorca.
May	British burn Portsmouth and Norfolk (Va).
(Summer)	Sullivan's ethnic cleansing of the Iroquois.
June	Spain declares war, siege of Gibraltar (ends February 1783).
July	Wayne raids Stony Point.
August	Fiasco at Penobscot Bay, 'Light Horse Harry' Lee raids Paulus Point.
Aug/Sept	Spanish Louisiana Governor Gálvez captures Baton Rouge.
September	John Paul Jones' battle with HMS *Serapis* off Yorkshire coast.
Sept- Oct	Unsuccessful siege of Savannah (Ga) by Estaing and Lincoln.

1780

January	Continentals mutiny at West Point.
February	Russia proclaims Armed Neutrality against Britain, joined by Denmark, Sweden, Prussia, Portugal, Austria and Naples.
February	Clinton begins siege of Lincoln in Charleston.
March	Gálvez captures Mobile.
May	Continentals mutiny at Morristown (and again in January, May 1781). Fall of Charleston. Tarleton's Loyalists shatter Buford at Waxhaws Creek.
July	Arrival of French army under Rochambeau at Newport.
August	Gates routed by Cornwallis at Camden (SC), Tarleton ambushes Sumter's guerrillas at Fishing Creek.
September	Defection of Arnold, André hanged.
October	Ferguson's Loyalists destroyed at King's Mountain (SC).
December	Greene takes command in the South. Britain declares war on the Netherlands.

1781

January	Continentals mutiny at Pompton, march on Philadelphia. Tarleton's force destroyed by Morgan at Cowpens (SC), Arnold sacks Richmond.
February	Rodney seizes St Eustatius and St Martin (Dutch West Indies).

March	Cornwallis defeats Greene at Guilford Courthouse (NC), retreats to Wilmington and marches north to Virginia.
April	Greene defeated by Rawdon at Hobkirk's Hill (SC).
May	Gálvez captures Pensacola.
May-June	Greene's unsuccessful siege of Ninety-Six (SC).
August	Combined British forces under Cornwallis move to Yorktown (Va). French and American armies march to northern Chesapeake Bay. French fleet under Grasse arrives off Yorktown.
September	Greene checked by Stewart at Eutaw Springs (SC). British fleet under Graves repulsed by Grasse at battle of Virginia Capes. Franco-American army transported by sea to James Peninsula.
October	Siege and surrender of Yorktown.
December	Kempenfeldt captures twenty French transports bound for the West Indies off Ushant.

1782

January	British evacuate Wilmington.
March	Massacre of unarmed Munsees and Delawares at Gnadenhutten (Pa). North resigns. Rockingham/Shelburne ministry.
July	Rockingham dies, Shelburne continues without a majority.
April	Rodney defeats Grasse at battle of the Saintes (French West Indies).
July	British evacuate Savannah.
August	Kempenfeldt drowned when HMS *Royal George* capsizes.
November	Treaty of Paris concludes war between Britain and the United States.
December	British evacuate Charleston.

1783

January	Treaty of Versailles ends war with France and Spain.
February	Fox and North combine to force Shelburne's resignation.
April	Congress ratifies Treaty of Paris.
June	Continental Army disbanded.
November	British evacuate New York.

FOREWORD BY RICHARD HOLMES

While working on *Redcoat*, my study of the British soldier in what I loosely called the age of horse and musket, I was reminded that the War of American Independence was the one major conflict lost by the British during the entire period. So, when I was considering my television work for 2002–3 the opportunity to make a four-part documentary on the war for the BBC and WGBH Boston was too good to miss. I thought I knew the war reasonably well (a supposition which proved over-optimistic) and welcomed the opportunity to visit those battle-fields that I had not seen before. The only disadvantage to a project which would take me across the Atlantic for part of the year and involve me in much new work at a time when my writing diary was already full, with *Redcoat's* successor marching steadily to completion, was that I would not have time to do justice to the book of the series.

I rather bridle at the term 'television historian'. Of course the techniques involved in presenting history on radio or television, writing about it at the popular or scholarly level, or teaching it at school or university, are different. But there is no more 'television history' than there is 'book history.' Both the spoken and the written word have their part to play, all the more so because an audience weaned onto history by one will, all being well, deepen its interest through the other. It follows that the books of television history series should not simply expand the script to emerge, as they sometimes do, as just a printed record of a visual experience. They should go deeper, developing arguments more easily deployed in print than on the screen, and encouraging further reading.

It was clear that time was going to prevent me from doing justice to a book on *Rebels and Redcoats*, and I could have wished for nothing better than for Hugh Bicheno to take it on. He was one of the brightest stars amongst historians during my time at Cambridge; we both share an abiding interest in what happens when men confront one another in battle, a process he has described so well in his book on Gettysburg; and he had already visited most of the battlefields described in the pages that follow. I grow increasingly impatient with historians whose wars have no battles, or whose battles have no maps.

In the case of this particular war, central as it is to the powerful symbolism surrounding the birth of the United States, I am concerned that an understandable desire to celebrate an event that has had such a great (and largely benevolent) impact on world affairs has led to as much mythologising as historiography. Hugh Bicheno makes it as clear in this book as I do in the series that this was both a civil war (with the losing Loyalists almost expunged from history by the victors) and a world war, in which France made a decisive contribution, albeit at the cost of impoverishment which would pave the way for revolution in 1789. He is brutally honest in his assessment of the atrocities carried out, from time to time, by both sides, and in his reminder that, where sheer survival often counted for more than political ideals, neither side had a monopoly of morality.

I was delighted to see many old friends reappear in these pages. Although my redcoat instincts might bridle at his blue uniform, Joseph Plumb Martin of the Connecticut Line is a chatty guide to the regular army that did so much to secure American victory. His opponent Sergeant Roger Lamb, who served with those two fine regiments the 9th (East Norfolk) and the 23rd (Royal Welsh Fusiliers) gives us a wonderful account of the business of close-range battle when the opposing lines first came within musket-shot at Guilford Courthouse: how well I remembered his words as I walked the ground. Loyalist Lieutenant Anthony Allaire survives rifle-bullets during the Battle of King's Mountain and the hangman's rope afterwards, and Captain John Peebles of the inimitable Black Watch tells us about skirmishing on the Hudson and siege work at Charleston. There is a strong sense of place: we see well why the Hudson valley is indeed one of America's traditional 'war-paths'. And there is an equally strong sense of personality that matters so much in war. I might have been gentler with 'Gentleman Johnny' Burgoyne before prowling the Saratoga Battlefield, but now I agree that he was indeed more 'playwright and self dramatist' than a general to whom a nation's fortunes and men's lives should have been entrusted.

This was always Hugh's book: he worked on his words, and I on my images, at much the same time but often an ocean apart, with little more than the occasional phone conversation or faxed sheet to clarify issues. There will properly be moments (though surprisingly few) where our judgements will differ. This was always Hugh's book: but as I read its final proofs I cannot help wishing that it had been mine.

RICHARD HOLMES
Ropley, February 2003

The great question which, in all ages, has disturbed mankind, and brought on them the greatest part of their mischiefs, which has ruined cities, depopulated countries, and disordered the peace of the world, has been, not whether there be power in the world, nor whence it came, but who should have it.

JOHN LOCKE, *Two Treatises of Civil Government*, 1690

I doubt if the oppressed ever fight for freedom. They fight for pride and power – power to oppress others.

ERIC HOFFER, *The True Believer*, 1951

INTRODUCTION

While researching the iconic and actual realities of the battle of Lepanto for *Crescent and Cross* it often crossed my mind that the standard accounts of the Anglo-American civil war of 1775–83 are the most outstanding example of propaganda not merely triumphing over historical substance, but virtually obliterating it. No sooner was the Lepanto manuscript completed than my old friend Richard Holmes, who first awoke my interest in military history when we were undergraduates, told me he was to present a television series on the American war with the working title 'Brothers at War'. We both felt the time was ripe for a popular politico-military reappraisal, we were in general agreement about the line it should take, and other peremptory calls on his time made it impossible for him to write the book in time to accompany the series. Another common factor was irritation not so much with the banal stereotyping of the film *The Patriot* (2000) as by the tiresome argument that it was 'just entertainment'. It was not, any more than was its artistic template Sergei Eisenstein's film *Alexander Nevsky*, both being works of contemporary propaganda thinly disguised as historical drama. But the similarities end there, for the very existence of Eisenstein's Russia was under imminent threat by the Teutonic enemy Nevsky defeated, hardly the case of the United States vis-à-vis today's Britain.

The question this poses is why the cultural engine of a highly successful society finds it profitable to churn out a pseudo-historical fable in which a virtuously virile and unassuming hero dressed in homespun (with adoring slaves in the background), triumphs over freedom-denying red-coated thugs led by an effeminate psychopath. Particularly when those few Americans who still seek to live according to the principles of the founding mythology they are taught at school are denounced and vigorously persecuted by their own government. Although US scholars have distanced themselves from the canonical account, a lingering duality can be seen even in Ray Raphael's recent best-selling compilation, in which he tries to rescue some social redemption from the sordid reality his material highlights. The fore-word to the paperback edition laments the proliferation of accounts dwelling on the wisdom and heroism of the group of men collectively known as the 'Founding Fathers', asserting that 'by ignoring ordinary people, it reinforces their feelings of powerlessness'. This assessment may be true, but I believe it overlooks how extraordinarily important the Foundation Myth has been in the elaboration of the construct known as America (to the annoyance of everybody else who shares the continent), as a result of a prolonged period of isolated nation-building during which the reinforcement of a deliberately falsified past played a crucial unifying role.

Like an enterprising dog the diligent historian cannot refrain from bringing things to the attention of the public that many would have preferred left buried, nor from showing a routine irreverence even for monumental lamp posts. It may be considered *lèse majesté* to piddle on the pedestal of the beacon that has kept darkness at bay in my lifetime – and will probably continue to do so for my grandchildren – but it is surely to honour the spirit of the 1776 Declaration of Independence, which was largely a histrionic *lèse* of King George III's *majesté*. The document also denounced measures taken for the common defence, the preservation of public order and the value of the currency, which most would regard as minimum obligations of any government. Consequently the successful rebellion carried out in the name of that declaration by a minority of the colonists of a small part of North America created an institutional experiment doomed to crumble under the weight of its own contradictions, the last echo of which was smothered in the next civil war, four score and nine years later. It should therefore be possible to view the event as a discrete historical phenomenon without incurring charges of anti-Americanism on one hand, or on the other being obliged to spend time discussing whether the present power and prosperity of its successor state was, in a manner of speaking, genetically programmed.

While this book draws heavily on a number of excellent mono-graphs by US scholars it is dismissive of the messianic froth with which the independence war has long been cloaked, something those who live there are hesitant to treat so cavalierly. The reason is not hard to identify – the self-righteous wartime rhetoric of 1775–83 is still common political currency in the United States, many of its citizens finding it comforting to believe their society is great because it is good and always has been. Thus Al Gore of the Tennessee dynasty, who but for some aberrant Florida chads would now be (sound of trumpets) Leader of the Free World, pronounced in *Earth in the Balance*, the book he wrote to raise his profile for the 1994 election:

> From the beginning, our leadership of the world community has been based on much more than military and economic strength. The American drive to correct injustice – from the abolition of slavery to the granting of women's suffrage – has constantly renewed our moral authority to lead.

Alas, in the entire Western world only Brazil lagged behind the US in abolishing slavery and did so without fighting a civil war over it, while American apartheid with its attendant lynchings and castrations persisted into the 1950s, as any scion of Tennessee cannot fail to know from personal memory. Better, on balance, for members of the American oligarchy to be silent on the matter of historic moral leader-ship, to dwell instead on the creditable fact that, here and now, their nation is overwhelmingly powerful and abuses its power far less than it could. The problem which has always faced patriotic Americans is that the unvarnished history of their nation is impossible to reconcile with the lofty principles enunciated at the time of independence. Even then, the 'right' most prominently exercised by many of those styling themselves patriots was to torment and dispossess those of whom they disapproved and/or who possessed something they wanted. Long before formal hostilities began disgusting acts of civil disorder were commonplace in the North, as in the case of Dr Abner Beebe of West Haddam, Connecticut, whose only offence was to exercise his right of free speech to defend the king:

> He was assaulted by a mob, stripped naked and hot pitch poured upon him, which blistered his skin. He was then carried to a hog sty and rubbed over with hog's dung. They threw the hog's dung in his face and rammed some of it down his throat, and in that condition exposed him to a company of women. His house was

attacked, his windows broke, when one of his children was sick, and a child of his went in distraction upon this treatment. His gristmill was broke, and persons prevented from grinding at it, and from having any connections with him.

In the more recently colonized South a feral state of nature lurked beyond a thin coastal crust of ostentatious, slave-based civilization, while along the frontier arson, rape and murder were the common currency of social exchange between the white settlers and the Native Americans whose lands they coveted. Many of the south and middle colony frontiersmen were poor, fiercely tribal Presbyterians self-identified as the 'Scotch-Irish' to differentiate themselves from despised Scots and Irish Roman Catholic immigrants. They were conditioned by a history stretching from the bloody lowlands between England and Scotland through settlements in Ulster held by fire and sword. In America they tended to move on whenever social and legal constraints caught up with them and as a result, to borrow the immortal pun from 1066 And All That, how revolting they were was a function of how far inland they had advanced.

The obverse to Gore's faith in immemorial righteousness is a belief that any enemy of the United States is perforce evil incarnate, as dramatized in an episode in the film mentioned earlier where British troops burn a church full of noncombatants, an episode seemingly modelled on the massacre at Oradour-sur-Glâne in France by the SS in 1944. An identical outrage did take place during the war of independence, but it was committed on 7 March 1782 at the Moravian settlement of Gnadenhutten, by 'patriots' who clubbed to death ninety-three devoutly Christian and unarmed men, women and children of the Munsee and Delaware tribes, and took their scalps in order to claim the bounty paid by the Pennsylvania legislature. The next day they brought in more victims and added them to the pile of mutilated corpses inside the little schoolhouse and then burned it along with the rest of the village in a futile attempt to conceal their crime.

It may be quixotic to couch a printed lance against the big screen, but the Big Lie should never be left unchallenged. If the 1775 rebellion had indeed been combated with the systematic ruthlessness of Oliver Cromwell in Ireland in 1649–50, or William Tecumseh Sherman in

Georgia in 1864, it would certainly have been suppressed – temporarily. But it was not and although the struggle among the colonists themselves was one of terror and counterterror often no less merciless than it invariably was when Native and African Americans were involved, with a few exceptions the contest between the representative armies was fought according to the usages of 'civilized' warfare. This is not to suggest it was characterized by mutual regard and respect, or that it was ever easy to surrender in the heat of battle when most were under the influence of alcohol, or that prisoners were well treated, or that civilians were always respected. It is, however, military common sense to offer your opponents an alternative to fighting to the death, while both commanders knew systematic plundering or scorched earth policies would be counterproductive in the overall competition for popular support.

It is also absurd to enumerate atrocities as though they constitute a scorecard of righteousness in war, when it consists largely of acts that would give pause to a moderately fastidious hyena. But for those wishing to do so it should be self-evident that the Rebels, intent on simultaneously crushing Native and African American autonomy, and employing by far the larger number of irregular forces, must have committed the most offences against peacetime standards of decent behaviour. Irregulars do not 'play by the rules' and are loath to permit their mobility to be encumbered by prisoners, while alas for those who wish to think well of our species only iron discipline is likely to prevent random looting, rape and murder once you cry havoc and loose the dogs of war. If blame is to be allocated it must rest on those who loosed them, in this case the small group of conspirators to whom Benjamin Franklin, the eldest, often repeated the old saw that they must hang together or most assuredly hang separately.

As one born of British parents in Cuba and later, after many years working in the rest of the Americas, a naturalized US immigrant, I have a wider base than most from which to conduct triangulation on the historical peaks and troughs of my adopting country. Although proud to become a citizen, I was conscious the designation 'Resident Alien' remained a more accurate description. However I experienced the same sense of cultural apartness after I moved to Britain a few years ago, although it is the country where I spent most of my formative years, where five centuries of my ancestors lie buried not twenty miles from where I sit and where my sons have chosen to remain. An intimate outsider's affection for both countries grants me, I believe, a privileged platform from which to view the moment when they went their separate ways, while broad life experience outside the Anglo-American intellectual bubble is also helpful. Whatever the personal reasons, it has long been apparent to me that the independence war was the second of three domestic wars fought, broadly speaking, to establish a political framework suitable to a unique pre-existing culture of individualism, hyphenating the historical space between the English and US civil wars of 1638–52 and 1861–65 respectively.

More immediately relevant in the writing of this book than being a sort of cultural E.T. suspended over the mid Atlantic has been that in my early career as an intelligence officer I found it relatively easy to seduce people from their allegedly natural group allegiances, even as I learned how insignificant abstract ideas are in moving people to action. Desires precede the ideologies adduced to justify them, and without disrespect to the PR value of the Declaration of Independence it can be boiled down to a more universal principle – 'we believe we can get away with it' – or as the Elizabethan epigrammist Sir John Harington put it:

> Treason doth never prosper, what's the reason?
> For if it prosper, none dare call it treason.

My next occupation as an adviser to people victimized by extortionists nurtured a belief that it is usually impossible to draw an objective slash between hero/coward, patriot/traitor, freedom fighter/terrorist and government/organized crime. But of all these experiences, the most useful to me here has been that I was present on several occasions when seemingly stable societies broke down, when agitation over small incidents or changes suddenly acquired disproportionate momentum and a self-fulfilling aura of crisis developed.

It was not inevitable the different perspectives on either side of the Atlantic would generate a mood for war in the mid 1770s – but they did and thereafter both sides were dealing with rapidly changing circumstances as a failed police action escalated into a full-blown rebellion. The British government took too long to appreciate the seriousness of the challenge and as a result the layer of civilian authority that constitutes the glove on the fist of armed force was stripped away. The army made a very bad start and lost the ability to overawe, making a trial of strength inevitable. Of course peace could have been restored at any time by conceding all the Rebel demands – but so it can at any time and any place, and governments that openly surrender to street violence have a short life expectancy. Instead a very nearly successful strategy of alternating sharp military action with political concessions was adopted, probably the only one that might have separated the revolutionaries from their 'crowd cover'.

Only after France openly entered the war did the British play to their traditional strength by employing the tactics of blockade and coastal raid so successful in thwarting American reverse imperialism during Madison's War of 1812–15. However these were the tactics of international war, hence a recognition that an American nation had come into being, which might be defeated but no longer reintegrated. Like an earlier undeclared war between the USA and France, the war of 1812 revealed an unfounded conceit among the rulers of the new nation, born of denial of the uncomfortable fact that their independence was merely the by-product of a French geopolitical strategy aimed at crippling Britain. Left to her own resources America counted for little in world affairs and needed to be reminded of it. Understandably, the new oligarchy based its legitimacy on a myth of heroic leadership, although the only outright victory it could fairly claim was in a propaganda war so successful that its hyperbole and sonorous cant remains by far the largest obstacle to a cold-eyed assessment of the struggle.

'To put your enemy in the wrong', Samuel Adams wrote, 'and keep him so, is a wise maxim in politics, as well as in war'. Or as the late President Lyndon Johnson put it, forcing your opponent to deny he has had carnal knowledge of a pig is half the battle. The other half is to offer the uncommitted a worthwhile reason to support you. It would be hard to find a cause less inspiring than an assertion of Parliament's right to tax, on the understanding it would not be exercised. If stated ideals and principles decided conflicts, the redcoats would have departed America on the day after the Declaration of Independence, wafted on their way by gales of laughter. Instead they stayed and fought, alongside the Loyalist Americans who gradually assumed the main burden of combat, until the contest became one between wide-spreading disillusionment in America and a growing conviction in Britain that there was nothing to be gained by continuing the struggle. Thanks to massive French and some Spanish support the Rebels were able to win, but it was a very near-run thing. The setting event for the surrender of Cornwallis at Yorktown in October 1781, which finally tipped the scales in favour of a settlement, was the sole significant victory of the French over the Royal Navy since 1690. Had that not occurred, history's dominoes might have fallen in a different pattern.

Winston Churchill believed the defining difference between the Americans and the British was that the former acted in accordance with broad, sweeping principles and the latter did not. What he failed to address was why the ideas first expressed by the Englishman John Locke and developed by the thinkers of the British Enlightenment remain alive and central to political debate in the United States, whereas they have become vestigial substrata in their country of origin. This was not always the case. It is notable that when social scientists rank the nations of the world according to indicators of relative personal freedom, the only common denominator among most of those scoring the highest is that they were once governed by the British. In constrast, American attempts to transplant their institutions have generally failed. What tends to be overlooked in discussion of the war fought by the first European colonies to become independent is that, despite much continuing rhetoric about how the event supposedly set the world ablaze, the 'young' USA was totally self-absorbed throughout the following century. Meanwhile the 'old' colonial power, already outstandingly dynamic in every field of human endeavour, exported that dynamism around the globe.

The countries directly affected by British imperialism in due course adapted and modified their shared experience in accordance with local conditions and customs, in most cases reaching back past the interlude of empire not only to indigenous roots but also and particularly to a uniquely English libertarian tradition which all may fairly regard as a direct ancestor. The diagram below borrows a device used by evolutionary biologists, who wrestle with the progressive bias on a daily basis, to

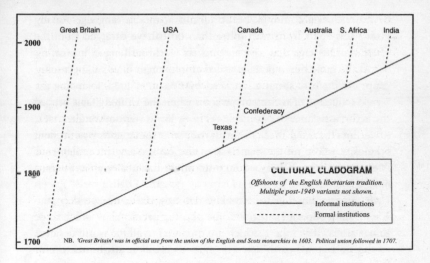

DIAGRAM ONE

emphasize that Great Britain is merely the eldest branch of a libertarian inheritance reaching far back into English history. Seen in this light, the imperial entities known as Great Britain and the United States are simply the two earliest surviving variants and the conflict of 1775–83 was between the two eldest children of one fecund tradition, not of parent and child. Sibling rivalry manifestly provides the better analogy for the simmering resentments that boiled over into war, the hysterical tone of the arguments that preceded it and the chip on the shoulder borne away by the triumphant but still aggrieved junior.

Both are also members of an extended family once dismissed contemptuously by Napoleon as a nation of shopkeepers. But while he pursued glory, the shopkeepers generated the cash flow to thwart him, as they had the kings of Spain and France before him and as they would his German and Soviet successors. Although siblings always squabble and the elder will naturally nurture ambivalent feelings when overshadowed by the younger, they instinctively close ranks against a common enemy. Despite the prominence of the self-anointed in both it is questionable whether the United States and grossly overcentralized Britain are politically compatible today. But they are drawn together by more than a common, beautiful and adaptable language, having grown less apart from each other than both have diverged from the libertarian heritage that gave them their world-girdling influence.

At the same time, the unguarded employment of appallingly inappropriate rhetoric about a 'crusade' by President Bush following the terrorist outrage of 11 September 2001, when the United States needed the active assistance of Islamic states in order to respond to the attack, underlines the much greater role played across the Atlantic by a strident religiosity whose roots reach back to the earliest English settlements. All too often this has lapsed into the most flagrant double standard and it is interesting to note as early as 1775 the English jurist Joseph Lind commenting how the Rebel leaders behaved as though they possessed 'some superior sanctity, some peculiar privilege, by which those things are lawful to them, which are unlawful to all the world besides'. In the US canon British defeat in 1775–83 is either attributed to – or held to constitute adequate proof of – the professional, intellectual and moral shortcomings of the directors of British policy. *Tu quoque* ('you're one too') is a hoary logical fallacy, but it is fair to hold people to the standards by which they judge others. Although the Founding Fathers were predominantly Freemasons (the eye and the pyramid on the great seal of the USA, still to be seen on the dollar bill, are Masonic cult objects), they found it convenient to pose as men touched by divine destiny to fulfil a preordained design and shamelessly falsified the record to give themselves starring roles in the teleological history to be written about the independence struggle.

It is legitimate, therefore, to point out that they were no less a self-perpetuating oligarchy than the British political establishment, neither elected nor respected by the majority of the people they claimed to represent, and that the whole enterprise nearly failed because of their corruption and incompetence. They had made no serious preparation for the war, found it almost impossible to make common cause during it and at times only the personal contacts and financial acumen of the English immigrant Robert Morris provided George Washington with just enough money to keep his ragtag army in being. Some years after the war Charles Thomson, Secretary to the Continental Congress throughout and uniquely qualified to leave an eyewitness account of the Fathers doing their Founding, refused to do so:

I ought not, for I should contradict all the histories of the great events of the revolution, and show by my account of men, motives and measures, that we arc wholly indebted to the agency of Providence for its successful issue. Let the world admire the supposed wisdom and valor of our great men. Perhaps they may adopt the qualities that have been ascribed to them, and thus good may be done. I shall not undeceive future generations.

Only the most devoted hagiographers have been able to stomach the personalities of Samuel Adams and John Hancock, the partnership that made the war happen. Adams was an obsessive who built a philosophy around bitterness at the loss of his patrimony when his father's venture into banking collapsed, and a failure at everything except the manipulation of public opinion. His cat's-paw Hancock inherited his wealth – as, indeed, did many other prominent separatists – and was easily led by appeals to his vanity. In addition James Otis, originator of the phrase 'taxation without representation is tyranny', suffered from mood swings so wild that a diagnosis of manic-depression seems amply justified. This is not remarkable – the 'well-adjusted', almost by definition, will be those at peace with the established order. The point is not that the American revolutionaries were more psychologically flawed or self-interested than any other group of men in similar situations – it is that they were no less.

On the other hand, iconoclasm rapidly becomes tedious to anyone not force-fed the Foundation Myth. Only one determined to apply to the past the incestuous sensibilities of the modern American academy would find it remarkable that Washington liked the company of decidedly pretty young men – so did his opponent William Howe, of whom his ribald soldiers sang that he spent more time in the saddle with one Mrs Loring than he did on campaign. Nor does it affect the validity of the sentiment 'that all men are created equal, that they are endowed by their Creator with certain unalienable Rights, that among these are Life, Liberty and the Pursuit of Happiness', to know that its author, Thomas Jefferson, was a life-long economic and sexual exploiter of slaves, who kept his own children by Sally Hemmings in bondage until his death. The historical presence of Benjamin Franklin is not reduced by his membership in the notorious Hell Fire Club and a taste for girls he indulged to an overripe old age. Unless brought up to believe in them as marmoreal paragons it comes as no surprise to learn they were men of human flesh and passions, albeit such as would require an army of spin doctors today.

Likewise it is shocking only to those who wish to believe that, like Athena, America sprang forth fully armed to discover that the great and largely silent majority of the colonists was resolutely uncommitted and went along with whoever seemed to be winning at any given moment, or at least paid in hard currency. More intriguing is the manner in which even some very prominent Rebels kept a foot in the enemy camp. That Franklin himself remained in contact with the British secret service proves only a desire to conduct confidential exchanges in which it suited neither side to be seen to be engaged. But it may be significant that when the British Army was advancing on Philadelphia in 1776 he entrusted his personal archive to his friend Joseph Galloway, a prominent Loyalist and a man he knew to be an agent of the British. Also most of the members of the delegation Franklin headed in Paris, including his close friend Dr Edward Bancroft, were in the pay of British secret service chief William Eden and kept London fully apprised of the covert dealings between the Rebels and the French throughout the war.

Although it depended on discretionary funding voted by Parliament the 'secret service' was not a formal institution, rather the conduit of untraceable money to buy the influence and information designed to strengthen the government of the day. Since those involved seldom committed anything incriminating to paper, or else employed organic concoctions requiring special treatment to reveal what was written, we will never know how many prominent American patriots hedged their bets. Overt paper trails generally lead to those reporting to military officials, who handled their intelligence operations with less discretion. Poor tradecraft led to the unmasking of Dr Benjamin Church, a member of the inner circle of Massachusetts conspirators, chief medical officer to what soon became the Continental Army and also General Thomas Gage's chief informer, while a failure to observe the most basic precautions cost Major John André his life and the British the fruits of General Benedict Arnold's defection in 1780. Eden and his operatives probably ran, without discovery at the time or revelation since, many more like Bancroft, whose role was only revealed by a document uncovered 150 years later.

We can, however, acquit the Founding Fathers of failing to live up to the inchoate desires projected upon the nation they created by those fantasizing about a fairer, less sordid world. Americans rightly bridle at those who briefly descend on their shores and go forth to condescend forever, such as Ireland's national poet Thomas Moore who wrote in 1806:

> While yet upon Columbia's rising brow
> The showy smile of young presumption plays,
> Her bloom is poison'd and her heart decays.
> Even now, in dawn of life, her sickly breath
> Burns with the taint of empires near their death;
> And, like the nymphs of her own withering clime,
> She's old in youth, she's blasted in her prime.

Unfortunately it remains true that any criticism of the United States is likely to be answered with a recitation about how much worse everywhere else is and always has been, a reflex drawing much of its vehemence from the Foundation Myth. One definition of immaturity is an inability to grasp that one's birth did not transform the world, thus the following from the website of the Sons of the American Revolution, with reference to the skirmish at Lexington on 19 April 1775 extravagantly known as 'the shot heard around the world':

> That shot was the bold challenge of the New World to the Old World. It heralded the beginning of the end of the old order, a world where servility to a hereditary monarch, class, privilege, and family connection were everything and no man could acquire land or wealth unless he was born to it.

This rings a trifle hollow when we have a President George Bush Junior echoing the call of President George Bush Senior for a New World Order, after an embarrassing interregnum by one for whom the word 'classless' might have been coined. The old world was never so old, nor the new so new, and it was only after the former crumbled amid the genocidal folly of the Great War that the United States began to exercise an international influence commensurate with its economic power. Pausing only to throw the match of self-determination into

REBELS AND REDCOATS

the European tinderbox of intermingled peoples, America withdrew into itself once more and did not assume its long-anticipated role in human affairs until the end of World War II. Until then the only liberating shots heard around the world came from the guns of the Royal Navy, as it unilaterally suppressed piracy and the slave trade. In 1823 President James Monroe enunciated his 'Doctrine' about European noninterference in the Americas, but it was the British who enforced it and Foreign Minister George Canning who in 1826 declared he had thereby 'called the New World into existence, to redress the balance of the Old'. Of course he had done no such thing, his aim throughout being to prevent the United States expanding to fill the political vacuum left by Spain, and Monroe would have been justified to answer him as Hotspur did Glendower:

> G: I can call spirits from the vasty deep.
> H: Why, so can I, or so can any man;
>   But will they come when you do call for them?

Bless them, they finally did – but in saving Western Europe from Hitler and from the no less monstrous Stalin Americans paid the price of loosening the bars of the cage wisely built around political power by their Constitution. Being the sole outright victor in World War II also thrust them into the role of global policemen, much as the British were by the Seven Years War or War for Empire of 1756–63. The parallel came to life, and provided the catalyst for an overdue revision of the Foundation Myth, when America became involved in Vietnam. Uncomfortable though they were to admit, the similarities in the situations faced by the oppressive redcoats in 1775–83 and the champions of freedom in Southeast Asia during 1964–73 were too striking to be denied. The discovery that one could lose a war despite having overwhelming might on one's side was also particularly wounding to a society inclined to see 'winners' as manly and virtuous, and 'losers' as conversely effeminate and unworthy. But it is not a nation much given to introspection and the revisionism never really progressed beyond the military superficialities to confront the equivocal motives and unsavoury methods employed by the Founding Fathers.

Only one genuinely great man emerged from the independence war and despite the thriving cult of personality built up around him

xxxviii

during it, his full stature only became apparent afterwards. Although George Washington desperately wanted to prove Americans could beat the British Army in the field, he lacked any natural gifts for generalship and was neither granted nor able to create the necessary circumstances to acquire them. Nonetheless his refusal to succumb to the temptation of personal dictatorship when it was his for the taking contrasts favourably with the response of Oliver Cromwell, an outstanding military leader, to much the same situation after the English civil war. If the greatest of Washington's military achievements was keeping some semblance of an army together despite the shattering defeats of 1776, during the same period he was the outright victor in the more demanding political struggle waged against domestic forces of political and social decomposition. Very few appreciated this at the time, least of all the British officials who might otherwise have played him differently.

Most Americans know the tribute proposed by 'Light Horse Harry', Robert E. Lee's father, which was adopted by Congress upon the death of the country's first president ('First in war, first in peace, and first in the hearts of his countrymen'). But few will be aware that he was paid an even greater compliment by the monarch whose authority he did more than most to overthrow. When he learned of Washington's refusal to stand for a third term as president in 1796, a delighted George III pronounced him 'the most distinguished character of the age'. Against all realistic expectation, the outcome of a war begun by rabble-rousers and terrorists proved to be neither anarchy nor dictatorship, but instead a stable and profoundly conservative regime. There were few in Britain in 1775 who did not share the king's view that the colonists' defiance of the sovereignty of Parliament was a mortal threat to a unique constitutional balance evolved over centuries. But fewer still would have disagreed with him twenty-one years later when he gracefully admitted his original error of appreciation, and expressed forthright admiration for the man who proved his fears unfounded.

This, then, is an account of a war which in 1776 saw a sympathetic Whig general halfheartedly directing a professional British Army in operations against an ever-changing band of miserably supported amateurs led by one who, in England, would have been considered a Tory, after all the Rebels' stated war aims had been granted save recognition as a sovereign state. In 1778, when even that would have been conceded, the Rebel leaders condemned their country to five more years of increasingly destructive war in the expectation that their alliance with France would enable them to gain Canada cheaply. They were to be as disappointed in this as they were in their calculation that a long war would strengthen their standing in the community. What could have been more American – or more representative of the old English principle that a man's home is his castle – than the New Jersey farmer who bestowed a fart on an outraged congressional collector of fines and bade him bear it to the Founding Fathers in Philadelphia? He was no 'Loyalist', merely an ordinary man as unimpressed by the new elite as he would have been by the servants of the king had they come to his door demanding money.

It cannot be emphasized enough that if the line of cleavage between 'Loyalist' and 'Rebel' had been the matter of autonomy there would have been extremely few of the former. The colonists had always governed themselves and throughout the eighteenth century they humbled royal governors who thought otherwise. At issue was *how* they should govern themselves now the rising population and increasing complexity of colonial society required more regulation than they were accustomed to. The institutional sclerosis of Westminster could not supply any useful answers to the novel situation of a free people at once requiring and rejecting government. In the end Lord North's administration demanded no more than a recognition of the principle of parliamentary supremacy, which not even the most fervent supporters of the colonial cause in Britain thought it legally possible to abandon. Alas, by then confrontation had changed the questions, sweeping along some who would have been happy to accept North's formula even a few months earlier. But not all, for many who valued their personal autonomy also perceived that a theoretical sovereignty residing 3000 miles away was preferable to practical authority exercised near at hand by men they knew well and held in low esteem.

As though to prove them right, the war pushed the yeomen farmers who first put teeth into the rebellion to the brink of ruin and notoriously created far greater social and economic inequalities than had ever existed previously. It also ensured the divisions among the colonists became so deep that the winners could expropriate the losers without compensation, a key feature in most independence struggles.

The British oligarchy learned some useful lessons about colonial government later applied elsewhere and was to benefit from what turned out to be a dress rehearsal for the mobilization required to meet the challenge of the collectivist French Revolution. That in turn came about because the shaky finances of the *ancien régime* were exacerbated by the American war, in which France expended a vast amount of treasure without gaining any geopolitical advantage. To the chagrin of the French statesmen who confidently predicted further debilitating strife between Great Britain and her ex-colonies for dominion over the rest of the continent, the British got out of the way of western expansion by the United States, while strengthening the borders of Canada with displaced Loyalists and Native Americans.

A final word on methodology – I believe prominent historical figures should be judged by the foreseeable consequences of their actions within the contemporary context. In particular for this period, to put any trust in letters written by men for whom dissembling was a way of life and who often edited them with an eye on the historical record, is to build on quicksand. I have sought to satisfy both the casual and the serious student by letting the Chronology, Maps and Appendices (including short biographies of the main actors), do the heavy factual lifting, freeing the text for argument. In the absence of footnotes the Bibliography starts with a short list of books I have found exceptionally useful overall and I pay tribute in the text to others that strongly influenced my interpretation of particular episodes. Lastly, my cavalier treatment of 'von' and 'de' in German and French names follows the English norm, whereby after a first mention the Marquess of Wherever is referred to as 'Wherever'.

Overviews must be selective and all have a guiding agenda. I have declared mine here to get it out of the way, for once one has dismissed the roseate glow of myth with which some invest the past for present purposes, what emerges is far more interesting. The independence war is a far more topical event than it has been portrayed in what Michael Kammen politely calls the 'creative interpretations' to which it has been subjected. My aim is to focus across the centuries on people much as we are, all of them counters in a game in which only a few were players, doing the best they could in demanding times. They were men who were often blood kin, with more in common with each other than they had with any other people, who clawed at each other in an eminently avoidable war born of the impatient ambition of some and the determination of others to thwart them. In this, at least, it was no different from any other.

1

CAUSES

THE SPIRIT OF the times was captured by Adam Smith's *Wealth of Nations* and the first volume of Edward Gibbons' *Decline and Fall of the Roman Empire*, both published in 1776. These reveal a common belief among the educated and thoughtful that the freedom to make money and dispose of it as each saw fit was not only fundamental to the liberties set out in the 1689 English Bill of Rights – upon which, sometimes word-for-word, the US Bill of Rights of 1791 was based – but had also divided the prosperous from the indigent since time immemorial. The major difference between the two Bills was religious tolerance, an indulgence the English could not afford in 1689 with only nineteen miles of water separating them from France, the would-be hegemonial power in Europe and standard-bearer of imperial Roman Catholicism. As Linda Colley convincingly argues in her landmark study of the emerging British identity: 'As members of the chosen land they might, were indeed virtually bound to have lapses and their periods of failure. But almost by definition they were blessed, and these blessings had a material as well as a spiritual form. An extraordinarily large number of Britons seem to have believed that, under God, they were peculiarly free and peculiarly prosperous'. What she tactfully refrained from suggesting was that it defined the American identity even more precisely, and still does.

It is imprudent to attach too much importance to the concepts bandied about in the cloud of political pamphlets published in the colonies during the immediate pre-war period. Most of them betrayed only a crude understanding of the political issues they dealt with and were generally rather poor echoes of similar English works published before, during and after the British civil wars. In his meticulous survey of these ephemera Bernard Bailyn summarizes the distinguishing theme of the American pamphlets as 'the fear of a comprehensive conspiracy against liberty throughout the English-speaking world – a conspiracy believed to have been nourished in corruption and of which, it was felt, oppression in America was only the most immediately visible part'. The eminent Columbia historian Richard Hofstadter dubbed this 'the paranoid style in American politics', arguing that it emerges when members of a particular social interest are shut out of political decision-making, feeding an underlying conviction that the world of power is satanic. When one party achieves this frame of mind the other can do nothing right and even inaction will be construed in a sinister light.

The Founding Father of the paranoid style and the foremost advocate of violent confrontation with Britain was the Bostonian Samuel Adams. Provincials will always find more than enough to condemn in the metropolis, but the puritanical Adams was consumed by hatred for the bawdiness and corruption of the British ruling elite, which in his eyes justified any misrepresentation, no matter how gross, to shed the worst possible light on what was usually no more than bumbling incompetence. During the pre-war decade he single-handedly generated a vast number of subversive 'letters to the editor' contriving spurious debates in which he would write both sides under different aliases, until at last the sparks he struck found some tinder.

The ideological seam Adams mined was a definition of liberty with uniquely English roots, in opposition to the emergence of a new, British identity, struggling to devise a coherent administration for the territorial gains of the Seven Years/War for Empire. In all probability the effort was doomed from the outset, for the war had also removed the threat from the Roman Catholic French in Québec and Spanish in Florida, which had previously bound together the interests of Britain and her super-Protestant colonies. It had also nurtured a competing imperial mentality. Adams gloated 'providence will erect a mighty empire in America; and our posterity will have it recorded in history, that their fathers migrated from an *island* in a distant part of the world', whose worthier citizens would necessarily flee its 'luxury and dissipation', leaving it to sink into 'obscurity and contempt'. The theme also jumps off the pages in George Washington's correspondence, in which the words 'empire' and 'nation' are employed interchangeably. The underlying argument was that while 'England' was an absolute standard, the concept of 'Great Britain' was open to challenge from those who believed a more pristine Englishness survived on their side of the Atlantic.

A belief that the emergence of the new British mentality threatened liberty was not confined to America. Many in Britain believed the country had taken a fatally wrong turn, the wars with France serving mainly to strengthen the hold on power of a corrupt oligarchy much like the Long Parliament, whose members grew fat during the English civil wars until expelled in 1653 by Cromwell. The most telling assaults on British moral authority in the colonies were reprints of broadsides with a wide circulation in Britain. Perhaps the most savage was written by James Burgh in 1746, reprinted in Philadelphia the following year by Benjamin Franklin, which bitterly denounced: 'luxury and irreligion ... venality, perjury, faction, opposition to legal authority, idleness, gluttony, drunkenness, lewdness, excessive gaming, robberies, clandestine marriages, breach of matrimonial vows, self-murders ... a legion of furies sufficient to rend any state or empire that ever was in the world to pieces'. *Plus ça change . . .*

Burgh's litany of social pathologies are, however, the dark side of individualism, itself the essence of an Englishness believed by many on both sides of the Atlantic to be more perfectly expressed on its western shores. Contrary to the Romantic myth linking the American rebellion to a notional libertarian Saxon heritage struggling to emerge from under the feudal Norman boot, the concept of land as a commodity, owned by individuals who could buy, sell and bequeath it freely, took hold in the century after the Norman conquest and marked a break with the collective ownership that properly defines the term 'peasant'. When Major-General John Burgoyne, on his way to America, learned the garrison in Boston was besieged, he commented to his cheering troops, 'What! Ten thousand peasants keep five thousand King's troops shut up? Well, let us get in, and we'll soon find elbow room'. He was a trifle behind the times – the besiegers were not peasants, nor had their ancestors been for half a millennium. The assertion of new and collective imperial obligations offended against deep currents of custom among people who no longer had the present danger of rival empires to persuade them any such changes were necessary.

Then as now, people knew individual freedom without self-imposed restraint must result in antisocial behaviour, requiring constraints that infringe on liberty. An acute awareness of this constitutes the philosophical mainstay of what some have dubbed the 'religious Right', whose more thoughtful representatives express the belief that unrestrained private behaviour has public consequences inimical to freedom. Between 1765 and 1775 Samuel Adams focused this concern on the British, but his task was made immeasurably easier by the volatile nature of a rapidly expanding society in which half the inhabitants were under sixteen years of age. Although writing about the late twentieth-century United States, James Q. Wilson observes that young people in all cultures and every age test the limits of acceptable behaviour: 'Testing limits is a way of asserting selfhood. Maintaining limits is a way of asserting community. If the limits are asserted weakly, uncertainly, or apologetically, their effects must surely be weaker than if they are asserted boldly, confidently, and persuasively'.

The hesitant exercise of British authority in the colonies, strikingly evident before and continuing into the war itself, perfectly fits this description. By contrast the Rebel leaders acted ruthlessly to enforce their own control, even hanging some pacifist Quakers to emphasize that neutrality was not an option. Warfare, given more or less equal numbers and technology, is a matter of the will to dominate, and while the directors of the British war effort were no less determined to prevail than their American counterparts, they had to answer to a parliamentary opposition that espoused the Rebel cause for its own partisan ends. In addition British ministers had to act through local commanders whose political affiliations gave them the status of independent contractors. Above all, British power was attenuated by distance and distracted by more pressing matters of state nearer home, so that sustained, concerted action by the self-appointed leaders of the thirteen colonies must have brought the war to a rapid conclusion. It dragged on as long as it did because Rebel no less than British writ ran only where there were armed men to enforce it, with the result that the

Rebel provincial authorities gave priority to the pay and equipment of their local Militias, whose primary function was to suppress domestic opposition, to the detriment of the collective force devoted to combating the British optimistically named the 'Continental Army' in 1775.

When measured against the performance of their British peers elsewhere the lack of a sense of loyalty and obligation among the leading American landowners and merchants can be seen as part of the social and economic wallpaper of the time. The foremost slave and plantation owners, 'land rich' but relatively cash poor, were George Washington of Virginia, Charles Carroll of Maryland and Henry Middleton of South Carolina, all important movers and shakers once the rebellion began. Washington's view that 'the Parliament of Great Britain hath no more right to put their hand in my pocket, without my consent, than I have to put my hands into yours for money' could have been written by any of the British West Indies plantation owners, who also talked a good libertarian line while refusing to pay towards their own defence, traded freely with the enemy and profiteered shamelessly from the armed forces sent from Britain and America to protect them. Finally, not even the subtlest ethicist could differentiate among the moral qualities of the Yankee merchants and the leading citizens of the great British seaports.

The difference was one of scale. The enormous profits generated by the British merchant houses, by corporations such as the East India and Hudson's Bay Companies, and by the West Indian planters, bought them a political influence in London to which their less wealthy and often heavily indebted North American peers could not aspire. For them the calculation that local government could be bought more cheaply led compellingly to thoughts of independence, as it did to those locally eminent men denied membership in the class an aggrieved Washington called 'our lordly masters'. It was also appealing to late converts such as John Adams, once they perceived that separatism offered the prospect of greater social prominence than the colonial relationship permitted. Money, no matter how earned, was always a more certain means to membership in the British oligarchy than merit and the colonists simply did not have enough of it. We may wonder whether the war might have been averted by spreading the net of patronage wider and by awarding knighthoods (the Order of the Bath, revived in 1725) to men like Washington, but the Crown was in no doubt about it. The Order of Saint Patrick was founded in 1783 to remedy this deficiency in Ireland, but it was not until the Order of Saint Michael and Saint George was established in 1818 that the British establishment fully recognized the need to honour imperial service.

The fish most clearly torn between the large and small ponds was Franklin, the only American who could aspire to significant status in either. He was pushed off the embankment and lost his sinecure as Assistant Postmaster-General in early 1774, when Solicitor-General Wedderburn excoriated him in the Privy Council over some dubiously acquired letters written some years earlier by the men who later became the governor and lieutenant-governor of Massachusetts, which Franklin had sent to the seditious Committee of Correspondence in that colony for use against them. The attack had some justification beyond the purloined letters, as in his private correspondence Franklin was a pot-stirrer quite on a par with Samuel Adams, like him carefully tailoring his message to whatever audience he was addressing. But in an age when the courtesies were observed even between mortal enemies, a man with a solid international reputation was treated like a thieving servant in the presence of the great and the powerful, without one of them seeking to moderate Wedderburn's intemperate language. This underlined a contempt for all things American vengefully resented by a broad range of prominent provincials who did not share Franklin's ambivalence about the size of the pond that best suited them.

Nonetheless they would not necessarily have been moved to armed rebellion had it not been that their own status in colonial society was threatened by incendiary proselytism and unchecked mob action. By the time the government of Lord North was moved to take action against rising disorder in the colonies with the words 'it is not political convenience, it is political necessity that urges this measure', many judged it too little and much too late. Among the upper and middle classes of colonial society, one of the clearest dividing line between Rebels and Loyalists was that by 1775–6 the former believed the British incapable of maintaining order and stability, and the latter did not believe the Rebels wanted to.

From the British side of the Atlantic there was another priority. When the House of Lords rejected a proposal made in January 1775 by William Pitt, Earl of Chatham, which would have recognized the fact of colonial self-government, Franklin commented they 'appeared to have scarce discretion enough to govern a herd of swine'. But within the economic and political understanding of the time their lordships were correct. The Acts of Parliament demonized by the American separatists could only be construed as the symptoms of a conspiracy by overlooking that 'planning' has always been the antonym of 'British way of doing things'. What they did betray was fear Britain might lose and its enemies gain the benefit of a transatlantic trade amounting to one third of all its international commerce, and of colonial iron, timber and shipbuilding resources believed essential for continued maritime superiority. Not many of the colonists shared Samuel Adams' burning desire to destroy, but with only a handful of exceptions all those living in Britain believed the loss of the colonies would leave them at the mercy of France. Until the sharp recovery of direct and indirect trade with the colonies during the war made it apparent, very few on either side of the Atlantic appreciated that a commonality of interests and tastes, and Britain's unique ability to supply the manufactured goods the colonists craved, would maintain and indeed increase trade after independence. The many prominent separatists who had hoped to repudiate their debts by declaring independence, or to diminish them through inflation by printing paper money, soon found the laws of commerce more binding than those of political affiliation.

There was a conspiracy, but it was not in London. The French insisted on the British keeping Québec province at the 1763 Peace of Paris in the confident expectation it would encourage separatism in the British colonies. Their ploy prompted the chief British negotiator to worry 'whether the neighbourhood of the French to our North American colonies was not the greatest security for their dependence on the mother country, which I feel will be slighted by them when their apprehension of the French is removed'. That concern was exacerbated by knowledge that French agents, including the spuriously titled Bavarian Baron de Kalb who was to die as a major-general of the Continental Army at Camden in 1780, had been dispatched to make contact with colonial dissidents within months of the treaty. Governments always have a problem defending policies based on the hints and nuances of secret intelligence, but behind the evasive public utterances of the Lord North administration lay well-founded suspicion that covert French encouragement lay behind the rising tide of unrest in the colonies.

Secret intelligence aside, Franklin's action over the purloined letters was just one of many indications that his apparent moderation was simply a smokescreen, even if his supporters among the opposition Whigs found it convenient to believe there was still enough common ground to preserve a figleaf of parliamentary supremacy. The words 'loyal' and 'opposition' would not have been linked by any observer of British politics in the eighteenth century and in this respect as in so many others the actions of the American dissidents were unremarkable in an age before the French Revolutionary and Napoleonic wars uncorked the malignant genie of nationalism. But it is thought-provoking that some of those who claimed to be the champions of English liberties and Protestant purity were in treasonous contact with absolutist, Roman Catholic France many years before the guns began to shoot. Not that it has ever stopped anyone, but it is not ethically sustainable to claim the high moral ground while practising realpolitik.

There is a reason why both Americans and Britons love to hate 'the French', and it has nothing to do with the real French people. 'The French' is a construct, an idealized enemy of infinite cunning and resource implacably committed to the subversion of the English-speaking peoples' heritage of freedom. Just like poor old Lord Raglan in the Crimea, the enemy is still 'the French' even when they happen to be our allies and they can't hoodwink us with their collectivist talk of liberty, equality and fraternity. Given that it is approaching two centuries since either the British or the Americans were involved in active hostilities with them it is not difficult to imagine how intense such feelings were at the time when France really was the mortal enemy of Protestant England and its quirky but freedom-enhancing political institutions. For the British government it made no difference whether the American dissidents were consciously or unconsciously serving French interests, but for the colonists to reconcile their self-righteousness with a war waged in alliance with France against Britain, it was necessary to invest 'the British' with all the negative associations of 'the French'.

The process of demonization was assisted by the treaties signed by the British with the Native Americans during the Seven Years War. These were regarded as meaningless by the colonists once the war was won, but were perceived as a firm basis for policy by the young King George III and the Earl of Bute, once his tutor and now his First Minister. The result was the Proclamation Line of 1763 (see MAP 1), which sought to limit the colonies to the space between the Appalachians and the Atlantic. It came too late to prevent the damaging uprising misnamed after the Ottawa leader Pontiac, in which the main protagonists were Delawares who had wisely departed Pennsylvania (those who remained and became Christian farmers were massacred by the Scotch-Irish 'Paxton Boys'), the Shawnee and the Seneca. The idea of a stable frontier also prompted Bute to propose the colonists should pay £225,000 per annum to defray the cost of maintaining a garrison force to guard it, the first of the substantive dominoes to fall in the sequence to war.

Although the peace-keeping rationale for the Proclamation Line was valid, when later in the decade London declared all territory west of the Proclamation Line to be Crown Lands and in 1774 extended the boundaries of Québec to include the American Midwest, it outraged a host of land speculators, notably George Washington and Benjamin Franklin. It also signalled the adoption by London of the traditional French policy of containment, thereby making enemies of the frontiersmen who might otherwise have made useful allies against the Rebel coastal elite. Vermont was a de facto independent republic from 1777 until it became the fourteenth state of the Union in 1791, Tennessee became the fifteenth in 1792, Kentucky the sixteenth in 1796, each representing a victory by the frontiersmen over the legal claims of New York, Pennsylvania and Virginia respectively. Furthermore, by allying with the Native Americans the British repudiated ties of blood and kinship and did more to unite the faction-ridden Rebels than all their disputed revenue acts put together.

Probably not taken very seriously at the time, but of lasting significance in America's carefully crafted self-image, was the projection of blame onto the colonial power for the signature vices of the colonies. A splendid example of the sophistry involved can be seen in the most underlined clause in Jefferson's first manuscript draft of the Declaration of Independence:

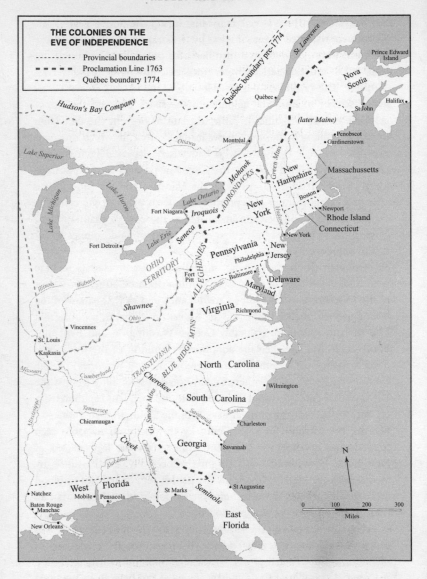

THE COLONIES ON THE EVE OF INDEPENDENCE

------- Provincial boundaries
━ ━ ━ Proclamation Line 1763
- - - Québec boundary 1774

MAP 1

He [George III] has waged cruel war against human nature itself, violating its most sacred rights of life & liberty in the persons of a distant people who never offended him, captivating & carrying them into slavery in another hemisphere, or to incur miserable death in their transportation thither. This piratical warfare the opprobrium of <u>infidel</u> powers, is the warfare of the <u>CHRISTIAN</u> king of Great Britain. Determined to keep open a market where MEN should be bought & sold he has prostituted his negative for suppressing every legislative attempt to prohibit or to restrain this execrable commerce: and that this assemblage of horrors might want no fact of distinguished die, he is now exciting those very people to rise in arms among us, and to purchase that liberty of which <u>he</u> has deprived them by murdering the people upon whom he also obtruded them: thus paying off former crimes committed against the <u>liberties</u> of one people, with crimes which he urges them to commit against the <u>lives</u> of another.

Jefferson noted the clause 'was struck out in complaisance to South Carolina and Georgia, who had never attempted to restrain the importation of slaves, and who on the contrary wished to continue it. Our Northern brethren also I believe felt a little tender under those censures, for tho' their people have very few slaves themselves yet they had been pretty considerable carriers of them to others'. Not a word about the ruling made in June 1772 by Lord Mansfield, Chief Justice of the King's Bench, in the case of an escaped slave claimed by his owner in England:

The power claimed by this return never was in use here. The state of slavery is so odious that nothing can be suffered to support it but positive law. We cannot say that the cause set forth by this return is allowed or approved by the laws of the kingdom and therefore the man must be discharged.

But as all politicians know, the executive truth is what people can be persuaded to believe long enough to commit them to a course from which there is no easy retreat. As to culturally useful misrepresentations, one of the few original American contributions to philosophy was made by the 'Pragmaticists', of whom the best known was John Dewey (1859–1952), who believed 'ideas are true if they are successfully employed in pursuit of human goals and interests'. On the face of it blatantly totalitarian, the precept seems less appalling when we consider the *civilizing* role of the Foundation Myth during the lifetime of the Pragmaticists, as the benchmark for the higher social and cultural aspirations of a society in a state of rapid and seldom edifying expansion.

Ideas can be instrumental in creating a bellicose frame of mind and may even get men into uniform, but they do not maintain cohesion in times of hardship or stiffen resolve in battle. That is a function of training, discipline and leadership. Although bad experiences when fighting alongside the redcoats in previous campaigns inclined many colonists with active military experience to favour the rebellion, they remained deficient in all these categories throughout the war. One of the New Yorkers taken prisoner when Major Patrick Ferguson's Loyalist command was destroyed at King's Mountain reported his captors, the deadly 'Over Mountain Men', demanded to know how Ferguson had turned despised coastal lowlanders into effective soldiers. They answered their own question by disbanding and returning home instead of following up their victory – they fought as individuals and once the immediate threat to their own turf was neutralized, they had little interest in the greater conflict. That attitude, of course, was what made London's efforts to make the colonists pay something towards the costs of Empire so profoundly misconceived – but it also explains why the Rebels in turn found it so difficult to organize effective collective resistance.

The contest was more equal than it is usually portrayed. In 1775 the American colonies had a population of about two and a half million whites and 550,000 blacks, while Great Britain had a population of about seven million, approximately half in England (of which 750,000 in London), a quarter in Ireland and the remainder divided between Scotland and Wales. In the preceding decade immigration and the birth rate of a young population enjoying the highest standard of living in the world had increased numbers in the colonies by 35–40 per cent, while the British population grew by only 10 per cent. The economic product of the colonies was two-fifths that of the British Isles and growing faster, and although the industrial revolution in Britain was in the process of altering the traditional relationship among land, population and wealth, it had not yet done so to any considerable degree. What levelled the playing field was that Britain had to guard against a hostile France (with a population of twenty-four million), and was separated from America by 3000 miles of often turbulent ocean.

In early 1775 the British Army numbered only 48,650 of all ranks in 103 regiments, one in three maintained by annual votes of the Irish Parliament. By 1782 the figure had risen above 140,000 (excluding about 40,000 Militia on stand-by for home defence), but in the meantime the Irish had demanded and received the liberties offered the Americans in the peace proposals of 1777 and 1779, Britain had gone to war with France, Spain and the Netherlands, while Russia, Prussia, Austria, Denmark, Sweden and Sicily had formed the hostile League of Armed Neutrality. From a base line of 7000 in 1775, the number of troops in North America, about a third of them German mercenaries, peaked at 43,500, a little under half the worldwide total, in 1778 before the French openly entered the conflict. Thereafter 'effectives' (as the able-bodied were described in contemporary returns) hovered between 28,000 and 33,000, with a further 7000–10,000 in Canada, and declined sharply as a proportion of the total. Fifty-one of seventy-three prewar British infantry regiments served in America, few of them ever attaining full strength (494 of all ranks per battalion) and some so reduced by disease they were dispersed to other regiments.

On the other side, enlistment figures for the Continental Army were 231,771, the great majority paid substitutes, while about 145,000 served in the Militia units that came and went as they saw fit. Without attempting to estimate how many of these were fraudulent, many men legitimately re-enlisted several times and gross enlistment figures must be reduced by a third to achieve numbers approximately in line with the generally accepted estimate of 250,000 who may have actually served at one time or another. Of these nearly 7000 died of battle wounds, over 10,000 died of camp diseases and 8500, of about 20,000 who surrendered, died in captivity. The largest total authorized by Congress was a 46,900-man Continental Army and 42,700 Militia in 1776, and the highest number formally enlisted in the Continental Army was 35,000 in November 1778, at a time when the main British Army in New York was depleted to 17,500 by the demands of war against France. However neither in 1776, when Washington had in excess of 40,000 men nominally under his command, nor even at the peak of long-term enlistment in 1778, were these consolidated. The largest force ever directly under his command was about 19,000 Continental Army and Militia during the 1777 campaign in Pennsylvania.

Without slighting the significance of the Militia in denying territory and free movement to the enemy, the serious fighting was done by the long-service soldiers of the Continental Army, described by Sergeant Jeremiah Greenman of the Rhode Island contingent in mid 1777 as being, 'all most ye biger part of them old Country [British born] men which are very bad we are to flog them night and morning'. Things had not improved three years later, when Connecticut Private Joseph Plumb Martin described some of those fighting for the cause of liberty and virtue as 'a caravan of wild beasts ... their dialect, too, was as confused as their bodily appearance was bad and disgusting. There was the Irish and Scotch brogue, murdered English, flat insipid Dutch and some lingoes which would puzzle a philosopher'. In sum, the formal military contest was not one between highly motivated citizens and soulless mercenaries. It was between similar groups of men, only one of which was properly trained, led and bound together by the ties of ritual and elite group pride necessary to make the plans of generals succeed, or to retrieve their errors, on the battlefield.

The members of the Continental Congress had little practical experience of war and seem to have imagined the numbers they authorized in 1776 were sufficient to guarantee victory. When they voted in favour of the Declaration of Independence it was certainly calculated to burn bridges, but it was done from what they believed to be a position of strength. As well as hopelessly underestimating the qualitative factor, they miscalculated on both sides of the numerical equation, for the spontaneous mass uprising of 1775 in Massachusetts was never repeated and Britain sent a far larger army than they had anticipated. The early appearance in American military history of estimated 'body counts' as a measure of combat success, despite the fact the Rebels seldom held the field after a battle and were thus unable to do any actual counting, was deeply misleading. Attrition, particularly among officers who led by example, did not work to the advantage of the less cohesive and disciplined force. A similar miscalculation of profit and loss lay behind the belief that the interruption of transatlantic trade would hurt Britain more than it would the colonies, a fallacy to which Jefferson was to succumb again when President from 1800 to 1808 and as the Confederacy was to do again in 1861–62.

Concerning the reasons why the war lasted as long as it did, accepting for argument's sake the dubious proposition the rebellion would have started without the promise of French support, it would almost certainly have ended with a compromise settlement in 1777–78 if France had not intervened overtly. Even then it might have been suppressed if the British had fully embraced the elements hostile to the rebellion within America. Beyond the office holders and some Anglican clergy who saw their livelihoods disappear, loyalty to the crown was not as important as revulsion at the bully-boy tactics employed by the Rebels, pre-existing local animosities, hatred of demagoguery and fear of violent revolution. Edmund Burke, writing later about the French Revolution with a clarity of vision veiled by partisan considerations in his comments on the American, was struck by the prominence of 'the fomenters and conductors of the petty war of village vexation', marginal lawyers with no stake in the status quo:

> They must *join* (if their capacity did not permit them to *lead*) in any project which could procure to them a *litigious constitution*; which could lay open to them those innumerable lucrative jobs which follow in the train of all great convulsions and revolutions in the state, and particularly in all great and violent permutations of property.

In America such people were venomously active at the local government level, where real power lay and where both their desire to strut their oratory and their malice towards their betters overflowed once the shooting started. Their behaviour provoked a strong reaction even among those inclined at first to support the revolt and lay behind the later disaffection of prominent Rebel leaders, most notoriously General Benedict Arnold of Connecticut. It is impossible to estimate what proportion of the white population lost faith in the revolution as the war dragged on. However, the generally accepted figure for those who – from the start – either chose or were forced to reject the rebellion openly is about 20 per cent of the white population, 500,000 men, women and children, of whom 100,000 eventually chose exile rather than remain under the dominion of the victors, to the very great benefit of Canada where most of them settled. We can only speculate whether, if properly encouraged and organized from the beginning, they might have constituted a sufficient mass base for a successful counter insurgency campaign. What is indisputable is that the British authorities could not ignore their clamour for protection in 1774–76, nor later simply abandon them to their fate.

More than 50,000 Loyalists took up arms in a growing force of 'Provincial' and the more prestigious 'American' regiments, some of which received the ultimate accolade of acceptance into the Regular Army. Their numbers, large though they were as a proportion of the overall British effort, understate their significance, for with the exception of the 17th Light Dragoons, the only cavalry available to British commanders in America during the latter years of the war was Provincial. Nor should we forget the naval dimension, where privateers paid for and manned by Loyalists began to exercise some of the functions of a blockade even before the Royal Navy abandoned the calculated forbearance shown by Admiral Lord Richard Howe until 1778. No less important was the contribution of African Americans, who provided that rare commodity, genuine volunteers for service in the Royal Navy, where they were generally fitter, better motivated and more skilled than those pressed into service. On land, only about 5000 African Americans served in the Continental Army, whereas as many black as white Loyalist men served the British cause and were resettled elsewhere with their families after the war. They served mainly as scouts and foragers, who if captured by the Rebels were hanged out of hand, and as labourers responsible for building roads, bridges, fortifications, barracks, etc. They also served in the ranks of the Regular Army and provided highly regarded bandsmen for many smart regiments, including the Hessian grenadiers whose all-black band became a tradition. Too often disregarded, African American women also provided invaluable domestic support services to the British, whose lack was always apparent in the ragged and dirty Continental Army.

The role of Loyalist Militia and Local units was far less significant than on the Rebel side, for apart from a few circumscribed areas they had been driven from their homes and were therefore unable to exercise the social control John Shy identifies as the crucial factor in the

Rebel success. Nonetheless, without these Americans the British Army could have undertaken only very limited operations after the French entered the war, when what might have been a mobile reserve of 5150 men was detached to defend the West Indies and a further 4760 to the losing struggle for Florida. Three thousand of the latter were Loyalists or regiments formed from Rebel prisoners or deserters and it is no exaggeration to say the British position in the Caribbean would have been lost without them. There are many examples of British distrust of the white Loyalists and callousness towards the African Americans who joined them, but despite this the traffic in refugees was overwhelmingly away from Rebel-held areas for the duration of the war. Even the French returned from their southern expedition in 1781 with hundreds of escaped slaves who sought their protection. Like the British, they refused to return them to their furious owners.

The crucial question about the Anglo-American civil war is why those in favour of maintaining the association with Britain were fatally more passive than those seeking rupture. The answer is implicit in the question – those who respect established authority and value order are at a severe disadvantage when these come under assault, because they look to the authorities they respect to restore the order they value. British failure to do this before the war greatly reduced the potential Loyalist pool, while as soon as hostilities broke out insurgent forces moved swiftly to impose their own authority, even in places like Georgia and the Carolinas where a majority of the inhabitants was Loyalist. The latter included Scots Highlander immigrants with ample reason to hate the House of Hanover, among them Flora MacDonald, who had smuggled Bonnie Prince Charlie 'over the sea to Skye' in 1746. There was also a substantial Loyalist majority in New York and New Jersey, in part arising from a history of abusive foreclosures by large landowners who generally favoured the rebellion. Most of the citizens of Boston, Newport, New York, Philadelphia, Charleston and Savannah remained and prospered under British occupation, and many sailed away with the army when it departed. But they did not play an active part in the defence of their interests and so they lost to those who did.

Against this, had the Rebel cause enjoyed the popular support, nobility of purpose and divine blessing that constitute three sides of the Foundation Myth pyramid, a devout and effective force of property owners akin to Cromwell's Ironsides should have emerged to build the fourth. That it did not, among people highly conscious of the historical parallels they were invoking by personalizing their dispute with Parliament in the figure of the king, tells us much. Cromwell, with no previous military experience, recruited 'men of spirit, that is likely to go as far as gentlemen will do . . . I raised such men as had the fear of God before them, as made some conscience of what they did, and from that day forward they were never beaten'. He would have found no lack of suitable recruits among the men who savaged the British column on the road from Concord to Lexington and who defended Breed's Hill to the last. But an elite force was the last thing any of the Rebel politicians wanted, for they were also highly conscious of the sequel to the English Civil War, and the fate of the Long Parliamentarians they resembled.

Theirs was not a nation, but thirteen thinly populated mini-states and four proto-states, the smaller distrustful of the larger and the larger jealous of each other, whose internal trade and communications were less significant than the maritime links they all had with Great Britain. If in the years before the revolt exploded the British authorities had employed against the colonies the tactics of divide and rule they used to such good effect against 'natives' everywhere else, the war would have been prevented – but there might now be two or three countries occupying the space of the United States. The colonies were Great Britain's to lose and it lost them by the unique combination of wishful thinking, ad hoc policy-making and futile bluster that is the historic hallmark of the British politician, and which has proved a greater guarantor of the liberties of the people of Britain than any conceivable suite of institutional checks and balances.

What British politicians did not do was provoke a peaceful people to revolt. Unless we are to suppose they were suffering from ennui and thought a little trouble in the colonies would liven things up, there is no reason to believe they would knowingly have embarked upon a course of action that would spark a rebellion they had no immediate means of combating and which must weaken them in the confrontation with Bourbon France and Spain at a time when Britain was without allies. All the ingredients that boiled together – ethnic hatred, religious totalitarianism, merchant greed, landowner debt, social and political frustration – were familiar to the rulers of Britain. What they failed to anticipate was that a sizeable number of people freer than any other in history would rebel against the nation that had nurtured the liberties they prized so highly, in alliance with empires long devoted to their suppression. They also scoffed at slave-owners who expatiated about freedom and human rights, forgetting the institution had underpinned the Greek and Roman empires, which all educated people were taught to admire.

Geoge III later lamented 'we meant well by the Americans – just to punish them with a few bloody noses, and then to make laws for the happiness of both countries'. Although he prided himself on being the first Hanoverian who felt himself to be British, George III was not English. As a result he failed to understand that for the bulk of his subjects, on both sides of the Atlantic, bloody noses only reinforced an ancestral bloody-mindedness more potent over time than mere skill at arms. Even if the king's schoolboyish vision had corresponded more closely to the sociological realities, few pugilists would argue in favour of thrusting your face into your opponent's fist. Yet as we shall see next, this was what the flower of the British officer corps decided was the best way to start round one of the contest for America.

2

OPENING SHOTS:
MASSACHUSETTS

IN JOHN ADAMS' SUCCESSFUL LEGAL defence of the British soldiers who killed some members of his cousin's rent-a-mob in the so-called 'Boston Massacre' of 5 March 1770, he argued they had been assaulted by a 'motley rabble of saucy boys, negroes and mulattoes, Irish teagues and outlandish jack tarres'. However, the sort of person who is bold in civil disorders seldom makes a good soldier and one looks in vain for members of the urban rabble described by John Adams among those who stood their ground against redcoat muskets and bayonets in 1775. In what proved to be a transient but myth-defining phenomenon, the Massachusetts conspirators were able to mobilize the moral authority residing in the small land-holders of their colony against a British military governor renowned for his personal decency and political moderation, who was moved to take action against their stockpiling of arms and ammunition only by peremptory orders to do so from London. John Shy styles Lieutenant-General Thomas Gage the 'Weak Link of Empire' and blames his vacillating performance first as C-in-C of the British Army in North America (1763–75) and then as governor of Massachusetts (1774–75) with starting the war, 'under ambiguous circumstances, at the heart of Rebel strength, in an area that could only be a dead end for British strategy, and with a series of humiliating setbacks for His Majesty's arms'. As to the first three counts, he was trapped into a no win situation by the conspirators and it is difficult to see how he could have acted otherwise. The last charge is the strongest, because he was extremely well informed by a wide network of spies and informers and had been involved in blood-soaked episodes that demonstrated the vulnerability of regular soldiers in broken terrain, as well as the ruinous cost of storming fieldworks. Yet he sent a column under the command of an officer almost too fat to ride a horse on a raid to Concord through densely wooded territory in April 1775, and consented to the frontal assaults on Breed's Hill in June that decimated (for once, literally) the only substantial British land force in the whole of North America.

Although clearly he had been promoted above his level of competence, a feature of the British Army in America before the war was that the only senior officers willing to remain in the colonies were those like Gage who had married and acquired lands there. In addition a rising proportion of the troops was enlisted locally, most of them men whom Gage permitted to transfer out of departing regiments when they were rotated back to Britain. In a society where such a large number were recent immigrants, unless we accept the syllogism that the only people entitled to be called 'Americans' were those who conspired and fought for independence, and their opponents perforce 'British', the fratricidal nature of this war was apparent from the first. It was arguably far more of a civil war than the conflict of 1861–65, still known to Southerners as the 'War between the States'. In the later war only the border states and territories were as evenly divided internally as most of the colonies were in 1775–83, and there were more clearly defined cultural differences between the two sides. More poignantly, although the South was militarily defeated it retained a separate and hostile identity for much of the following century. An awareness that this would be the certain result of a purely military 'solution' to the rebellion in the colonies seems to have paralyzed Gage, and to have greatly inhibited both his successors as commander-in-chief.

Not so the conspirators, of whom Thomas Hutchinson, the American-born Massachusetts governor whose authority Benjamin Franklin had helped to destroy, observed:

> ... [they] had gone too far to recede. If the colonies were subject
> to the supreme authority and the laws of Great Britain, their

offences, long since, had been of the highest nature. Their all depended upon attaining to the object which first engaged them. There was no way of attaining to it but by involving the body of the people in the same circumstances they were in themselves. And it is certain that ever after this time an opinion was easily instilled, and was constantly increasing, that the body of the people had gone too far to recede, and that an open and general revolt must be the consequence.

As we have seen more recently in Northern Ireland, it is relatively easy for a tiny number of determined subversives to create an atmosphere in which others are drawn into their nightmare world. And as we can see in Palestine, even those who target swiftly and repress ruthlessly are hard put to cut off the heads of the Hydra fast enough once they begin to proliferate. Was it really 'weak' of Gage and his political masters to refrain from assassinating the agitators, or from punishing their communities in order to isolate those determined to provoke violence? If not, then they deserve some sympathy for respecting the standards of civilized behaviour in the face of provocation by those not similarly inhibited. Full-blooded repression usually works, and by comparison with the norms of European warfare in the eighteenth century, not to mention the methods employed by the American Rebels, the British Army in America was remarkably well behaved. Too well, obviously – it is a measure of how counterproductive 'niceness' can be in hard-edged times that the Massachusetts conspirators judged they could push Gage and the government he represented into pre-emptive surrender.

In modern army parlance the British foray that resulted in the first battle of the independence war would form part of the bulging file marked 'SNAFU'. Uncannily similar in some respects to the ill-fated penetration into the heart of Mogadishu by the US Rangers and Special Forces on 3–4 October 1993, the operation included such hardy perennials as underestimation of the enemy, lack of contingency planning, and failures of staff work, command and coordination. Gage had warned the Earl of Dartmouth, Secretary of State for the Colonies, 'if force is to be used at length, it must be a considerable one . . . for to begin with small numbers will encourage resistance, and not terrify'. But on 16 April 1775 he received a reply that ridiculed his estimate of the troops required (more than 20,000) and ordered him to arrest the members of the illegal Provincial Congress, which he knew from several well placed informers was meeting in Concord, some sixteen miles away from Boston along a winding road with 'ambushment' points at every turn (see MAP p. 24).

Gage's spies had also told him a considerable supply of arms and military stores was cached in Concord, including three 24-pounder cannon whose significance has gone strangely unremarked by historians. These were 5600-pound monsters requiring eight to ten men to serve them and a team of six horses to pull them, and although their maximum accurate range was 1500 yards, at full elevation they could fire a ball twice as far. They were siege guns, not field artillery pieces, and how they came to be buried in the courtyard of Concord jail is a mystery. Whatever else the raid did not accomplish, until March 1776 it deprived the Rebels of the means to fire upon the Boston Peninsula or to threaten the shipping channel leading to it. The big guns can have had no other intended purpose, and if we examine the geography of Boston harbour (see MAP p. 25) we can see Gage had much to fear from guns with the range to fire into the peninsula from more places than he could hope to garrison. Major John Pitcairn of the Royal Marines ordered the gate to the jail broken down and held a pistol to the head of the jailer to force him to reveal their location, the only occasion force was employed against a civilian during the five-hour occupation of Concord. As to why Gage did not mention them either in his written orders to the corpulent Lieutenant-Colonel Francis Smith, who led the raid, or in his reports to London, he may have wished to conceal a detailed knowledge that could only have come from the innermost Rebel councils (he would have instructed Pitcairn privately), and there was little point in reporting specifics to political masters who rejected his accurate and well-founded general assessments as the vapourings of an 'old woman'.

The cannon fitted the jigsaw in another way. The conspirators were desperate to provoke some bloody event to polarize opinion, and the French would have regarded a brace and half of 24-pounders as seed corn. Pitcairn was killed at Breed's Hill two months later, Gage never thought the raid needed any explanation and Samuel Adams very carefully selected what items of correspondence he would leave

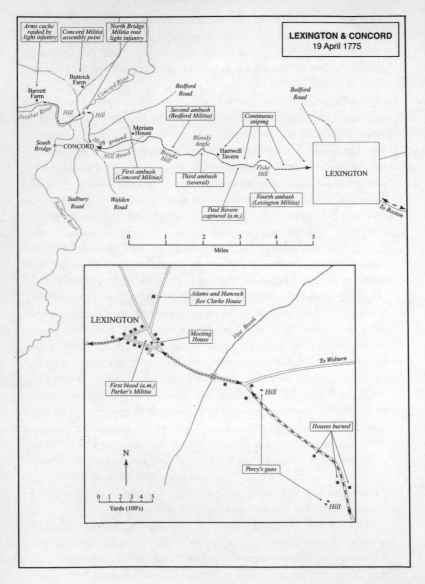

LEXINGTON & CONCORD
19 April 1775

Arms cache raided by light infantry

Concord Militia assembly point

North Bridge Militia rout light infantry

Buttrick Farm

Concord River

Barrett Farm

Assabet River

Bedford Road

Bedford Road

Hill

Hill

Second ambush (Bedford Militia)

Continuous sniping

Meriam House

Bloody Angle

South Bridge

CONCORD

High ground

Mill Brook

Brooks Hill

Hartwell Tavern

Fiske Hill

LEXINGTON

First ambush (Concord Militia)

Third ambush (several)

Fourth ambush (Lexington Militia)

To Boston

Sudbury Road

Walden Road

Paul Revere captured (a.m.)

Sudbury River

0   1   2   3   4   5
Miles

Adams and Hancock flee Clarke House

LEXINGTON

Vine Brook

Meeting House

To Woburn

First blood (a.m.) Parker's Militia

Hill

Houses burned

N

Percy's guns

Hill

0 1 2 3 4 5
Yards (100's)

MAP 2

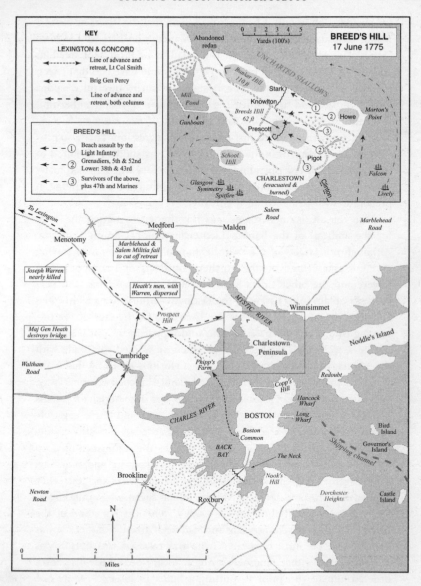

KEY

LEXINGTON & CONCORD

Line of advance and retreat, Lt Col Smith

Brig Gen Percy

Line of advance and retreat, both columns

BREED'S HILL

① Beach assault by the Light Infantry

② Grenadiers, 5th & 52nd Lower: 38th & 43rd

③ Survivors of the above, plus 47th and Marines

0 1 2 3 4 5
Yards (100's)

BREED'S HILL
17 June 1775

Abandoned redan

UNCHARTED SHALLOWS

Bunker Hill 110.0

Stark

Mill Pond

Knowlton

① Howe

Morton's Point

Breeds Hill 62 ft

Gunboats

Prescott

②

③

Pigot ②

③

School Hill

Falcon

Glasgow
Symmetry
Spitfire

CHARLESTOWN
(evacuated & burned)

Clinton

Lively

To Lexington

Medford

Malden

Salem Road

Marblehead Road

Menotomy

Marblehead & Salem Militia fail to cut off retreat

Joseph Warren nearly killed

Heath's men, with Warren, dispersed

Prospect Hill

MYSTIC RIVER

Winnisimmet

Maj Gen Heath destroys bridge

Cambridge

Phipp's Farm

Charlestown Peninsula

Noddle's Island

Waltham Road

Redoubt

Copp's Hill

Charles River

BOSTON

Hancock Wharf

Long Wharf

Bird Island

Governor's Island

Boston Common

BACK BAY

The Neck

Shipping channel

Brookline

Nook's Hill

Castle Island

Newton Road

Roxbury

Dorchester Heights

N

0 1 2 3 4 5
Miles

MAP 3

25

for posterity, observing as he destroyed them that the letters he burned would have damaged the reputations of men who had trusted him. Proof of secret contact between the paladins of Protestant freedom and virtue and the French prior to 1775–76 would have had that effect, even decades after the war. The existence of such powerful weapons at such a place and time of itself is one of those ugly facts so harmful to beautiful theories, in this case the myth of peace-loving farmers spontaneously rising up against unprovoked aggression. They also provide an explanation why the cautious Gage was suddenly inspired to undertake a high-risk operation deep into territory where he had many informers and must have known the local Militia had been drilling in preparation for just such an eventuality.

The role of Samuel Adams was not limited to setting the stage for the ambush of the hapless Lieutenant-Colonel Smith's column. Although not targets of the raid, he and John Hancock were staying at the Clarke House on the northern outskirts of Lexington when Revere and the other riders came through. It was Adams who persuaded Captain John Parker of the Lexington Militia to recall his men and to form battle lines across the Common in the face of the oncoming column of redcoats; he who told John Hancock 'it is not our business, we belong to the Cabinet' when he wanted to parade with the Militia; he who gloated, 'Oh what a glorious morning this is for America' when he heard the firing as he and Hancock scurried away. Who fired the first shot at Lexington is therefore immaterial, for Adams had made sure it would be fired, if not then and there certainly somewhere along the road. Two groups, the redcoats furiously resentful of being spat upon and mocked for years, the colonists puffed up by the impunity with which it had done the spitting and mocking, came together and the discipline of the former failed the test. They opened fire on the dispersing Militia, killing seven and wounding as many more. One of the 'freedom riders' who carried news of the British raid into the countryside and had been arrested earlier (as was Paul Revere, the most celebrated, who was released *sans* horse), was also now killed, either genuinely trying to escape or because his guards ordered him to run prior to putting a bullet in his back. Only one redcoat was wounded, in the leg. Pitcairn was obliged to ride in front of the men to halt the firing and his report was damning: '. . . without any order or regularity, the light infantry began a scattered fire and continued in that situation for some little time, contrary to the repeated orders of both me and the officers that were present'. Among the latter, Lieutenant John Barker of the King's Own excused his failure to maintain control by stating the men were 'so wild they could hear no orders'.

Not merely their discipline and leadership but also their training was to be found seriously deficient in the day's fighting. Smith's 600/700-man raiding party consisted of the flank companies from nine of the eleven regiments in Gage's command, that is the two companies in each regiment selected for their imposing size (grenadiers) and marksmanship (light infantry). The grenadiers appear to have behaved well, but in addition to providing the *casus belli* the light infantry failed to hold the North Bridge at Concord, failed to keep the Militia at a distance during the march back, and might well have surrendered if the sight of one of their wounded mutilated at the bridge had not convinced them the Rebels would slaughter and scalp them. The corrosive effect of garrison duty was evident, but the poor quality of the junior officers upon whom success in skirmishing absolutely depends is no less apparent from the telling statistic that, of the nineteen officer casualties among the 73 killed and 174 wounded (there were also 26 missing, mainly wounded men shamefully left behind), none was hit while away from the main body. The tradition of vigorous leadership among the subalterns of the British Army soon revived, but it seems to have been in abeyance on 19 April 1775.

After an unconscionable delay of five hours caused by mislaid orders, a support column of four full regiments of foot and ten companies of Royal Marines, 1200 men with three light guns, set out from Boston under the command of Brigadier-General Hugh, Earl Percy, heir to the dukedom of Northumberland and an unusually conscientious professional soldier. He had carefully mapped the roads of Massachusetts, and this as much as his handling of the troops under his command caused the casualty pendulum to swing against the Militia. The change in momentum began after a cannonball fired through the Meeting House (church) in Lexington announced that Smith's column had come under the shelter of Percy's guns, posted on hills overlooking the town. He also burned three houses around his position and sent his flankers wide of the line of return march with orders to take no prisoners among those lying in ambush.

Rebel casualties for the day were still only 49 killed and 39 wounded, but if Percy had been given command of the original raiding party the body count would have been more balanced, as he would surely have held the North Bridge until the main force left Concord. Abandoned prematurely, several hundred Militia crossed it to set up the first devastating ambush at the Meriam House. He would not have permitted his men to bunch up like a herd of sheep in the killing grounds overlooked by Brooks and Fiske Hills, and he would certainly have identified the narrow, high-banked zigzag of the Bloody Angle as a perfect ambush point, to be by-passed by marching across country. He might also have torched Lexington to give his pursuers something else to think about. Possibly that is why the totally unsuitable Smith was selected to lead the raiding party instead – Percy was a direct descendant of Shakespeare's wild Hotspur, and must have been an alarming subordinate for the mild Gage.

British memoirists reported the Rebels called out 'God save King Hancock', but the great man was by then on his way to Philadelphia in the handsome uniform he had designed in anticipation of being nominated commander-in-chief of the Continental Army. There were nonetheless five general officers among the Rebel forces, as well as countless colonels, majors, captains and lieutenants, most of whom contributed nothing to the battle. One who tried was the area Militia commander-in-chief, Major-General William Heath, who tore up the bridge over the Charles at Cambridge and tried to block Percy's retreat at Prospect Hill (see MAP 3). He was joined by Dr Joseph Warren, who was possessed of the real authority that came from being the most public face of resistance to British rule, and who had already felt a bullet part his hair in a failed ambush just outside Menotomy in which seven Militiamen died. One shot from a 3-pounder opened the way to Charlestown Peninsula for the exhausted redcoats, for Percy knew that to attempt to return via Cambridge would put his command in a trap. By now, powerful Militia forces from as far afield as Marblehead and Salem were approaching (they, too, had made a late start), and the cannonball that scattered Heath's men was one of the last left. All in all, one cannot disagree with Arthur Tourtellot's conclusion that, with the sole exception of Percy's leadership, 'as an example of military skill [the day] spoke poorly indeed for the Anglo-Saxon people'. The earl was kinder in his assessment of the Militia:

> Whoever looks upon them as an irregular mob, will find himself much mistaken; they have men amongst them who know very well what they are about, having been employed as rangers against the Indians and the Canadians, and this country being much covered with wood and hilly, is very advantageous for their method of fighting. You may depend on it, that as the Rebels have now had time to prepare, they are determined to go through with it, nor will the insurrection here turn out so despicable as it is perhaps imagined at home.

The informer Benjamin Church, fresh from reporting to Gage about the results of the raid, rejoined the conspirators' Committee of Safety and was put in charge of drafting the first propaganda broadside on the subject, a document so overwrought and mendacious that one is compelled to wonder if he was not subtly trying to sabotage it. More effective was the clarion call produced by Dr Warren, in which he warned that women and children *would* suffer at 'the butchering hands of an inhuman soldiery, who, incensed at the obstacles they met in their bloody progress, and enraged at being repulsed from the field of slaughter, will, without the least doubt, take the first opportunity in their power to ravage this devoted country with fire and sword'. This was widely believed to have already happened, not only in the Colonies but in England where Edmund Burke coined the phrase 'drunken and licentious soldiery', a source of perverse pride to the British Army ever since. At the same time, while not wavering in his determination to complete the rupture towards which he had been working for several years, Warren was manly enough to write an apology to Gage:

> Your Excellency, I believe, knows very well the part I have taken in public affairs: I ever scorned disguise. I think I have done my duty: some may think otherwise; but be assured, sir, as far as my influence goes, every thing that can be reasonably required of us to do shall be done, and every thing promised shall be religiously performed ... I have many things that I wish to say to Your Excellency, and most sincerely I wish I had broken through the

formalities which I thought due to your rank, and freely had told you all I knew or thought of public affairs; and I must ever confess, whatever may be the event, that you generously gave me such opening as I now think I ought to have embraced.

Unlike Samuel Adams, Warren seems to have been genuinely worried that conflict in America would weaken Britain in the confrontation with France, but otherwise his moderation is in the same category as Benjamin Franklin's. Neither wanted bloodshed, but both wanted what only war could now achieve. What distinguished Warren was his frankness and courage, both moral and physical, which shine like a beacon across the centuries. He was one of the very few in this wretched conflict whose natural nobility put to shame many of those born to the purple. It was a tragedy for Massachusetts, and probably also for the United States, that this talented and charismatic man felt obliged, perhaps as a subconscious act of expiation, to take his place as a common soldier among the defenders of Breed's Hill two months later, although he had by then been elected president of the Provincial Assembly and a major-general. He was dressed in his best and, if he did not seek it, he did not flinch from the death that found him. His body was later identified by Paul Revere from some dental work he had performed, the first recorded example of what is now a commonplace of forensic medicine.

Some six weeks later Gage at last received substantial reinforcements from Britain with the less welcome accompaniment of the two major-generals who were to succeed him for the duration of the active war, and a third who did more than most to lose it early. In order of seniority they were William Howe, younger brother of Admiral Lord Howe, who together with his brother implemented a doomed policy of limited warfare to encourage reconciliation; Henry Clinton who took over from him and drifted from stalemate to defeat; and John Burgoyne who was to sacrifice an army to his vanity. In the meantime a fire-eating Connecticut Militia captain called Benedict Arnold, who was to play a leading role in the defeat of Burgoyne, had obtained a commission from the Massachusetts Committee of Safety (now the collective commander-in-chief of the 20,000 New Englanders camped around Boston) to seize the British arsenal at Fort Ticonderoga. We shall return to the overtly imperialist aspects of the early rebellion in a later chapter, turning now to the battle that rivals Washington's crossing of the Delaware in late December 1776 as the most iconic event of the whole war.

The imminent arrival of the convoy from Britain was almost certainly the other reason why Gage sent half his garrison to Lexington and Concord. The prospect of reinforcements may have emboldened him, but more likely he feared Howe would be arriving with a commission to replace him, and this goaded him into obeying the categorical instructions from London to disarm the colonists by force, with which he disagreed so profoundly. Before and even more so after the Concord expedition Gage was inexcusably passive in preparing Boston for war, even abandoning a redoubt built by his subordinates on Bunker Hill to close off the Charlestown Peninsula. The construction of a battery on Copp's Hill in Boston, an inadequate substitute for the abandoned work, and of a redoubt on Noddle's Island, was the work of his nominal subordinate Admiral Samuel Graves, whose further advice to seize the Dorchester Heights Peninsula was rejected as 'too rash and sanguinary'. Graves was an officer who lacked courage, professional ability and minimal probity, and this gives us a fair contemporary yardstick against which to measure Gage.

The following is a condensation of the main items in Norman Dixon's study of the psychology of military incompetence. Most of them can be grouped under the general heading of moral cowardice and any one of them can lead to defeat, while a combination of several ensures it:

1. Failure to practise economy of force, in particular to accept heavy immediate casualties in order to save lives and resources in the long term.
2. Clinging to traditional forms/rejection of new ideas.
3. Refusal to accept/suppression of information at variance with preconceived opinion.
4. Underestimation of the enemy/overestimation of one's own capabilities.
5. Indecisiveness/abdication of effective command.

6. Bull-headedness: failure to perform adequate reconnaissance; preference for frontal assaults over manoeuvre; persistence in a course of action after it has failed.

7. Distrust of 'cleverness'/refusal to employ surprise or deception.

8. Penchant for blaming others and/or bad luck for failure.

On the other hand avoiding all these pitfalls does not guarantee success, for the hallmark of great commanders is their ability to infuse an army with their spirit, a genius for war that cannot be learned. Therefore the cold light of hindsight should be used sparingly when judging the performance of one of the most demanding duties known to man, and credit given to those who failed, but did not do so because of egregious professional shortcomings. The commander of the assaults on Breed's Hill on 17 June 1775, generally regarded as among the most bull-headed operations in military history, was the intelligent and competent William Howe. The explicit contradiction between his known qualities and the way the battle was fought is not addressed by the standard critique, which states he should have acted more quickly once dawn revealed the Rebels busily constructing a redoubt on the hill, or landed a force behind them, or waited a little longer until the guns firing from Copp's Hill and the Royal Navy ships in the Charles had shattered the morale of the defenders. He was perfectly aware of these options and chose to reject them. Nor can it be seriously argued that the skill he subsequently showed in amphibious operations, deception and manoeuvre was somehow learned at Breed's Hill. It follows he must have been trying to achieve something more than the mere capture of an enemy post and the recovery of a peninsula that should never have been abandoned.

There is little doubt the first item on Dixon's list provides the answer. Howe was seeking by a single, almost theatrical act to restore the prestige of British arms frittered away by Gage, and to convince the Rebels they could not stand against the regulars. This was not an ill-founded assumption – the Militia seldom stood in the face of a steady advance, not through lack of personal courage but because collective cohesion and steadiness under fire is a great deal more than the sum of the individual parts. Myth also has it that on Breed's Hill the advance of the dim British automata was stopped by clever colonials who sniped their officers. Although the Rebels no doubt included many excellent marksmen, they famously held their fire until 'they could see the whites of their eyes', by which time the British officers would have been behind their troops with the NCO file closers, maintaining line discipline. Furthermore, after the first volley there was little chance of selective fire on the smoke-shrouded black powder battlefield, particularly on a still and oppressively hot day. The severe attrition among British officers has the more simple explanation that when the assaults faltered they had to pull rather than push their men back into action, and were therefore the first back into point-blank range.

Although the engagement was seen as a humiliating defeat by the Rebels at the time, giving rise to a surge in desertions and the court martial and dismissal of a colonel and five captains, it was a moral victory of the highest order for the men who held Breed's Hill, despite shameful lack of support from their fellows at Bunker Hill and on the mainland. The conclusive argument in favour of this verdict is that it was so perceived by the British high command, which now resigned itself to a wider war. It was one thing for troops who had lost their combat edge in prolonged garrison duty to be pecked at from cover as they marched along a country road under the command of a third rate officer, another altogether for the heart to be torn out of regiments fresh from the British Isles when they were doing what they were trained to do under the direction of some of the best officers in the army. With the new arrivals the army in Boston numbered about 10,000 – nowhere near enough to occupy the colony – and it seemed worthwhile to gamble a quarter of them to overawe the dangerously numerous armed rabble surrounding the city. To a degree it did so, for the Rebels undertook no further active operations against Boston. But it was not the striking and overwhelming success that might have made them all think better of their naïve enthusiasm for war.

When asked why the Confederates lost at Gettysburg, General Pickett dryly answered he had always thought the Yankees had something to do with it, and they had plenty to do with the outcome at Breed's Hill. The redoubt itself and the supporting breastworks were well laid out, and the man who supervised the work and directed the defence was Colonel William Prescott, a man offered a royal commission when he was only nineteen for service at the 1745 siege of Louisbourg. He had chosen instead to return to farming and now, like Cincinnatus, he was in arms again at the behest of his fellow citizens. Holding three triangular fieldworks (*flèches*) covering the refused flank to the north of the hill and a hastily reinforced fence running down towards the Mystic River was Captain Thomas Knowlton, sent forward from Bunker Hill by General Israel Putnam, both Connecticut officers. Lastly, holding the beachfront behind a rudimentary breastwork was the personal following of John Stark, who had been second in command of Rogers' Rangers during the French and Indian War. Although he later relented, at this early stage of the war his contempt for politicians was so uncompromising that he had refused a commission from his native New Hampshire, and so had no formal rank.

About two-thirds of the 4000 Rebels on the peninsula manned the front line, armed with a logistician's nightmare of assorted calibre muskets, and at the last moment abandoned by their artillery support. The men on Breed's Hill itself had gone forward before anyone else, worked all night, bore the brunt of the bombardment and were the focus of the assaults. That they stood is testimony to the example set by Prescott and his fellow colonels, six of whom were among the 138 killed, 276 wounded and 36 captured. Along the refused flank, where Howe directed the main thrust of his first assault, the light infantry and grenadiers sent against Stark and Knowlton were shattered, with some companies reduced to less than a dozen men. The casualties bear witness to the determination with which they pressed home their attack, but their opponents were fresher, unharassed by artillery, and had come forward through the crowds at the neck of the peninsula and Bunker Hill, where the faint-hearted had dropped out.

Of the 2300 British troops involved in the assault, 226 were killed outright and 828 wounded, of whom a much higher than usual proportion died of infected wounds. Army surgeons blamed this on the metallic debris fired by the Rebels, indicating many were using shotguns or antique blunderbusses. Among the dead were twenty-seven officers, including the gallant Pitcairn as he led his Marines in the last assault on the redoubt, and a further sixty-three were wounded. All of Howe's staff were killed or wounded as a result of his decision to step out ahead of the men in the second assault, and he himself was splashed with their blood. Francis, Lord Rawdon, whom we shall meet again, had a ball graze his scalp as he was pinned down next to the wall. 'Our men grew impatient', he recalled, 'and all crying "Push on, push on," advanced with infinite spirit to attack the work'. Now it was bayonet time, and the defenders had none so at last they broke. Despite Putnam's efforts to hold a second line of resistance, the men on Bunker Hill fled across the narrow neck of the peninsula, swept by the 9-pounders of the shallow draft *Symmetry*, and the individual 12-pounders mounted on two gunboats that had given Howe's troops the only close supporting fire they received all day. With their right flank in the air, Knowlton's and Stark's men fell back in good order, even salvaging one of the cannon abandoned at Bunker Hill, and Burgoyne noted it was 'no flight: it was even covered with bravery and military skill'.

Howe had sent in the first and second assaults with the men carrying heavy knapsacks containing supplies for several days, evidently intending to press on after the walkover he expected. The knapsacks along with that illusion had been discarded before the third assault, and now there was little hope of mounting the vigorous pursuit urged by Clinton, who had crossed to Charlestown without authority from Gage and led a company of bandsmen and walking wounded back to battle. But there was no enthusiasm for it among the exhausted men taking stock of their losses on the ramparts of Breed's Hill. With so many commissioned and noncommissioned officers down, the battle was finally won by the grit and determination of the common soldier. They seldom left historians much to work with, but the dying John Randon spoke for them all through gasps of pain in his last letter to his wife and children:

> I have received two balls, one in my groin and the other near my breast. I am now so weak with the loss of blood, that I can hardly dictate these few lines, as the last tribute of my unchange- able love to you. The surgeons inform me that three hours will be the utmost I can survive.

For all the outstanding courage of the attackers, the defenders finally broke because they were low on ammunition, unsighted by smoke and felt abandoned by the rest of their army. They had not been brought under effective artillery bombardment, always a winner against raw troops, and if the British commanders had anticipated the tenacity of the resistance they would encounter, no doubt Graves would have been asked to bring the 32-gun broadside of his flagship HMS *Somerset* to bear on the redoubt, instead of hiding her on the other side of Boston. However it was not the Royal Navy that needed to reassert its prestige, and nine days after the tragedy Gage wrote his professional epitaph to the Secretary of State for War:

> These people show a spirit and courage against us they never showed against the French, and everybody has judged them from their formed appearance and behaviour when joined with the King's forces in the last war; which has led many into great mistakes. They are now spirited up by a rage and enthusiasm as great as ever people were possessed of, and you must proceed in earnest or give the business up. A small body acting in one place will not avail. You must have large armies, making diversions on different sides, to divide their forces. The loss we have sustained is greater than we can bear. Small armies cannot afford such losses, especially when the advantage gained tends to little more than the gaining of a post . . . We are here . . . taking the bull by the horns, attacking the enemy in their strongest parts. I wish this cursed place was burned. The only use is its harbour . . . but in all other respects it is the worst place either to act offensively from, or defensively. I have before wrote your Lordship my opinion that a large army must at length be employed to reduce these people, and mentioned the hiring of foreign troops. I fear it must come to that, or else to avoid a land war and make use only of your fleet.

He would have been fully justified in adding an 'I told you so' paragraph or two. But Gage needed his army income to sustain him through a retirement made bleak by the loss of his American investments. If this influenced him to send the fateful expedition to Concord and to assent to Howe's plan for Breed's Hill against his better judgement, the responsibility rests with the government that chose to ignore his warnings but not to relieve him for so many years. He politely pointed the finger at their unwillingness to think things through in the passage cited above, and might have added that many officials in

London, notably the new Colonial Secretary Lord George Germain, tended to trust to their own experience of war in Europe over the expertise of officers who had done their best soldiering in America.

The way to deal with Massachusetts had always been to enforce restrictions on its trade while relaxing them in the other colonies, thereby subverting colonial solidarity. By seeking a quick military fix instead, the reverse occurred. The Continental Congress adopted the army around Boston and, to the palpable chagrin of Hancock, selected Virginia's favourite son George Washington to command it. There could be no other choice – Virginia was not only much the most populous colony but was also vital to ensure the other southern colonies did not go their own way. The new commander-in-chief was shocked by what he found when he took up his appointment, and further discomfited by a mutiny in the sole regiment present from Virginia, a tough crew that rose up in arms to break some of their comrades out of the prison to which they had been consigned for . . . insubordination. In letters to confidants written at the end of August (here run together), and in language that reminds us how little knowledge of, or liking for each other, the colonists had at the start of this war, Washington sniffed:

> I dare say the men would fight very well (if properly officered) although they are an exceedingly dirty and nasty people; had they been properly conducted at [Breed's] Hill or those that were there properly supported, the regulars would have met with a shameful defeat, and a much more considerable loss than they did . . . such a dearth of public spirit, and want of virtue, such stock-jobbing and fertility in all the low arts to obtain advantages of one kind or another in this great change of military arrangements, I never saw before and pray God I may never be witness to again . . . it is among the most difficult tasks I ever undertook in my life to induce these people to believe that there is, or can be, danger until the bayonet is pushed at their breasts; not that it proceeds from any uncommon prowess, but rather from an unaccountable kind of stupidity in the lower class of these people which, believe me, prevails but too generally among the officers of the Massachusetts part of the army who are nearly of the same kidney with the privates.

John Burgoyne would not have changed a word – before 17 June. And surely no British aristocrat in 1775 could have improved on the words written in 1789 by John Adams' wife Abigail, to describe Captain Daniel Shays, who had fought at Breed's Hill, and the yeomen of Massachusetts when they rose up under the banner of no taxation without representation against the exactions imposed on them by the Boston merchant oligarchy and its unconditional servant Samuel Adams. They were, she wrote, 'ignorant, wrestless desperadoes, without conscience or principles, who have led a deluded multitude to follow their standard, under pretence of grievances which had no existance but in their immaginations'. Thus the brave new dawn of liberty and virtue – the same ineffable attitude with worse spelling.

3

NEW YORK AND NEW JERSEY

H OWE TOOK OVER in October 1775, at a time when the military
intelligence available to him was sharply reduced by the un-
ravelling of Gage's network of informers. One of Benjamin Church's
reports was intercepted in July, and he was imprisoned after the cipher
was cracked in October. At about the same time Benjamin Thompson's
cover was blown,* but he escaped and made it to Boston by sea
from Connecticut. His final report to Howe makes fascinating reading,
especially as it so closely echoes Washington's comments on the dirti-
ness and insubordination of the Rebel army, 'notwithstanding the
indefatigable endeavours of Mr Washington and the other generals,
and particularly of Adjutant General [Horatio] Gates'. However the
crucial piece of intelligence it contained was that the Rebel army was
ravaged by disease:

> But the number of soldiers that have died in the camp is compara-
> tively small to those vast numbers that have gone off to the
> interior parts of the country. For immediately upon being taken
> down with these disorders they have in general been carried back
> ... to their own homes, where they have not only died themselves,
> but by spreading the infection among their relatives and friends
> have introduced such a general mortality throughout New Eng-
> land as was never known since its first planting.

Both Gage and Howe wanted to evacuate the army from Boston
to Halifax before the winter, to make an early start in 1776 against
New York, but a shortage of suitable shipping made it impracticable.

* See Appendix A for a brief summary of the life of this extraordinary man.

39

Thus while 9000 men were inactive in Boston, fewer than 1000 were available to defend Canada against the opportunistic Rebel invasion mounted at this time, and when the evacuation at last took place, the Rebels perceived it as the much-vaunted British Army being driven out and were correspondingly heartened. This was thanks to an obscure Maine-born bookseller named Henry Knox, who by Herculean exertions brought forty-three cannon overland from Fort Ticonderoga, among them a few 24-pounders and a larger number of mortars. Howe awoke on 5 March 1776 to find the Rebels had done it again and built an artillery fort overnight, on Dorchester Heights, and subsequently another on Nook's Hill where it could bring the fortifications at the Boston Neck under fire. What he did not know was that Washington had supplemented his lack of large cannon with some convincing dummies, and lacked the mortar bombs and even the powder to undertake a serious bombardment.

Twelve days later, after a half-hearted plan to storm the Heights was aborted by bad weather and under an informal agreement with Washington not to torch the city in return for a cease-fire, the army and navy along with more than 1000 Loyalists sailed out of Boston harbour, never to return. The British initiative that followed this extremely bad start was one of those 'solutions' posited on domestic considerations cringingly familiar to all who have ever served their country abroad. The North administration compounded its selection of William Howe, an MP who had once assured his constituents he would not serve against the colonists, by appointing his like-minded elder brother Admiral Lord Richard Howe to command the North American fleet. Both were able officers, and under a political governor general might have devised a winning strategy. But they were also appointed peace commissioners, although granted no discretion over the terms they might offer to achieve it, surrendering the 'good cop, bad cop' negotiating option, and undermining military effectiveness with no compensating political advantage. Lastly, the appointment of the Howes as the supreme authority in both the military and the political spheres blatantly offended against the strict separation of the two powers that was one of the core principles of the Glorious Revolution of 1688, thereby making the Rebels and their supporters in Britain the gift of a highly emotive propaganda issue.

It might have been possible to combine the political and military functions against an uncertain enemy, but the Rebel leaders had already raised the stakes by invading Canada and now forced the issue with the Declaration of Independence. It was accompanied by a pogrom against Loyalists and of the property redistribution that is the cement of all revolutions, and by the first appearance of that signature American device, the extraction of oaths of allegiance amid deliberately incited public hysteria. The Declaration itself was little more than a drawing together of various strands of Rebel propaganda, with particular emphasis on the fears of the moment. Among these were the German mercenaries known to constitute a significant proportion of the force approaching New York under the command of the Howe brothers, the largest expedition Britain had ever sent overseas, and the greater success enjoyed by the British in recruiting Native American auxiliaries. Originally a broadside signed on 4 July only by John Hancock as president and Charles Thomson as Secretary of Congress, the Declaration represented an irrevocable act of treason, causing reluctance even among those who voted for it to append their signatures. Some never did and one, the New Jersey delegate Richard Stockton, later revoked his signature and swore loyalty to the king in order to get out of a British prison. With the exception of Samuel Adams they were men of means with much to lose, but in the end they voted and signed not according to interest, but because they were backed into the corner created by their own rhetoric.

On the other side of the Atlantic, despite pressure from the king who for some time had believed the colonists must submit or triumph and who rejected a last-minute 'Olive Branch' petition from Congress, Lord North still flinched from irreversible confrontation. The peace proposals he authorized the Howe brothers to offer granted the colonists' right to tax themselves in exchange for the maintenance of notional British sovereignty, by this time wholly inadequate as an incentive and highlighting how deepy unsuited North's skills as a parliamentary manager were to the conduct of a war. George III tried to supply the guiding will that might have imposed strategic coherence and cannot escape blame for the outcome, but the main burden lies with an oligarchy passing through a period of unusually venomous factionalism. It is impossible to accept the sincerity of the support for the Rebel cause expressed by opposition spokesmen such as Barré, Burke, Fox and Wilkes. They were all protégés of Shelburne and Rockingham, who had shaped the policies the Rebels rejected, and their commitment to truth, justice and the American way was shown when Fox formed a government with North in 1783–84, fairly denounced by the king as 'the most unprincipled coalition the annals of this or any other nation can equal'. Although the war conducted by Sandwich at the Admiralty, Germain at the Colonial Office and the Howes in America could undoubtedly have been waged better in the absolute, they were among the most able men of their class at this time, and there is little reason to believe any other combination – under North – would have produced a better result.

The Boston army went first to Halifax, where the Loyalists disembarked, reinforcements arrived from Britain, and the army was reorganized to contribute to the relief of Québec (see Chapter Five), to send an expedition south to join with further reinforcements (see Chapter Seven), while the main force prepared to descend on New York. The first landing was on Staten Island, where hundreds of Loyalists welcomed it. Unwisely, in some cases, for the troops had been cooped up for a long time, and Lord Rawdon commented 'a girl cannot step into the bushes to pluck a rose without running the most imminent risk of being ravished'. Howe's order book records a surge of floggings and hangings, but these were usually for looting, reminding us that even the civilian penal code at this time prescribed the death penalty for quite minor offences against property, while taking a broader view of personal violence. On 12 July his brother arrived with an even larger fleet, 150 ships to add to the 138 already present, and three more convoys shortly added to the total, including the expedition returning from Charleston.

William Howe had already sent frigates up the Hudson as far as Tappan Bay, but the narrow access to the port of New York was guarded by several artillery forts. The highest, and hence most dangerous to shipping while being least vulnerable to naval bombardment, was on the Brooklyn Peninsula overlooking the narrowest point between Manhattan and Long Island, where the Rebel army had not been idle since marching down from Massachusetts. The peninsula was enclosed by redoubts linked with ramparts, bristling with trees

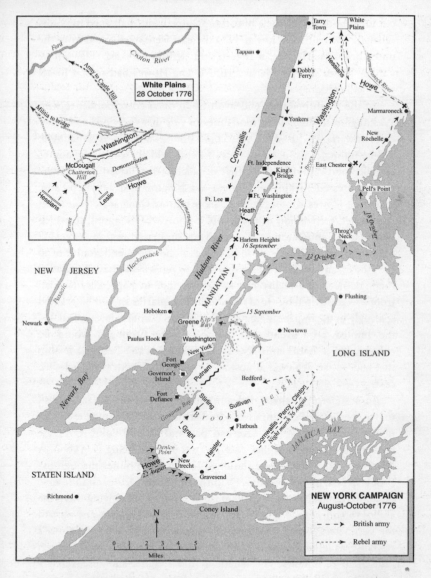

White Plains
28 October 1776

Ford

Croton River

Army to Castle Hill

Militia to bridge

Washington

McDougall

Chatterton Hill

Demonstration

Leslie

Howe

Hessians

Bronx

Marmaroneck

Tarry Town

White Plains

Tappan

Dobb's Ferry

Hessians

Howe

Marmaroneck River

Yonkers

Marmaroneck

New Rochelle

Cornwallis

Washington

Bronx River

Ft. Independence

King's Bridge

East Chester

Pell's Point

Ft. Lee

Ft. Washington

Heath

Throg's Neck

16 October

Harlem Heights
16 September

12 October

NEW JERSEY

Hackensack

HUDSON RIVER

Flushing

Passaic

Hoboken

MANHATTAN

Kip's Bay

15 September

Newark

Greene

Paulus Hook

Washington

Newtown

New York

LONG ISLAND

Fort George

Putnam

Bedford

Governor's Island

Stirling

Sullivan

Brooklyn Heights

Fort Defiance

Gowanus Bay

Grant

Flatbush

Cornwallis - Percy - Clinton
Night march 26 August

Heister

Newark Bay

STATEN ISLAND

Denice Point

Howe

22 August

New Utrecht

Gravesend

JAMAICA BAY

Richmond

Coney Island

N

NEW YORK CAMPAIGN
August–October 1776

- – – → British army
- - - - → Rebel army

0 1 2 3 4 5
Miles

MAP 4

cut to point downhill, their branches stripped and sharpened to points (abatis). The cultivated lowlands to the east were overlooked from the outer Brooklyn Heights, a rugged and densely wooded ridge whose narrow passes were similarly fortified. The Howes had reason to act with deliberation.

In the meantime they endeavoured to open correspondence with Washington to discuss the modalities of prisoner exchange and other rules of warfare, with which they could not be sure he was acquainted. To the ultimate cost of thousands of Rebel soldiers who were soon to be killed and captured, the initiative failed at first because the letters were addressed to him as 'George Washington Esq.', then because when the Howes consented to address him as General he claimed it constituted recognition of the lawful authority of Congress, to which he owed his appointment. To receive a shysterish response to what they regarded as a mark of indulgence cannot have endeared him to the Howes, and the light-heartedness of his replies may have persuaded them he needed a reality check. British and, in particular, Hessian troops were advised by word of mouth that quarter should be granted sparingly in the impending battle. The Howes may also have calculated the limited attractiveness of North's peace proposals would be enhanced by a sharp reminder of the costs of war to a Rebel leadership that had, so far, achieved almost all its political objectives at negligible cost.

In a superbly orchestrated amphibious operation on 22 August, 10,000 men with attendant cavalry and artillery landed along the stretch of Long Island between Gravesend Bay and Denice Point. Over the next three days the number rose to 23,000 men, facing 12–13,000. A third of the defenders were stationed to cover the routes through the Brooklyn Heights at Gowanus, Flatbush and Bedford, the rest in reserve on and around the Brooklyn Peninsula, interior lines giving them the ability to concentrate quickly to counter a thrust against any part of the perimeter. It was a textbook deployment, and so might Howe's response have been had it not been for Clinton, who took it upon himself to reconnoitre the length of the Heights and discovered a fourth, unguarded pass two miles east of Bedford, which would permit the entire Rebel position to be outflanked. Much though William Howe had come to dislike the second-guessing of his second in command,

Clinton's proposed route offered the only alternative to a protracted siege operation.

Accordingly Clinton led 10,000 men with thirty guns to this pass during the night of 26–27 August. The next morning, Heister's 5000 Hessians and Highlanders pinned Sullivan at the Flatbush Pass while the same number under Grant, later joined by 2000 Marines, attacked the Gowanus Pass defended by William Alexander, who styled himself Lord Stirling although the title had been denied him by the College of Heralds. While the defenders were thus engaged, Clinton's cavalry burst out of Bedford behind them. Thanks to the sacrificial heroism of Stirling and the socially elite battalions from Maryland and Delaware under his command, Grant's jaw of the pincer was held open long enough to permit some of the defenders to escape. Only one officer and nine men of Maryland's 'Dandy Fifth' got away, leaving behind 256 dead and 150 captured, most of them wounded. Stirling had roused them to fever pitch by reference to a speech given in Parliament by Grant in 1775, in which he swore to march across America with 5000 men. Earl Cornwallis, commanding the British brigade to his front, was pleased to find himself fighting against gentlemen and respectfully observed 'General Lord Stirling fought like a wolf'. However it seems Stirling's enthusiasm for war did not survive this dreadful encounter, and he was never to be so effective again.

Howe reported 3300 Rebel casualties, practically the whole of Sullivan's command, among them chillingly few living wounded and only 1097 prisoners. In return the British lost five officers and fifty-six men killed in Stirling's desperate rearguard action. The Hessians reported groups of men who pretended to surrender, only to open fire when they approached, but this was an excuse for the murder of men who had genuinely ceased to offer resistance, proof of which is that the Hessians only suffered two fatal casualties. As an officer of the 71st explained, 'we took care to tell the Hessians that the Rebels had resolved to give no quarter – to them in particular – which made them fight desperately, and put all to death that fell into their hands ... it was fine sight to see with what alacrity they [and our brave Highlanders] dispatched the Rebels with the bayonets after we had surrounded them so that they could not resist'.

It was a comprehensive rout, but Howe checked the assault before it could crash into the lines across the peninsula, which in the opinion of his senior field officers could have been carried without great loss. That is why armies have commanders-in-chief – an unplanned assault on 9000 men behind strong fieldworks would certainly have been expensive and might well have failed. Controversy over whether or not this was a lost opportunity tends to divert attention from the more evidently questionable behaviour of Howe's opponents. Washington and his most trusted subordinate Nathanael Greene, a Rhode Island anchorsmith with no previous military experience, had spent two months organizing the defences and should therefore have fought the battle. Instead Sullivan took over on Long Island on 20 August after Greene developed an illness that lasted precisely as long as the battle, while Washington appointed his rival Putnam to overall command on the 24th, when Howe's army was already knocking at the door.

The heavy losses suffered by the Connecticut Militia at Brooklyn Heights, after which a further 6000 went home, seems to have triggered a rapid process of disaffection in a colony until now second only to Massachusetts in popular support for the rebellion. By the end of the war coastal Connecticut was trading so freely with the enemy that it can be regarded as part of the hinterland from which the British Army in New York drew supplies and forage, without which it could not have remained. Some evidence that the rot set in before Brooklyn Heights can be gleaned from the memoirs of Joseph Martin, a teenager enrolled in a Connecticut regiment of the Continental Army, who recalled a 'fine' lieutenant 'snivelling and blubbering' before the battle, begging forgiveness of his men for offences Martin did not specify, and presumably fearing a shot in the back. In the next paragraph he noted:

> The officers of the new levies wore cockades of different colours to distinguish them from the standing forces, as they were called; the field officers wore red, the captains white, and the subaltern officers green. While we were resting our Lieutenant-Colonel and Major (our Colonel not being with us), took their cockades from their hats; being asked the reason, the Lieutenant-Colonel replied, that he was willing to risk his life in the cause of his country, but was unwilling to stand a particular mark for the enemy to fire at.

Had any German or British officer removed distinctions of rank he would have been obliged to resign his commission by the ostracism of his peers. Those of the Rebel army were less demanding of each other, but the private soldier's universal rule is that only courage gives executive substance to rank and privilege in battle. The lieutenant-colonel mentioned above does seem to have retained his epaulettes, for Martin approvingly noted that one of them was shot off his shoulder at Harlem Heights, where the Rebel rearguard under Connecticut's Knowlton, hero of Breed's Hill, and the Virginian Andrew Leitch checked the British pursuit. Washington wrote that the skirmish 'inspired our troops prodigiously, they find that it only requires resolution and good officers to make an enemy (that they stood in too much dread of) give way'. However both Knowlton and Leitch were killed, underlining that the inspirational leadership required to make untrained soldiers stand against regulars came at a high cost.

The stand at Harlem Heights closed an otherwise disastrous chapter for Rebel arms begun by a landing at Kip's Bay behind the main Rebel force on 15 September. Washington had successfully evacuated the Brooklyn Peninsula during the night of 29–30 August thanks to a north wind and adverse tide that kept the Royal Navy from patrolling the straits. It was on these shaken men, with Greene back in command, that the next blow fell. The assault was commanded by Clinton, who defined himself in a revealing diary note: 'My advice has ever been to avoid even the possibility of a check. We live by victory. Are we sure of it this day? I doubt it'. Although the shoreline was rocky and fortified, and the first wave of Hessians, crammed like cattle in the assault barges, sang the German equivalent of 'Nearer my God to thee', naval bombardment put the defenders to flight. Martin again:

> Every man that I saw was endeavouring by all sober means to escape from death or captivity ... the men were confused, being without officers to command them – I do not recollect of seeing a commissioned officer from the time I left the lines on the banks of the East River, until I met the [one who suggested he abandon a wounded comrade because 'the country will be rid of one who can do it no good'] in the evening.

47

Once again outflanked at a place they had not thought practicable, this time with nobody else to blame, Washington and Greene became paralysed after trying unsuccessfully to rally the men, and the stunned commander-in-chief was finally led away by his aides. Reports that he exclaimed, 'Are these the men with which I am to defend America?' are rightly dismissed by his biographer – he was a better man than that. Putnam galloped back to New York and ordered the retreat of the 10–12,000 men posted there, along with most of Knox's artillery corps. Those who believe Howe missed an opportunity to cut them off should ask themselves what would have been the likely fate of 4000 Hessians, even if joined by the leading elements of the 9000-man British second wave, had they got between this force and the 9000 men under the command of Heath at the northern end of Manhattan Island. As it was the Rebels abandoned their main supply depot and all the heavy artillery in the redoubts around the southern end of Manhattan, with negligible loss to the British Army until the rearguard action at Harlem Heights.

Before the Kip's Bay landing William Howe had once again tried to parley with the Rebels, this time with their political leadership. Congress sent John Adams for New England, balanced by Edward Rutledge from South Carolina, whose contempt for the 'low cunning and levelling principles' of the Yankees was no secret, and Benjamin Franklin for the middle colonies, the latter known to Howe from social contact in London. Neither he nor they had been granted any discretion, so the meeting was a waste of time, but Howe was sufficiently nettled by one of Franklin's witticisms to blurt out 'I suppose you'll endeavour to give us employment in Europe'. This was a slip of the tongue – he was not supposed to know the old man had finally prevailed upon a reluctant Congress to send a representative to Paris. But it also betrays his astonishment that men whose cause had just suffered a resounding defeat should have treated even the meagre carrot he had to offer with light-hearted disdain. The reason appears to be that both the political and military leaders of the rebellion believed the huge mobilization they had authorized would stop Howe, or at least inflict disabling losses on him, product of a dangerous complacency arising from the early engagements in Massachusetts.

We do not know what fluttering there may have been in the

congressional dovecote after Kip's Bay, but at ground level the mood among the guano-spattered men was surly. During the Harlem Heights fight a general's aide, alas unidentified, drew his sword on a Connecticut sergeant whom he accused of cowardice. The man, who had been sent to the rear to fetch ammunition, cocked and levelled his musket, for which he was later arrested and condemned to death. Martin observed it was as well he was reprieved at the last minute, 'for his blood would not have been the only blood that was spilt – the troops were greatly exasperated, and showed what their feelings were by their lively and repeated cheerings after the reprieve, but more so by their secret and open threats before it'. The morale problem was entirely the result of indifferent leadership, for at this time the men were still properly paid, clothed and occasionally well fed, and there was no shortage of artillery, small arms and ammunition. Myth has it these were either personal weapons or stocks seized from poorly guarded depots, but even if we are to suppose that every colony gave up every weapon it captured in 1775–76, more cannon were lost by the Rebels during the New York campaign than the British Army had ever felt it necessary to store in the colonies. It is impossible to reconcile the spontaneous uprising thesis with this proof of serious long-term planning and preparation.

In addition to a patchy but adequate supply situation, the men were inclined to be tolerant of those officers who did not presume too much on their rank, recognizing that in an army of amateurs all were learning their trade as they went along. Nonetheless, generals who send men to defeat lose authority, no matter how wonderful their characters, while those who lead them to victory are adored, even if they have the personal qualities of a warthog. The next test of Washington's leadership was at White Plains, at the crossroads of highways between several ferries across the Hudson River and Connecticut, and between upper and lower New York. This is another under-studied engagement, possibly because it never developed into a full-blown battle, but it deserves closer inspection as an example of the chess-like manoeuvring to isolate enemy strong points so characteristic of eighteenth century European warfare.

Faced with a strong defensive position across the neck of northern Manhattan, and the formidable natural barrier of the channel between

Manhattan and the mainland crowned by artillery redoubts, all backed by what was still a large Rebel field army (see MAP p. 43), Howe mounted another amphibious operation. Encountering opposition at Throg's Neck, he found a disembarkation point more to his liking further north at Pell's Point, and drove the local defenders away. The ailing Heister had gone home after disagreements with Howe and Knyphausen led the spearhead. The force eventually numbered about 13,000, half of them Hessians, but instead of trying to cut off the Rebel army Howe conducted a parallel pursuit to Marmaroneck, brushing aside Militia as he went, until he learned where the enemy intended to make a stand. The Rebel vanguard was led by Lord Stirling, who had been exchanged for Cortlandt Skinner and Montfort Browne, royal officials taken hostage in New Jersey and the Bahamas respectively. He had orders to hold White Plains, at the strategic crossroads of the highways to northern New York and to Connecticut, and fortified a line across the headwaters of the Bronx and Marmaroneck Rivers (see inset MAP p. 43). After Washington arrived with the bulk of the army, he ordered a further line of fortifications to be built on higher ground beyond but still commanding the crossroads.

The Rebels may have had a numerical advantage, but estimates of their numbers are at best an educated guess, not only in this campaign but throughout much of the war, because of the often great discrepancy between men on the books and those fit to fight ('effectives'), and because the Militia component was always undercounted by Continental officers, including Washington, with the intent of persuading Congress to provide them with a long-service, 'proper' army. It is intriguing that the two Rebel generals who held the Militia in the highest regard were the most experienced in formal warfare. Horatio Gates and Charles Lee were ex-British Army officers who dismissed the possibility the Rebels might create a field army capable of defeating their old service, and advocated a 'cloud of mosquitoes' approach to harass the enemy and limit his territorial control to the ground he occupied. Lee went further and recommended the adoption of a scorched earth policy. Precisely such tactics had thwarted French armies in Germany earlier in the century, but the concept was too radical for Washington and the class he represented to stomach. Since at this stage he trusted neither his troops nor his own generalship to fight a battle of manoeuvre, Washington's sole thought was to put the men behind breastworks and wait for the British to attack them.

However Washington had not understood the need to entice his opponent to act as he wished, for the White Plains position was so strong that even a commander a great deal more bull-headed than Howe would have hesitated to mount a frontal assault. Instead he made a demonstration with the bulk of the army in the valley to pin the defenders of the first line, and outflanked it by seizing Chatterton's Hill, a dominant feature which neither Stirling nor Washington had thought to fortify until the eve of battle. The hill was held by a mixed force of Continental Army and Militia under John McDougall, a pre-war political activist whose previous command experience had been limited to privateering during the War for Empire, and who made it abundantly plain he was out of his element this day. The eyewitness account of Captain John Peebles of the 42nd (Black Watch) provides a valuable insight into the impression left upon the British Army by the first pitched battle Washington directed personally:

> When our troops moved down, the enemy rushed towards the highbanks of the Bronx in great numbers and kept up a very heavy fire upon them as they passed the river which they kept up all the time they were forming and moving up the steep hill on the other side but the steadiness and intrepidity of our troops beat them from their strong grounds where they had taken the advantage of fences and stone walls, and made them retire back on the remaining body that was posted on the hill, who immediately turned tail with the fugitives and ran off in the greatest confusion to their works on the other hill [in front of White Plains] ... and exhibited to our whole army (who were looking on) a recent proof of their inferiority in courage and discipline.

Unobserved by Peebles and the rest of the army, Howe had detached a Hessian division to advance on the western side of the Bronx River. It was this, not the expensive British assault, which caused the defenders to abandon the hill in such haste. In contrast, Joseph Martin's view was that he and his fellows had fallen back after stopping an attack that threatened to outflank the main Continental line, after which 'the British were very civil, and indeed they generally were, after they had received a check from Brother Jonathan for any of their rude actions; they seldom repeated them, at least not until the affair that caused the reprimand had ceased in some measure to be remembered'. Thus one side saw an easy victory, the other a creditable holding action, followed by an orderly withdrawal to the lines behind White Plains, and then across the Croton River to a yet stronger position at Castle Hill.

Leaving 5000 men under Heath to prevent an advance up the Hudson Valley that Howe had no intention of undertaking, Washington crossed the Hudson and hurried south to the now-isolated twin forts named for him and for Lee, his second-in-command, whom he also detached with 6000 men at Tappan. The hope of repeating Breed's Hill now led him to commit the crowning error of the campaign by failing to evacuate Manhattan while he still had the chance. The Rebels held the northern end, with Fort Washington itself the central keep of extensive fieldworks festooned with dense *abatis* taken from the carefully cleared killing grounds to their front. Faith that the shovel could beat the bayonet was dispersed forever by the clinical efficiency with which the fort and its surrounding works were taken, as described succinctly by Peebles:

> It was near noon when a signal was made for Gen. Knyphausen to begin his attack on the enemy posted on the high ground nearest the Hudson River. He . . . sustained a very heavy irregular fire for above 20 minutes [until] the Hessians who are slow but steady troops . . . at last gained the summit of the hill. In the meantime the Light Infantry and Guards were landed at the foot of the high ground [along the Harlem River] and dashed up the hill with great alacrity, driving the enemy before them . . . While these operations were going on to the northward, Lord Percy was advancing [from the south], and the 42nd [Peebles' regiment] crossed Harlem River 4 miles below King's Bridge, where they were opposed by a considerable body of the enemy posted on those steep hills who began their fire upon them before they landed. By about 3 o'clock in the afternoon all the attacks had succeeded and we were in possession of all the high grounds in the environs of Fort Washington, having taken and killed a good number . . . and driven the rest into the fort: Gen. Knyphausen

proceeded with his Hessians to the very barrier of the fort which being surrounded on all quarters they beat a parley and desired to capitulate ... about 2600 [nearly 2900] of their best troops were here and most of them riflemen, Col. McGaw [an old acquaintance of Peebles] commanding officer.

At Fort Lee, on the other side of the Hudson, Washington 'seemed in agony as he saw the fort surrendered'. There followed one of those evasions of responsibility that cast a shadow on his reputation. He wrote, 'I had given it as my opinion to General Greene, under whose care it was, that it would be best to evacuate the place; but, as the order was discretionary, and his opinion differed from mine, it was unhappily delayed too long, to my great grief'. This was indefensible, as was permitting Greene to leave the fort when it came under attack. On the other side sixty-year old Knyphausen led his grenadiers, tearing down barriers with his own hands, and we may be sure the contrast was in the minds of the men marched through the streets of New York, amid the execration of the civilian population. Pennsylvanian Captain Alexander Graydon observed 'it was obvious in the calculation of this assemblage of female loyalty, the war was at an end, and that the whole of the Rebel Army, Washington and all, were safe in durance'.

Among the less attractive aspects of the canonical accounts is that every defeat is attributed either to treachery, or to lack of spirit among the 'losers'. Both have been advanced to explain this debacle, and neither applies. The defenders were Washington's best men, in his estimation 'trained with more than common attention', and the value of the information provided by deserters was somewhat naturally over-stated in their claims for compensation. The simpler truth is there were too few troops to stop four converging attacks, and no lives should have been risked to defend a fort whose inability to stop the Royal Navy navigating the Hudson had already been demonstrated. The loss of Fort Washington was the culmination of a series of gross command blunders, all deriving from an amateur's underestimation of what a properly handled professional army could do.

Thus far Rebels seeking to surrender had found themselves on the wrong side of the rules that governed professional warfare, and the quality of the mercy shown to them had been further strained by their resort to arson on Long Island, followed by what may have been an accidental fire that burned more than 500 houses in New York during the night of 20–21 September. Washington chortled about this, but it was fatal for the volunteers he had sent to gather intelligence, among them Nathan Hale, a young member of Knowlton's Rangers, who was among those rounded up that night and hanged. The normally unemotional Captain Johann Ewald, a Hessian Jäger officer, upon seeing Loyalists' houses systematically torched around White Plains, 'was so enraged ... that I decided to follow the enemy further than I should have, in order to get my hands on some of these home-burners, whom I was willing to throw into the flames'. Ewald levelled civilian housing without hesitation if it was necessary to improve a defensive position, or if someone used it to fire on his men. But the spiteful, militarily pointless destruction of homes made him want to commit a sadistic atrocity, and it is not difficult to imagine the consequences had the Rebels continued to employ these tactics.

Now, for reasons that are not obvious, the unwritten rules changed. Graydon recalled as his column of prisoners emerged from the works, an overexcited British officer rode up: 'What? Taking prisoners? Kill them! Kill every one of them!' When Graydon called out that he placed himself under his protection, 'no man was ever more effectually rebuked. His manner was instantly softened [and] after a civil question or two, as though to make amends for his sanguinary mandate, he rode off'. It is possible that as more British officers had encounters like this, and realized they were dealing with men very like themselves, they found it impossible to sustain the necessary hatred. Conversely Washington was markedly less off-hand in his future correspondence with Howe, and his troops thereafter refrained from wanton incendiarism.

Three days after the fall of Fort Washington, Cornwallis crossed the Hudson from Yonkers and marched on Fort Lee, which was abandoned with yet further loss of artillery and stores, and Washington's much reduced army was followed rather than pursued across New Jersey to Pennsylvania. The retreat involved four major river crossings at any one of which he could have been trapped and destroyed (see MAP p. 55). Howe's excuse for failing to do so was that an army burdened with lumbering wagon trains on roads barely worthy of the

Pleased at Princeton – George Washington inclined to smile

Constitutional Majesty – young George III in coronation robes

RIGHT Reluctant War Lord – Frederick North, Earl of Guilford

BELOW LEFT Naval Supremo – John Montague, Earl of Sandwich

BELOW RIGHT Impatient Scapegoat – George Germain, later Viscount Sackville

'The most distinguished character of the age' crossing the Delaware

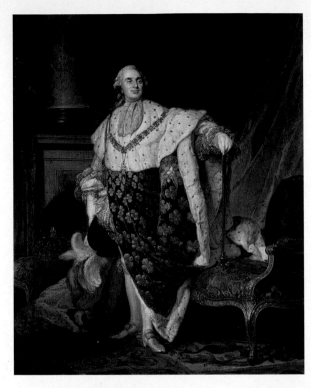

LEFT Hapless Absolutist – Louis XVI in coronation robes

BELOW LEFT War's Architect – Charles Gravier, Comte de Vergennes

BELOW RIGHT Soldier Diplomat – Jean de Vimeur, Comte de Rochambeau

above Pioneer PR man – Benjamin Franklin

top right America's Abu Nidal – Samuel Adams

right Natural Nobleman – Dr Joseph Warren

below The Trap Baited – skirmish at Lexington

'At best a necessary evil' – the murder of Jane McCrea

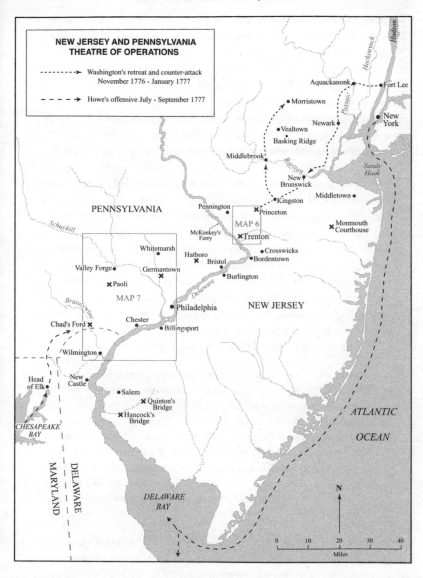

NEW JERSEY AND PENNSYLVANIA THEATRE OF OPERATIONS

------> Washington's retreat and counter-attack
November 1776 - January 1777

- - - -> Howe's offensive July - September 1777

MAP 5

name was certain to be outmarched by a Rebel force travelling light. Much was later made in Parliament and by Rebel propaganda of indiscriminate plundering by the Hessians ('blame the foreigner' being a constant in allied warfare), which supposedly turned New Jersey against the British. First of all it did not, and New Jersey was and remained even less devoted to the Rebel cause than Connecticut became. Secondly, while living in the path of mass troop movements is a fraught experience even in peacetime, it should be obvious that the army in retreat, without a supply train of its own, must have been the main offender.

We are approaching the moment with the best claim to marking the watershed of the war, when a thoroughly beaten Rebel army struck back to destroy a brigade of Hessians at Trenton, then made a fool of Cornwallis by marching around him to strike again at Princeton, before finally taking up winter quarters at Morristown in northern New Jersey. At a stroke this symbolically recovered much of the ground and prestige lost, while dispelling the carefully won British reputation for invincibility. But before that Howe had let Washington escape across the Hackensack, Passaic and Raritan Rivers, at any one of which he could have been trapped by a vigorous pursuit. As the British took up winter quarters around New Brunswick Ewald noted:

> Several distinguished persons arrived from Pennsylvania, who implored [Howe] to press General Washington as closely as possible so that we might overtake him in the vicinity of the Delaware, by which his retreat would be cut off. There we would surely destroy or capture his disheartened army. Indeed one of them, Mr [Joseph] Galloway, was so enraged over the delay of the English that he said out loud, 'I see, they don't want to finish the war!' . . . One had to conclude, therefore, that we had hopes of ending the war amicably, without shedding the blood of the King's subjects in a needless way.

That, of course, is only one side of the coin, if a rather shinier one than normally to be found in accounts of men at war. There can be no doubt the Howe brothers felt the sharp shock already administered was enough, and that the correct strategy now was to open their arms to receive back the errant colonists. This received its clearest expression in Admiral Howe's instructions for the application of a highly porous blockade, through which the Rebels rapidly recovered the material losses of 1776. The aim, he wrote, was to, 'cultivate all amicable correspondence ... and to grant them every other indulgence which the necessary restrictions on their trade will admit, in order to conciliate their friendly dispositions and detach them from the prejudices they have imbibed'. The Howes deserve more credit than they have been given for seeking to recover dominion over the colonies without leaving a legacy of bitterness that would have made it a hollow achievement. To say they should not have been given incompatible political and military instructions is one thing, but to assert there was any other way they could have hoped to bring about a solution that would not have demanded an indefinite and unsustainably large British military presence in America is quite another.

The other side of the coin is that Washington, by leaving the generals with independent prestige in the north and retreating towards Philadelphia, where the Continental Congress provided such legitimacy as the rebellion possessed, ensured that Samuel Adams and others like him would not create a divided command. Lee, whose radicalism appealed to Adams and to whom Joseph Reed, Washington's friend and adjutant-general, had written saying he (Lee) was the only likely saviour of an otherwise lost cause, simplified matters by getting captured on 13 December. Lee had been dawdling in response to Washington's orders to join him south of the Delaware and had got no further than Vealtown. From there he rode to Basking Ridge with only a personal escort, possibly to explore the possibility of a surprise attack on the British lines of communication. He was instead himself surprised by a troop of cavalry under the command of Ensign Banastre Tarleton. One of two French colonels with him was killed, the other captured, their presence coming as no surprise to the British. Just before capture Lee had written to Gates, in command of yet another force further north:

> The ingenious manoeuvre of Fort Washington has unhinged the goodly fabrick we have been building. There never was so damned a stroke. Between ourselves, a certain great man is most damnably deficient. He has thrown me into a situation where I have my choice of difficulties. If I stay in this Province [New Jersey] I risk

myself and the army, and if I do not stay the Province is lost for ever . . . Tories are in my front, rear and on my flanks. The mass of the people is strangely contaminated.

Lee was to remain in British hands until March 1778, and Washington's political position was further improved when Congress set a lamentable example by scampering off to Baltimore, speeded on its way by a dispatch from Washington alleging he had 'positive information' about enemy intentions to winter in Philadelphia, when he surely knew only the vanguard under Cornwallis had crossed the Raritan. He also claimed to be withdrawing 'so as to lull them into security', a line many a retreating general has employed. He had no reason to anticipate an opportunity to hit back in any significant way, but with winter upon him and the remains of his army approaching the end of its enlistment period he was desperately anxious to do so.

When the moment came he was saved because armies are like enormous dogs, anxious to believe their master knows what he is doing and heartbreakingly willing to give him another chance even after he has repeatedly abused their trust. The glory in the events that followed was not that Washington managed to redeem months of defeat and retreat with a resounding victory at the eleventh hour, but that when he decided to strike back there were just enough men willing to follow his lead. There should be a monument to them standing proud of all the other memorials in the capital named for their general, because his fame, that city, and all it contains, stand on their faithful shoulders.

4

PENNSYLVANIA AND
NEW JERSEY

IF WASHINGTON IS TO BE held accountable for the loss of stock-piled stores and the dispersal of the largest army the Rebels ever fielded, he must also be given full credit for rebuilding the army on a firmer footing, starting from the meagre base of the force still under his command at the end of 1776. This was also, of course, a necessary precondition for being able to exercise real executive authority. In a regularly constituted army his practice of summoning senior subordinates to councils of war before any engagement would have been the signature of a weak and indecisive general, and he was so seen by Lee, Gates and others. But in such an army he would have been able to give orders with some security they would be understood, and being understood acted upon. This was not his situation in 1776, as we have seen in the case of Lee, nor was it at the battle of Trenton, where the Pennsylvania Militia failed to act in accordance with his instructions, which against an alert enemy might have led to another defeat.

At the end of his retreat from the Hudson Washington was left with 2000 members of the Continental Army (hereafter 'Continentals'), most of them Virginians. Only about 500 came from threatened Pennsylvania, and the once proud Maryland and Delaware contingents were reduced to pathetic remnants by battle loss, disease and, latterly, desertion. The situation improved sharply when he was joined by the remnant of Lee's command, 2–3000 New Englanders now under Sullivan, and by 600 men commanded by Gates, all Philip

Schuyler felt he could spare from upper New York. The indefatigable Knox had managed to salvage 10–12 field pieces, half of them 6-pounders, but when a disappointing turnout of only 1500 Philadelphia Militia arrived under John Cadwalader, they did bring with them two five-inch howitzers, two 6-pounders and three 4-pounders. The sixty-day period of enlistment for the Militia ended on New Year's Day, as did the six months of many of the Continentals. Most of the New York and New Jersey contingents had deserted to avail themselves of the amnesty offered by Howe, to the fury of the Loyalists. Furthermore Howe would not permit those who had suffered insults and injuries in the king's name to seek revenge, because mob rule under British auspices would have undermined the order and stability he had come to restore. However he could not restrain the violence of Loyalists in faraway Delaware, who took back the court-houses, cut down the Liberty Poles and drove away the hated 'Whigs'. Alarmed, the Rebel leaders in neighbouring Maryland instructed their Congressional delegates to vote for the acceptance of Howe's proclamation.

Howe's desire for order made good military sense as well, because regular armies by their nature cannot wage revolutionary war. Those that have tried, as Cornwallis was obliged to do in the South in 1780–81, soon discover that the requisite delegation of authority to junior officers and dependence on irregular forces is deeply subversive of hierarchy and discipline. This is the reason why insurgents target magistrates and the police, because without them the army is called upon to perform functions – such as crowd control – for which it is unsuited, which have a high probability of generating civilian resentment, and which distract from its primary function. Wherever the British Army remained for any length of time, such as New York, Philadelphia, Savannah and Charleston, the infrastructure of civilian government was quickly re-established and the military task correspondingly simplified.

Because in the end they lost, it is easy to see how these considerations complicated the task of the British commanders-in-chief, less so to appreciate that Washington faced a similar dilemma. If his class were to be so discredited by defeat that it forfeited the right to lead, there would be no restraining the levellers and demagogues whom he feared as much as did any British aristocrat. The trump card, possession of which Washington felt justified in defending by any means necessary, was that Congress without the Continental Army would be revealed for the futile talking shop it was. Despite the subversive presence of Gates, who travelled to lobby Congress on his own behalf against Washington's wishes, even Samuel Adams could see that to change commanders-in-chief at this stage would snap the tenuous threads still holding the army together, after which other colonies would soon follow the example of New York and New Jersey. In addition to wounded Connecticut, the shakiness of Rhode Island had been revealed by the welcome given to Howe's occupying force at Newport, its largest town, which controlled Narragansett Bay and therefore cut off the Rebel stronghold of Providence from the sea (see MAP 16). And as we have noted, there was by now scant enthusiasm for war in Pennsylvania, Delaware and Maryland.

On 27 December Congress declared that, 'having perfect reliance on the wisdom, vigour, and uprightness of General Washington', it vested him with near-plenipotentiary powers for six months. As soon as they learned of Washington's victory at Trenton on the 26th the delegates made a weasel-worded partial retraction that further detracted from their authority. Joseph Reed commented, 'when I look round and see how few of the number who talked so largely of death and honour are around me, I am lost in wonder . . . Your noisy Sons of Liberty are, I find, the quietest in the field'. Robert Morris, one of the three congressional delegates who stayed in Philadelphia to organize support for the army, wrote in shame that 'many of those who were foremost in the noise, shrink, coward-like, from the danger, and are begging pardon without striking a blow'.

The future relationship between Washington and Congress was akin to that of a constitutional monarch with a government enjoying little popular support. Congressmen might scheme and commit minor acts of insubordination, but they knew their prestige was less than his, and that their survival depended on him rather less than viceversa. He became, in all but title, King George I of the United States, something Rebels raised in the monarchical tradition probably needed as much or more than they did a talented general. Paradoxically, this process was initiated by the major defeats of 1776, not the minor victory at the end of it, although it was more directly the result of Howe's reluctance to pursue a military solution to the rebellion by running down Washington when he had him in the open.

The hunting analogy is apt, for British officers at this time did refer to Washington as 'the fox', not because they esteemed him either clever or quick, but because they thought he had dived into his earth, whence the Hessian hounds would dig him up in the 1777 campaigning season. As a result the British suffered the totally unnecessary but richly deserved defeat the gods of war take such pleasure in inflicting on the arrogantly complacent. Howe, his mind occupied with arrangements for a comfortable winter in New York, wished to withdraw to cantonments along the south bank of the Raritan centred on New Brunswick, but Cornwallis persuaded him to leave advanced outposts along the north and eastern banks of the Delaware. This was a task for the light infantry, who like the grenadiers were organized into an independent brigade by Howe, but Cornwallis assigned it to six Hessian line regiments and their Jäger flank companies under Colonel Carl von Donop. He in turn wished to keep his seven regiments (the Black Watch was also attached) within close supporting range of each other around Bordentown, where there were ample quarters available in estates abandoned by wealthy Rebels.

Disastrously, Howe yielded to the request of Colonel Johann Rall for a larger command in recognition of the performance of his regiment at White Plains and Fort Washington, and he took up station at the village of Trenton with his own and the Knyphausen grenadiers, and Lossberg's fusiliers. Cornwallis, intending to return home to his dying wife on 27 December, devolved command on Grant, whose contempt for Americans had survived Stirling's attempt to educate him at Gowanus, and who announced he would 'undertake to keep the peace in New Jersey with a corporal's guard'. He remained at New Brunswick with the grenadiers and another brigade, and posted the light infantry at Princeton under Brigadier-General Alexander Leslie, an irascible Scot who was so irritated by the buffoonish behaviour of Rall that he withdrew the British outpost at Maidenhead, midway between Trenton and Princeton.

Rall's promotion had gone to his head, for as well as annoying Leslie he ignored orders from Donop to build artillery redoubts on

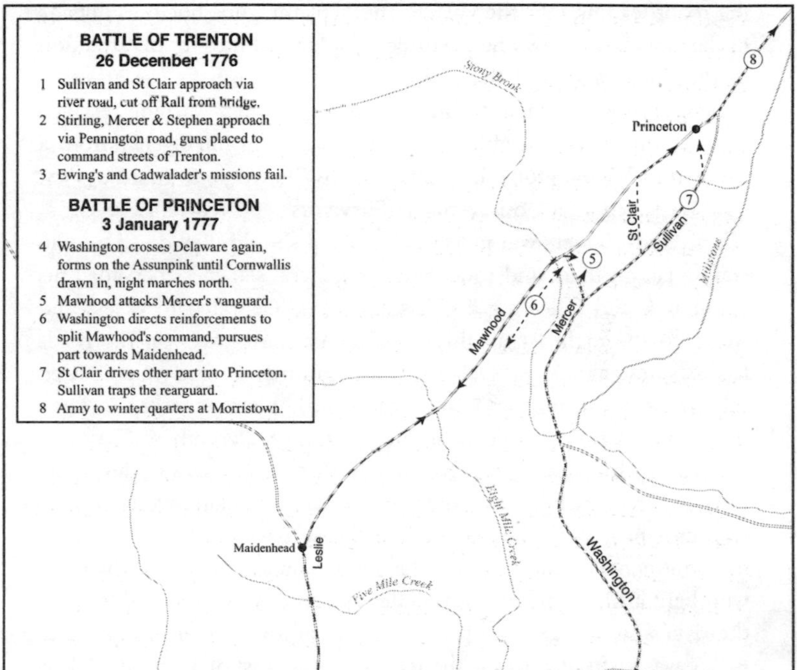
BATTLE OF TRENTON
26 December 1776
1 Sullivan and St Clair approach via river road, cut off Rall from bridge.
2 Stirling, Mercer & Stephen approach via Pennington road, guns placed to command streets of Trenton.
3 Ewing's and Cadwalader's missions fail.
BATTLE OF PRINCETON
3 January 1777
4 Washington crosses Delaware again, forms on the Assunpink until Cornwallis drawn in, night marches north.
5 Mawhood attacks Mercer's vanguard.
6 Washington directs reinforcements to split Mawhood's command, pursues part towards Maidenhead.
7 St Clair drives other part into Princeton. Sullivan traps the rearguard.
8 Army to winter quarters at Morristown.
Stony Brook
Princeton
St Clair
Sullivan
Millstone
Mawhood
Mercer
Washington
Eight Mile Creek
Maidenhead
Leslie
Five Mile Creek
Pennington
Washington & Greene
Shabbakonk
Assunpink
Cornwallis
McKonkey's Ferry
Sullivan
Sandtown
Delaware
Rall
N
Reed & Cadwalader (Bristol)
Ewing
Donop (Bordentown)
Crosswicks
0
1
2
Miles

MAP 6

the roads leading into the village, and kept the guns lined up outside his headquarters, where he postured and devoted most of his attention to the fine brass band that was soon to become a fixture at social occasions in Rebel Philadelphia. Rall also ignored a warning received from Grant on 25 December, explicitly based on intelligence from a spy within Washington's headquarters, to 'be on your guard against an unexpected attack on Trenton'. Survivors reported Rall's reaction: 'These clod-hoppers will not attack us, and should they do so we will simply fall on them and rout them'. A general slackness pervaded his command, and following a Christmas Day celebrated to excess and well into the night by all three regiments, the pickets on the roads leading west along the Delaware and towards Pennington allowed themselves to be surprised when the clod-hoppers emerged in force from a driving hailstorm in the morning of 26 December.

Washington had seized every boat along the Delaware and now intended to make full use of them in an elaborate plan involving three river crossings. While he marched northeast to McKonkey's Ferry with the Continentals and Knox's artillery, the main force of Pennsylvanians with light artillery under Cadwalader at Bristol was supposed to cross the river and engage Donop's command, and a smaller group under Ewing was instructed to use the ferry crossing west of Trenton to close off the drawbridge across Assunpink Creek. Fortunately for his peace of mind, Washington did not learn until later that Cadwalader had found it impossible to get his guns across and withdrew, and that Ewing had found it too difficult to cross the ice-choked river.

Washington's own crossing further up river is the subject of the most iconic painting of the war – deservedly so, for every man was a hero, not least the boatmen who managed to get 4000 men and Knox's cannon across, in clumsy flat-bottomed ore barges, in the dark, through pack ice. It was freezing, they had no proper clothing and some even lacked shoes, all of them were 'short-timers', some of them had seen and all knew what Hessian bayonets could do. There had been no rousing speeches, indeed no warning because Washington feared it would compromise the element of surprise, not knowing it was preserved only by the stupidity of his opponent. The men hugged their muskets to keep them dry, hunched their shoulders before the howling wind, and obeyed the hoarse command of the general they could barely see: 'Soldiers, keep by your officers. For God's sake, keep by your officers!'

It helped that some of those officers were superb. Captain John Glover's boatmen were from Marblehead in Massachusetts and had been in the fight from the beginning. They had already been the salvation of the army once before, when they evacuated the men besieged on the Brooklyn Peninsula. Two of the brigadier-generals were Scots immigrants, the wealthy Arthur St Clair of Pennsylvania and Hugh Mercer, a physician and member of the Virginia House of Burgesses. Two were Irish immigrants, Colonels John Haslet of Delaware (whose own regiment was down to six men from 700 in mid year) and Edward Hand of Pennsylvania, who had been a surgeon's mate with the Royal Irish until 1774. John Stark was there, still only a colonel despite his outstanding leadership at Breed's Hill. One of Knox's batteries was commanded by the West Indies-born New Yorker Lieutenant Alexander Hamilton, Philip Schuyler's son-in-law, and the Virginians included Captain William Washington (a distant cousin of the commander-in-chief) and his eighteen-year old lieutenant, future President James Monroe, both shortly to be seriously wounded in a crucial charge that silenced an enemy battery.

To say Washington's overambitious plan would have failed against a halfway alert enemy simply emphasizes the boldness with which he acted upon the detailed intelligence he received from John Honeyman, a Trenton resident. Not content with dividing his force once, Washington sent Sullivan and St Clair along the river road with instructions to seal off the Assunpink bridge if Ewing failed to do so, while he accompanied Greene's three brigades in a short march north to attain the Pennington road. The map (p. 63) does not quite do justice to the manner in which this approach gave him a commanding position at the head of a fan of roads through Trenton, an ideal artillery position now marked by the battle monument. Greene's brigades were commanded by Mercer, Stirling and the Virginian Adam Stephen, who sent an unauthorized patrol across the Delaware on Christmas Day that might have alerted an officer less complacent than Rall. Surprise also required a night approach, an advantage lost when the river crossing took much longer than expected. But in a crowning stroke of good luck a hailstorm intervened to provide alternative cover, with the added bonus that it blew into the faces of the defenders. On the following day Knox wrote to his wife:

> About half a mile from the town was an advanced guard on each road [which] we forced, and entered the town with them pell-mell; and there succeeded a scene of war of which I had often conceived, but never saw before. The hurry, fright and confusion of the enemy was like that which will be when the last trump shall sound. They endeavoured to form in the streets, the heads of which we had previously the possession of with cannon and howitzers; these, in the twinkling of an eye, cleared the streets ... During the contest in the streets measures were taken for putting an entire stop to their retreat by posting troops and cannon in such passes and roads as it was possible for them to get away by. The poor fellows [were driven through the town into an open area beyond and] saw themselves completely surrounded; the only resource left was to force their way through numbers unknown to them ... they did not relish the project and were obliged to surrender.

Trenton is a classic example of the effect of dislocation of expectations, and the ripple effect across the entire Hessian contingent was dramatic. Donop retreated without even considering a counterattack, and as Ewald commented sadly:

> Thus had the times changed! The Americans had constantly run before us ... and now we had to render Washington the honour of thinking about our defence. Due to this affair at Trenton, such a fright came over our army that if Washington had used this opportunity we would have flown to our ships and let him have all of America. Since we had thus far underestimated our enemy, from this unhappy day onward we saw everything through a magnifying glass. This great misfortune ... surely caused the utter loss of the thirteen splendid provinces of the Crown of England.

Not Trenton alone, however. As Cornwallis and Grant rolled ponderously south from New Brunswick, the Rebel army withdrew across the Delaware with a thousand prisoners and six brass guns. There Washington was reunited with Joseph Reed, whose home was in Trenton and whose faith in his friend was now restored. Between them they devised a yet more daring plan, to cross the river again, draw Cornwallis into Trenton, then march around him to Princeton to fall on his baggage train, and possibly also to raid his main depot at New Brunswick. Ignoring Donop's suggestion that he send a parallel column towards Crosswicks, Cornwallis thundered along the single axis of the Princeton road, goaded by the resolute rearguard action of riflemen commanded by Hand at the Five Mile Creek and Shabbakonk crossings. Although Washington now commanded about 8000 men, he had no desire for a pitched battle and would have retreated again had Cornwallis possessed even a tithe of Howe's battlefield skill – but it seems he knew his man.

He was also, once again, blessed by fortune. Bringing up the rearguard, Lieutenant-Colonel Charles Mawhood made a very early start from Princeton in the morning of 3 January with the 17th, his own regiment, and the 55th, leaving the 40th to follow with the baggage. He was past the Stony Brook Bridge, heading south to join Leslie at Maidenhead, when he saw the Rebel vanguard under Mercer marching north on the road running alongside the brook. Had Mawhood left later, Washington would have discovered that a town held by three fully alert regiments was an altogether nastier proposition than his success at Trenton may have led him to believe. As it was, Mawhood countermarched and hammered the Rebel vanguard at a slight rise still known as Mercer's Heights, for the Scotsman died there, bayoneted after his horse was crippled, while the gallant Haslet, almost the last Delaware representative left in the Rebel army, was shot as he tried to reform the men driven from the hill. Mawhood overpursued, leaving the 55th to hold the hill while with the 17th he chased Mercer's Virginians back to the Sandtown–Princeton road, and was fortunate the next force to confront him was Cadwalader's Pennsylvania Militia. They drove him back on the 55th, only to break in turn when raked by fire from the British regulars, who had added two captured Rebel guns to their own pair.

But then the main force directed by Washington himself came up and wrapped around the hill, and it was Mawhood's turn to flee and lose his guns. The 17th and part of the 55th broke out to recross the bridge, hotly pursued for a few miles until Washington called it off, while the rest fell back to a stream just south of Princeton, where they formed with the 40th. Outflanked again, they broke and most kept going through Princeton towards New Brunswick, leaving about 200 men forted up in Nassau Hall, then the largest edifice in North America. Hamilton brought up his battery and fired one ball into the building, while a second ricocheted off the outside wall (the point of impact is still visible). It was enough for the shaken defenders, who promptly surrendered, a precedent that was to mislead Washington badly nine months later. He reported that with 500 extra men he would have marched to New Brunswick and 'finished the war' by capturing desperately needed hard currency, but with Leslie's and the remains of Mawhood's brigades about an hour behind him, it would have been insane to do so. Pausing only to loot Princeton comprehensively, the exultant Continental Army marched to the fertile Morristown Valley, where it spent the last comfortable winter it was to experience.

Washington did not neglect the opportunity to discredit another potential rival. Having saddled Connecticut's Putnam with the blame for Long Island, he now ordered Massachusetts's Heath to advance from Castle Hill to assault Fort Independence (see MAP p. 43), a task Heath could not persuade his men to undertake after the defenders refused his summons to surrender. Howe's private secretary noted, 'One Heath, once a butcher, now a Rebel general [actually, a prosperous farmer, pillar of his community and very well read in military matters], has left the army in disgust [not so], on account of some reflections thrown upon him by Washington for not attacking Fort Independence. He blamed his men, and his men, him; villains and cowards together'. Washington's brutal rebuke may perhaps be explained as the product of a surge of relieved overconfidence after Trenton, but in the light of his own errors and silence about the way men of his class like Cadwalader and Schuyler had let him down, not excused:

> Your conduct is censured (and by men of sense and judgement who were with you on the expedition to Fort Independence) as being fraught with too much caution by which the Army has been disappointed, and in some degree disgraced. Your summons, as you

did not attempt to fulfil your threats, was not only idle but farcical, and will not fail of turning the laugh exceedingly upon us.

Although Trenton saved the rebellion from military collapse, it was also teetering on the edge of financial disaster. Surprisingly, among men who had thought economic warfare was one of their strengths, the Rebels had failed to anticipate that both overseas and domestic suppliers would require cash payment once hostilities began. This rapidly drained coin from circulation, and the paper promissory notes printed by Congress and the individual colonies led to a depreciation so great that among the powers Congress vested in Washington was the right 'to take, wherever he may be, whatever he may want for the use of the army, if the inhabitants will not sell it, allowing reasonable price for the same; to arrest and confine persons who refuse to take the continental money, or are otherwise disaffected to the American cause'. For the duration of the war the Continental Army was obliged to take what it needed, while the cash-paying British Army obtained whatever it wanted from inhabitants who were restrained only by the threat of Rebel reprisals. Although Clinton and Cornwallis were later to find it a convenient excuse for inaction and surrender respectively, there was never any serious shortage of the necessities on the British side, while Washington's army was at times immobilized and wracked by mutinies because of constant want amid an indifferent or hostile civilian population.

The rebellion would have foundered in 1777 were it not for massive assistance from France. In January the French made the Rebels a lump sum grant of four million livres (£1,668,000, when £40 was a comfortable annual income for a family) plus an annual subsidy of two million livres more, and shipped an avalanche of surplus military materiel across the Atlantic. The French Army adopted a new musket in 1770, and its almost unused predecessor, the 1766 Charleville Léger, became the standard equipment of the Continental Army. The following contrasts it with the Second Model Land Pattern Musket, or 'Brown Bess' as it came to be known affectionately from about 1785, with which the British Army was equipped for more than a century following the introduction of the First Model in 1730.

	Calibre (in.)	Barrel length (in.)	Length overall (in.)	Weight (lb.)
Charleville Léger	0.69	44.75	60.00	9.6
Brown Bess II	0.75	42.00	58.25	8.8
Brown Bess carbine	0.75	30.50	46.90	7.7

The Charleville had a weaker firing mechanism and was more prone to fouling, and although marginally more accurate it had less stopping power than the Brown Bess. Whatever its faults, the Léger brought a standard calibre to a Continental Army hitherto cursed with a bewildering variety. The French Army was also in the process of standardizing its artillery under the direction of the great Jean-Baptiste de Gribeauval, and surplus cannon also made their way across the Atlantic. With them came an immense amount of clothing, boots, blankets and tents, a great deal of which the Rebels were unwise enough to store in a depot at Danbury, Connecticut, where it was destroyed on 27 April 1777 in an amphibious raid led by the Loyalist governor of New York, William Tryon (see MAP p. 129). A month earlier a smaller raid had destroyed substantial Rebel stores at Peekskill, in the area known as the Hudson Highlands. Much of the deprivation suffered by the Continental Army was the result of the never replaced loss of expensive materiel in 1776–77, and one has to wonder if the French did not finally declare war and send troops at least in part to ensure the supplies they sent, or the money they lent, did not always end up burned, carried away or paid to British merchants for civilian goods.

It is pointless to base an assessment of the Howe brothers' strategy on what they wrote. They would never have revealed their intentions to Germain and Sandwich, political opponents who could be depended upon to exploit any lapse into frankness. The Howes' private papers were lost in a fire, but in all probability they would not have been enlightening, because in an age when everybody spoke and wrote far too much, they were notoriously reticent. The British military establishment was well aware a purely military conquest of the colonies was out of the question, and from his words to Franklin at the Staten

Island meeting, we know William Howe was alert to the probability of French intervention. We know, now, that the consolidation of power in the hands of Washington and the morale boost of Trenton marked a watershed, but to any reasonable contemporary the former was a sign of political desperation, the latter a relatively minor reverse barely weighing in the scales against abundant evidence that the bubble of revolutionary enthusiasm had burst. Amid a flood of deserters bearing a unanimous message that the revolution had shot its bolt, there was no reason for the Howes to vary their strategy in 1777. The aim was not to annihilate Washington, something only relentless pursuit by a much larger cavalry force than Howe had to hand could have ensured, but to demonstrate he could not prevent the British Army from going wherever it wanted. It was reasonable to expect the middle colonies to drop out once their vulnerability became apparent, leaving Massachusetts in the north and Virginia in the south to be dealt with in detail. This strategy, it bears repeating, offered the only prospect of creating the preconditions for a durable settlement.

It also offers a credible explanation why, after failing to draw Washington into combat in New Jersey, Howe embarked 18,000 men on an amphibious expedition that sailed around Delaware and through the heart of Maryland to land at Head of Elk, when a landing at New Castle on the Delaware would have spared it several weeks at sea. To suggest he blithely overlooked the danger of additional exposure to disease and bad weather, or that he did not realize his horses would be unfit for service after such a long time at sea, is to push the 'bloody fool' interpretation of military history too far. With 40,000 inhabitants Philadelphia was the second largest English-speaking city in the world (all were, of course, dwarfed by London), it was where the Continental Congress uneasily sat, and Washington simply could not abandon it without a fight. It was, therefore, admirably suited to Howe's double objective of taking the second most populous colony out of the war – one, furthermore, which had remained lukewarm until a Rebel coup d'état in June 1776 – while demonstrating Washington's inability to stop him. It was also sensible to emphasize that he could have landed anywhere, leading the trembling Rebel authorities in Delaware and Maryland to clutch their own meagre defences, and withhold men who might otherwise have gone to strengthen Washington.

The trial of strength came along the Brandywine (see MAP 7), a minor tributary of the Delaware north of Wilmington. The position Washington occupied was strong, but not forbiddingly so, and behind him there were several other streams where he might confront Howe again should he take the direct line to Philadelphia. The city itself was moated by the broad Schuykill, with artillery forts and underwater obstacles blocking the Delaware just downstream of where the two rivers joined. These were good dispositions. Washington knew the British Army liked to advance along the banks of a river, with its supply line safely afloat and imposing no delays on land operations. What he did not anticipate was that the inhabitants around the head of the Chesapeake Bay would cheerfully sell Howe all the wagons, food and forage he required. Nor that those living at the point of intersection of the borders of Maryland, Delaware and Pennsylvania would guide his opponent unerringly around his flank. Any judgement of Washington's generalship that assumes he was always operating in supportive, friendly territory cannot fail to be damning. If, on the other hand, it is accepted that his army was less welcome than his cash-rich opponent's, and that he was on occasion more poorly served by local guides and informants, a deeper appreciation of his problems emerges.

The standard interpretation of the Brandywine fight, at the time and since, has been that Howe once again failed to display the killer instinct after outflanking his hapless opponent. This hinges on the fragile assumption that he expected his opponent not to notice as he marched half his army, in daylight, on a broad, leisurely sweep around his right flank, and that he could contemplate taking the casualties his army would certainly have suffered had he sought a battle of annihilation against equal numbers (both armies were 12–13,000 strong). If it had taken place in Europe, historians would record only that Howe manoeuvred his opponent out of a defensive position, and drove him to the southeast before himself marching northwest. That the battle was anything more than a skirmish came about because Washington's first reaction to news that Howe had divided his army was to exploit a local numerical advantage against Knyphausen's force, facing him across the Brandywine. He dispatched Sullivan's division to refuse his flank and ordered Wayne and Greene to assault across Chad's Ford, only to discover that the Hessian had retained most of the British

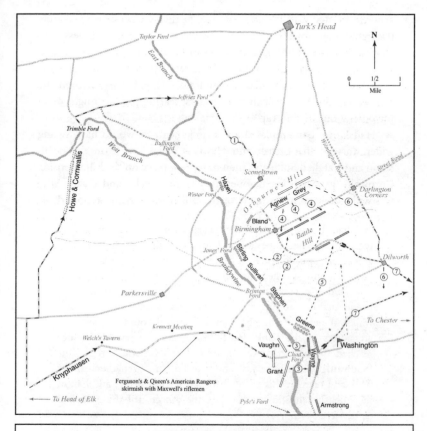

BATTLE OF THE BRANDYWINE
11 September 1777

1 Wide outflanking march by Cornwallis's division undetected by Hazen's cavalry pickets, only reported to Washington when it reaches Sconeltown at approximately 1200 hours. Deployed for battle on Osbourne's Hill by 1400 hours.
2 Washington orders Sullivan's division to refuse his flank along the Birmingham-Darlington Corners road.
3 Seeking to exploit Howe's divided forces Washington orders an assault across Chad's Ford, discovers that Knyphausen has most of the British artillery and abandons the attack.
4 General assault by Cornwallis drives Sullivan's men over Battle Hill.
5 Washington sends Greene's division to contain the collapse of his right flank, later rides there himself.
6 Guards, grenadiers and light infantry become disorganized in the woods, emerge too late to block the rebel retreat at Dilworth but take Wayne's rearguard division, retreating from Chad's Ford, in the flank.
7 Flight of both wings of the Rebel army leads to chaos on the Chester Road, but Howe lacks the cavalry to pursue.

MAP 7

artillery. Belatedly calling off the attack, he then sent Greene to support the right wing, which he reached after covering four miles in less than an hour. Before riding after him, Washington ordered the Pennsylvanians, Militia on his left and Continentals under Anthony Wayne at the ford, to begin a phased withdrawal. Knyphausen crossed the ford but stopped to await further orders, fearing pursuit might drive the enemy out of the trap.

Had Howe contemplated an encirclement, he would have swung wider. Instead the British and Hessians advancing from the north stood and watched Sullivan's men move into place on the hill opposite. Cornwallis growled 'the damned Rebels form well', and Ewald, who was with the leading elements of the British right flank, reported:

> We had hardly reached the village [Birmingham] when we received intense grapeshot and musketry fire which threw the grenadiers into disorder, but they recovered themselves quickly, deployed and attacked the village ... In the distance I saw red coats and discovered that it was General Agnew with his brigade. I requested him to support the grenadiers, and pointed out a hill which, if he gained it, the enemy [Stirling] could not take the grenadiers in the flank. He followed, and we had no sooner reached the hill than we ran into several American regiments [Sullivan], which were just about to take the grenadiers in the flank and rear. At this point there was terrible firing, and half of the Englishmen and nearly all of the officers [of the 44th and 64th] were slain.

What Ewald did not know was that in stopping this attack Sullivan had left his right unsupported, and only Greene's lightning march saved him from being pushed off Battle Hill towards the Brandywine. There followed a fighting retreat to Dilworth, where the Guards, grenadiers and light infantry emerged from the woods just too late to attack Greene's men. They were granted another opportunity against Wayne's rearguard, marching along a road south of the village, but night was falling and the engagement was inconclusive. Washington's army disengaged in reasonably good order, and although eleven guns were lost, only about 400 men surrendered. To remind us that even the eyewitness account of a professional like Ewald must be taken with a pinch of salt, British losses were only 89 killed and 488 wounded, against about 200 Rebels killed and 500 wounded. Generals do not make a habit of admitting that battles have not turned out as planned, and Howe boasted to Germain that 'the enemy's army escaped a total overthrow that must have been the consequence of an hour's more daylight'. Ewald was in no doubt the extra hour was not available because Howe deliberately moved slowly, 'so that the American army should not be destroyed to pay a fresh compliment to the Opposition Party [in London] and to bring forth a new [peace] proposal'.

Perhaps Howe was as Machiavellian as Ewald thought, but a more obvious explanation is that a small army very far from home simply could not afford to risk heavy casualties at the start of a campaign in the heart of enemy country, against an opponent who would always be able to disengage, regroup and come back for more. It was an unwelcome development to find Washington willing to offer battle at the first opportunity, and nearly precipitating a bloodbath by his naïve aggressiveness. A more experienced commander would have withdrawn upon finding himself outflanked, and both the slowness of the flank march and the hour or more spent making a display on Osbourne's Hill argues this was all Howe expected to achieve. He was now faced with an army that stood and fought, commanded by an unpredictable general, which introduced unwanted extra variables into what was already a complex equation.

Part of the reason for the improvement in the Continental Army was that it now contained a higher proportion of long-service men, who were subject to a military code of discipline almost as strict as the British. Another was that much of the swarm of posturing officers who were conspicuous by their absence in combat during 1776 had either resigned or settled into profitable administrative duties, in particular the sale of passes to merchants wishing to trade with the enemy. It was also more homogenous, with the mass of New Englanders and the contingents from New York and New Jersey now mainly serving in the north under Schuyler, Putnam and Heath. The chronic weakness of the army was at the junior infantry officer level, in part because those who styled themselves gentlemen demanded higher rank upon arrival, but mainly because Congress and people alike actively denied the army honour, of which regular pay is principally a symbol. On the British side, Peebles' diary is full of the daily rituals and regular collective celebrations which bound the army together, the purchase of commissions gave officers a personal stake in the army, political patronage was tied to performance in a way unknown to the Continental Army, and the two-way bonds of loyalty were constantly affirmed. Few British officers ever wavered from their conviction that the rebellion was a dishonourable cause, because they could see for themselves how badly enemy soldiers were treated by their own side.

Dr Benjamin Rush, a signatory of the Declaration of Independence and Surgeon General of the Middle Department, observed that wounded Continentals received better treatment in British hospitals than they could hope for in their own, not because of humanity, for 'they hate us in every shape we appear to them', but because that was the way things were done. It is notable that Washington was extremely loath to employ British deserters because he considered them to be dangerous malcontents who would infect the Continental Army, while Rush approvingly commented on the paternalistic enforcement of hygiene by British officers, and that their soldiers were forbidden to touch enemy blankets to prevent them catching 'Rebel distempers', a nice double entendre. Both sides segregated enemy deserters into separate units. The rate of return to their original service was higher among the British, but this may simply reflect that the American deserters were sent away from temptation to the West Indies. German deserters, of whom there were many, on the whole dropped out of the war altogether.

None of these background considerations simplified the problem confronting Howe following Brandywine, which was to reach Philadelphia and its large Loyalist population without fighting a major battle. Washington soon realized Howe was not going to do him the favour of advancing along the Delaware and headed north to mount a forward defence of the Schuykill crossings, first marching his army through the city, 'induced to do this, from the opinion of several of my officers and many friends in Philadelphia, that it may have some influence on the minds of the disaffected there'. On 16 September the two armies clashed again at White Horse Tavern, where Washington was outflanked on both sides before a torrential downpour halted the battle. Knox wrote 'nearly all the musket cartridges that had been delivered to the men were damaged, consisting of about 400,000. This was a most terrible stroke to us, and owing entirely to the badness of the cartouch-boxes which have been provided for the army'. Washington was obliged to get out of Howe's way and march to a depot at Warwick Furnace to resupply, before marching east again to take up a commanding position at Evansburg, from which he could descend to defend any of the several fords across the upper Schuykill.

He had left Wayne with more than 2000 men, Continentals known as the 'Pennsylvania Line', at the village of Paoli, named for the Corsican who led the first ever nationalist colonial revolt, which in 1755 had produced the first written constitution in history. The given reason was that Wayne was supposed to lurk until Howe's army passed and then fall on the baggage train, the more likely one that the Pennsylvanians wished to remain nearer their homes. Either way it was folly to divide the army, and Wayne's men paid a terrible price for it when Howe, advancing about one mile to every five marched by Washington, reached Valley Forge and sent a detachment to eliminate the threat. The force consisted of the 40th and 55th under Colonel Thomas Musgrave, and the light infantry battalion, 42nd and 44th under Major-General Charles Grey, who was in overall command. He ordered all flints removed from the muskets and conducted a night assault, arriving at the Rebel encampment at one o'clock in the morning of 21 September. Major John André, Grey's ADC, noted in his diary:

> The picket was surprised and most of them killed in endeavouring to retreat. On approaching the right of the camp we perceived the line of fires, and the Light Infantry being ordered to form to the front, rushed along the line putting to the bayonet all they came up with, and overtaking the main herd of the fugitives, stabbed great number and pressed on their rear till it was thought prudent to order them to desist.

The Pennsylvanians lost 250 men killed and mortally wounded, and some 30 captured, among them French Count Julius de Montfort, along with many loaded wagons and their cattle herd, against one British officer and two men killed and five wounded. Promptly denounced as a 'massacre' by Rebel propaganda, the operation did not dishearten the Pennsylvania Line, rather the opposite, and was to

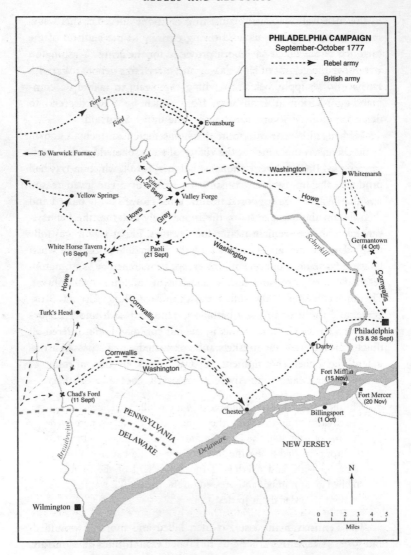

PHILADELPHIA CAMPAIGN
September-October 1777

Rebel army
British army

Ford

Ford

Evansburg

Ford

To Warwick Furnace

feint
(21-22 Sept)

Washington

Whitemarsh

Yellow Springs

Valley Forge

Howe

Howe

Germantown
(4 Oct)

Howe

Grey

Schuylkill

Cornwallis

White Horse Tavern
(16 Sept)

Paoli
(21 Sept)

Washington

Howe

Cornwallis

Turk's Head

Philadelphia
(13 & 26 Sept)

Cornwallis

Darby

Washington

Cornwallis

Fort Mifflin
(15 Nov)

Chad's Ford
(11 Sept)

Washington

Fort Mercer
(20 Nov)

PENNSYLVANIA

Chester

Billingsport
(1 Oct)

Brandywine

DELAWARE

Delaware

NEW JERSEY

N

Wilmington

0 1 2 3 4 5
Miles

MAP 8

have paradoxical repercussions the next time the armies clashed. But before then Howe had tricked Washington by marching northwest along the Schuykill until he induced his opponent to shadow his movement, then doubled back and, with a burst of speed not normally associated with his movements, got the whole army across without loss at a ford below Valley Forge. While a fuming Washington took up a position at Whitemarsh, the British vanguard under Cornwallis strolled into Philadelphia, whence Congress had fled, this time well inland to York, on the other side of the broad Susquehanna River. An unimpressed Peebles noted 'the streets crowded with inhabitants who seem to rejoice upon the occasion, tho' by all accounts many of them were publickly on the other side before our arrival'.

Eight days later, on 4 October, Washington's exasperation led him to waste a last opportunity to exploit his opponent's rapidly diminishing complacency at Germantown, where Howe was camped with the main body of his army, about 8–9000 men, some five miles north of Philadelphia. Washington claimed the same number of Continentals, plus some 3000 Militia, but there were certainly more. He had fallen back on troops posted along the Delaware, and had recently been joined by reinforcements from the Hudson Highlands, including Joseph Martin's regiment and another from Connecticut. Despite an evident desire to repeat the tactics employed at Trenton, it is most unlikely he would have dared divide the army as he did unless convinced he enjoyed a significant superiority in dependable troops, which in his own frequently expressed opinion did not include the Militia. Howe in turn was to allege he made his dispositions in order to invite an attack, but Ewald did not believe him and neither should we.

Lies told by both commanders for political reasons aside, the defining feature of the battle was a thick fog that reduced visibility to 30 yards or less. While this enabled the Continentals to surprise the light infantry pickets, even though they had been warned by deserters an attack was imminent, thereafter it reduced Washington's overelaborate plan to a shambles. He had sent the Pennsylvania Militia along both banks of the Schuykill, where they were to make demonstrations supposed to freeze Howe's left wing in place and discourage reinforcement from Philadelphia, and a detachment of Maryland Militia in a long hook to the north intended to distract attention from his main flank attack under Greene (see MAP 9). Alas, the larger Pennsylvanian Militia force under Armstrong took up a static defensive position across the Wissahickon stream, the smaller one was so obviously a feint that Cornwallis ignored it, while the Marylanders failed to come anywhere near the battle.

More damningly, neither Greene nor Washington and Sullivan, his subordinate commander, maintained control over their divisions, with the result that Wayne's Pennsylvania Line regiments, thirsting for revenge, overpursued the light infantry and were therefore attacked in the flank by Greene's right wing brigade commanded by Stephen, after which both groups dissolved in panic. The push along the Germantown road was stopped not so much by the determined resistance of Musgrave and part of the 40th forted up in the Chew House, as by Washington's personal decision to halt the advance and commit Knox's artillery and the reserve under Stirling in order to deal with it. This had produced a quick result at Princeton, but Musgrave's men proved a harder nut. Meanwhile the rest of Greene's attack was held by the Guards, 25th and 28th, joined by reinforcements from the left wing under Agnew, who somewhere along the way was shot and killed by a civilian. Finally outflanked by the Queen's American Rangers, forced-marched from Philadelphia by Cornwallis, Greene's command broke and ran. The same happened with less combat around the Chew House, the general collapse of the army attributed by Joseph Martin to lack of ammunition and faintness from hunger.

Colonel Timothy Pickering, at this time Washington's adjutant-general, lost faith in him at Germantown. His warning that the plan was overelaborate was ignored, as was his advice to mask the Chew House and regroup. More than 5000 men had driven in the light infantry pickets and the 40th, but in the process had become 'greatly broken and scattered, great numbers having left their corps to help off the wounded, others being broken by other means, or by carelessness; for officers and men got much separated from each other, neither (in numerous instances) knowing where to find their own'. It was on this disordered mob that the counterattack by Grant and Grey fell. Without mentioning that it contradicted Washington's version of events, Pickering slyly observed, 'this retreat surprised everybody (all supposing that victory was nearly secured in our favour); but I think

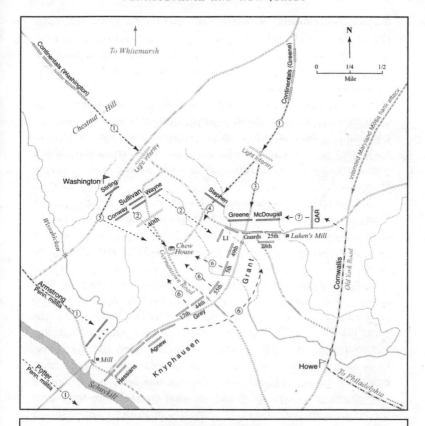

BATTLE OF GERMANTOWN
4 October 1777

1 Converging attacks in the morning fog by two of five columns drive in the light infantry (LI) pickets. Pennsylvania militia demonstrations on the Wissahickon and opposite Philadelphia intended to pin Knyphausen and Cornwallis.

2 Sullivan and Conway drive in the 40th, Musgrave with six companies fortifies the stone-built Chew House. Wayne's division, seeking vengeance for the Paoli raid, over-pursues the light Infantry.

3 Two of Greene's three brigades, led by McDougall, attack Grant's refused flank.

4 Stephen's brigade advances at an angle to Greene's general assault, mistakenly attacks Wayne's.

5 Washington brings up Stirling's reserve and the artillery but throws them into the assault on the Chew House.

6 Converging attacks towards the Chew House by Grant's 55th & 5th, Grey's 17th & 44th. Part of Grey's and Agnew's divisions sent to reinforce the right wing.

7 Cornwallis and the Queen's American Rangers (QAR) arrive after a forced march from Philadelphia, assault Greene's division in the flank at Luken's Mill. Both Rebel divisions fall back in disorder, pursued back to Whitemarsh.

MAP 9

the facts before mentioned will tolerably account for that event'. From this time also the Irish-French volunteer Thomas Conway, who commanded Sullivan's left at Germantown, became loudly convinced the Continental Army would never succeed under the direction of Washington. This, be it noted, the opinion of an officer who was to be made a Marshal of France in 1787. What elicited his and Pickering's contempt was that Greene and Washington once again evaded responsibility, Greene blaming Stephen, whose well-known fondness for the bottle was held responsible for the clash with Wayne's men, Washington alleging he had acted on advice from Sullivan not to leave 'a fortress to his rear'.

The canonical accounts contain altogether too much chat about the Continental Army drawing heart from moral victories, Germantown supposedly being one of them. The battle was fought at a time and place of Washington's choosing and ended with his army fleeing the field, having lost 650 killed and wounded, the only notable officer casualty being mortally wounded in an attempt to parley with the Chew House defenders. In addition more than 400 surrendered, among them 70 officers described by Peebles as 'shabby looking fellows', and the entire 9th Virginia. In return the British lost four officers (all senior) and 66 men killed, 28 officers and 419 men wounded, and 14 missing. It was a severe, demoralizing and predictable defeat that pitilessly exposed Washington's limitations. Two months later, in the midst of vain efforts to prevent the British clearing the Delaware forts, even the loyal Greene was moved to protest by his chief's unrealistically aggressive orders, in words that apply equally well to Germantown:

> Your Excellency has the choice of but two things, to fight the enemy without the least prospect of success, upon the common principle of war, or remain inactive, & be subject to the censure of an ignorant & impatient populace. In doing one you may make a bad matter worse, and take a measure, that if it proves unfortunate, you may stand condemned for by all military gentlemen of experience; pursuing the other you have the approbation of your own mind, you give your country an opportunity to exert itself to supply the present deficiency, & also act upon such military principles as will justify you to the best judges in the present day, & to all future generations.

To a commander-in-chief who could never be sure of the loyalty of an officer corps overflowing with opportunists who saw military service mainly as a means to other ends, the Rhode Islander's forthrightness and political naivety must have been immensely reassuring. What Greene did not appreciate was that Washington's main concern was what Congress, smarting from yet another flight from Philadelphia, might make of the contrast between his own humiliation by Howe, and the resounding victory in the North recently handed to his rival Gates by the playwright and self-dramatist John Burgoyne, every general's dream opponent.

5

THE VALLEY

BEFORE THE ADVENT of railways, significant military forces seldom strayed far from coasts and rivers. Nor did they need to, for human habitation and wealth was always concentrated in littoral areas. The 'roads' of America were primitive tracks, as they were everywhere else in the world at this time with the sole exception of the remarkable English turnpike system. The novelty was not that land communications were appalling but that they ran through woods of an extent and density not seen in Europe since the time of the Roman Empire. Far more significant to a maritime power like Britain were the four great hydrographic systems, the St Lawrence, the Hudson, the Delaware and the Chesapeake Bay catchment area. Of these, the first two were linked by an almost continuous ribbon of water reaching from Canada to New York along the Richelieu River, Lake Champlain and Lake George, which exerted a fatal fascination over strategists on both sides. Fatal, because the 'almost' in that description was a nearly impenetrable watershed between the ends of lakes and the northernmost curl of the navigable Hudson. Both sides were to find defeat by crossing it.

For the Rebels, a conquest of Canada depended on the fantasy that French Roman Catholics would rally to a furiously Anglo-Protestant cause. Even if they did, any gains would be unsustainable against a British counterinvasion along the St Lawrence. The reverse illusion that the Richelieu–Champlain–Hudson corridor could be used to amputate New England from the rest of the colonies was likewise based on wishful thinking. British naval control of the broad lower

Hudson did not prevent Washington from moving his army back to White Plains in August 1778, and the narrower upper reaches were even less of a barrier. Washington felt compelled to risk everything in the defence of New York and Philadelphia, but he was unmoved by the threat from the north, and left it to be dealt with by regional forces. Any link between the British strongholds in New York and Canada could only be extremely tenuous unless the woods and mountains through which it threaded were controlled by Loyalists.

The Rebels were the first to pour resources into this strategic black hole, encouraged by the capture of Fort Ticonderoga on 10 May 1775 by Ethan Allen, his cousin Seth Warner, and their 'Green Mountain Boys', declared outlaws by New York for their depredations in the area from which they took their name, now known as Vermont, then as the Hampshire Grants. They were enlisted in a private venture by a group of entrepreneurs including Silas Deane, whose close friend Benedict Arnold, also from Connecticut, joined the party armed only with a commission from the Massachusetts Committee of Safety, and was permitted to claim co-leadership with Allen. The small garrison was easily induced to surrender, after which another raiding party arrived with boats seized from the lake port bearing the name of the Loyalist John Skene. With these, Warner took possession of Crown Point, while Arnold led an expedition the length of Lake Champlain to capture Fort St Johns. After an ill-advised attempt to hold the fort against British troops from nearby Chambly, the Green Mountain Boys departed with their loot, leaving Arnold to hold Ticonderoga and Crown Point with a handful of men. Arnold had a gift for making enemies, and some he made during this venture dripped poison about his alleged political ambitions in the ever-receptive ears of the Massachusetts and Connecticut politicians, with the result that when reinforcements arrived they came with an officer who outranked him.

It would take several books to do justice to the snake-ball of ambitions and rivalries behind the Canada venture. As if it were not enough that the protagonists of the enterprise included Deane, Allen and Arnold, who all later conspired with the British against the rebellion, during Arnold's next expedition he commanded Lieutenants James Wilkinson and Aaron Burr, who later plotted with the Spanish and French to create separate nations in the southwest. An undiscussed

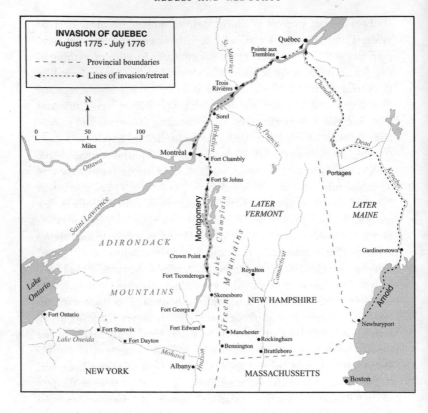

INVASION OF QUEBEC
August 1775 - July 1776

- - - - - ▶ Provincial boundaries
◀ - - - - - ▶ Lines of invasion/retreat

N

0   50   100
Miles

MAP 10

theme of this war is that any political entity born of treason has great difficulty in establishing its own legitimacy. Once broken, the bonds of individual and sectional cooperation for the greater good are not easily restored. Loyalty towards the United States, as such, grew very slowly, and in 1775–83, no less than during the second civil war of 1861–5, coercion alone ensured its survival. There was, unquestionably, an American identity before 1776 – but it was a sentiment hostile to nationalism, and was defined in opposition to the idea that the state could be more than simply a loose framework within which individuals made their own way.

Deep-seated individualism was not conducive to strategic coherence. It was militarily absurd to follow up the successes on Lake Champlain with a full-blooded invasion of Canada, although opportunity and motive were presented by the fact that General Guy Carleton, governor of Canada since 1766, had sent most of his troops to Gage in Boston and was the author of the hated Québec Act. The invasion was, however, politically astute because there was a danger the stalemate around Boston would lead to a general demobilization, as men returned to their farms for the harvest and had time to reconsider in the company of their wives and children. The removal of British authority to the north and west also appealed to the land speculators as a first step towards dispossessing the trans-Allegheny Native Americans, but the main purpose of the invasion, like the Declaration of Independence a year later, was to undercut those on both sides who favoured a compromise peace.

One of the invasions followed the traditional route through Lake Champlain, under the nominal command of Philip Schuyler, but in reality the work of his deputy, the Irishman Richard Montgomery, a recent immigrant who had been an officer in the British Army under General Jeffrey Amherst during his successful campaign along the same line of advance in 1759–60. Montgomery formally took over from the ailing Schuyler during the siege of Fort St Johns, which Carleton had garrisoned with 500 of the 800 regulars he retained and which held out from 5 September to 2 November. In the meantime Ethan Allen had been captured after he and his merry men, on their way to claim Montréal, ran into a small party of regulars.

Here again things get intricate. After the British evacuated Boston, Graves left no guard ships and some of the reinforcements arriving from Britain sailed into a trap, among them 200 men of the newly raised Fraser's Highlanders (71st) and their Captain Archibald Campbell of Inverneill, who was foully treated because of unfounded reports that Allen was being similarly misused. In fact, Allen was taken to London and given VIP treatment because he held out the prospect of bringing Vermont into the British fold. The two men were finally exchanged in 1778, Campbell to spearhead the successful British offensive in the south, Allen to use the assurances he had received from the British to strengthen his hand in dealing with Congress, to the fury of prominent New Yorkers who had legal title to the territory. Of more immediate importance for British plans in the area, however, was that while Allen assured them that the Green Mountain Boys were potential allies against the Rebels, leadership of them fell to Seth Warner, who was unaware of his cousin's machinations.

Montréal fell to Montgomery on 13 November 1775 without resistance. Carleton had found the French Canadians wanted little to do with this struggle among Protestants, and his salvation came from the two battalions of Royal Highland Emigrants (later the 84th) raised by Lieutenant-Colonel Allan MacLean from the inhabitants of Prince Edward Island, who like him had fought for the Stuart pretender in the Jacobite uprising of 1745–6. In a forced march from Sorel, MacLean just managed to reach Québec before the second prong of the American invasion, commanded by none other than Benedict Arnold, appeared out of the wilderness. Arnold had resigned his Massachusetts commission, but was appointed a colonel in the new Continental Army after he joined Washington at Boston. Washington knew British military engineers had surveyed a feasible overland route to Québec from the coast of Maine, and Arnold was a logical choice to lead the expedition, which set out from Newburyport on 19 September. Although we may question whether the many journals this venture produced could have been maintained by men experiencing conditions as desperate as they described, there is no doubting the outstanding leadership involved in getting half the 1100 mutually hostile Virginians, Pennsylvanians and New Englanders to Québec on 13 November. There Arnold called upon the defenders to surrender, received a terse reply from an 18-pounder, and fell back along the river to Trois Rivières, to await the arrival of Montgomery.

MacLean took over from the shaky lieutenant-governor until Carleton joined him, following a nightmare journey along the St Lawrence. He found a seventy-man remnant of the 7th, 200 of MacLean's Highlanders, 400 sailors and Marines from the Royal Navy ships in the ice-bound harbour, and about 300 undependable French Canadian Militia drawn from the 5000 inhabitants of the city, plus 184 cannon and enough powder and ammunition to permit him to be profligate in their use. With these he had to defend a wide perimeter in the face of about the same number of bold adventurers, winnowed by hardship to a hard core and led by some of the best officers the rebellion was to produce.

During New Year's night, under the additional cover of a snowstorm, Montgomery led his New Yorkers in a daring escalade against the southern end of the city walls, while Arnold led his men against the northern end. Montgomery was killed and his assault failed when he led it into an artillery trap, and Arnold was also wounded early. Despite being blown off his scaling ladder by the blast from a cannon at the first attempt, the Virginian Daniel Morgan took over leadership of Arnold's column and pressed on. The first barrier was breached and fifty men surrendered to him, but despite his conviction the city would have fallen if only he had not paused to regroup, his men sobered up to the reality of being isolated in a hostile city, at night. They chose to go no further, were surrounded, and surrendered.

Before Howe arrived in New York, Congress sent several thousand more soldiers and a delegation including Franklin and Carroll of Carrollton, the richest and sole Roman Catholic signatory of the Declaration of Independence. The reinforcements and the delegation arrived simultaneously with the thaw of the St Lawrence, along which sailed a fleet bearing 10,000 men under the command of John Burgoyne. Driven like cattle from Canada and down the Richelieu Valley, the Rebels made no effort to hold the forts along their way, and were it not for the exertions of Arnold would have abandoned Lake Champlain without a struggle. He constructed, from scratch, a serviceable little flotilla that imposed a three-month delay on Carleton, who stopped to build up an overwhelming naval force of his own. Arnold's flotilla was destroyed when the two fleets met at Valcour Island, but he had delayed the British long enough for the approach of winter to persuade Carleton to postpone operations to capture Fort Ticonderoga and prepare it as the forward base for a spring offensive in 1777.

Supposedly this prevented Carleton from making an early start to an invasion down the Hudson in 1777. There is, however, no evidence Carleton had any such intention. He was of the same mind as the Howes, and released Morgan and the rest of the Rebel prisoners on parole, with the avuncular comment, 'since we have tried in vain to make them acknowledge us as brothers, let us send them away, disposed to regard us as first cousins'. This indulgence was misguided in the case of the embittered Morgan, who had been flogged for punching a sergeant during the French and Indian War. But Carleton was not thinking beyond the defence of Canada, for which Ticonderoga was important solely to guard against another Rebel invasion along Lake Champlain. Thence into the wilds beyond was a step he would have undertaken reluctantly, and only if given specific orders. The invasion that followed was the product of Burgoyne's return to London, where he sold the idea to Germain.

In 1776 Washington's inexperience led him to ignore the principle of concentration and nearly brought the Rebel cause to ruin, but the British then handed the ball back by employing two armies in widely separated and nonsupporting operations during 1777. Piers Mackesy's masterful study of the war singles out chronic transport problems as the defining factor:

> It was the shipping shortage which had retarded Howe's reinforcements from Europe, further delaying his offensive. It was very probably the pressure on the dockyards which had prevented Carleton from being supplied early and adequately with the means of commanding Lake Champlain. Perhaps the influence of the ocean was never again to appear in so visible a form during the course of the war. But always the cold wastes of the Atlantic were to exert their invisible stranglehold on the British operations.

While lack of available shipping helps to explain why the troops no longer required for the recovery of Canada were not sent to join Howe, for Germain in London the temptation to use those troops anyway was great. It was made greater because it enabled him to slight Carleton, whom he detested and hoped to provoke into resignation, and because it held out the prospect of prompt vengeance against the New Englanders. A year earlier Burgoyne had submitted a paper entitled 'Reflections upon the War in America' in which he praised the Rebel soldier as 'his own general, who will turn every tree and bush into a kind of temporary fortress, from whence, when he hath fired his shot . . . will skip as it were to the next, and so on for a long time until dislodged either by cannon or by a resolute attack by light infantry'. His views on Native American auxiliaries were sharply at variance with those of Germain, Carleton and the once and future

Governor Tryon of New York, who were convinced the answer to Rebel tactics was to employ Native American warriors to clear the woods and sow terror in advance of the army. Burgoyne believed they were, 'at best a necessary evil, their services to be overvalued; sometimes insignificant, often barbarous, always capricious, and that the employment of them was only justifiable, when by being united to a regular army, they could be kept under control'.

But he did not succeed in controlling them, and by uniting them with the Regular Army he made himself responsible for their actions, in particular the cause célèbre of Jane McCrea, the fiancée of a Loyalist officer marching with Burgoyne's column, who was killed and scalped for her long auburn hair when on her way to join him. Burgoyne disastrously failed to punish the perpetrator, for fear the rest would turn against him. The episode encapsulated the folly of hiring the services of the hereditary knight Saint Luc de la Corne, fiend incarnate to the colonists for the imaginative sadism and cannibalism of the Seneca operating loosely under his direction during the Seven Years' War for Empire, whose view was that 'it was necessary to brutalize matters'. Employing him and his out-of-area warriors, who drove the terrified local tribes to seek shelter with the Rebels, was an egregious emphasis on the very elements in British prewar policy most unanimously rejected by the great majority of the colonists. It also made a mockery of Burgoyne's wordy proclamation that he had come to restore order and civility, provided fuel for Rebel propaganda and caused the flow of Militia away from the Northern Department to reverse. In return the military advantages were slight, for the British were never able to emulate the deadly French ability to combine native auxiliaries and regulars in the field.

This colossal miscalculation aside, the defining feature of the campaign was Burgoyne's desperation to achieve either a striking success or heroic failure. The plan he submitted to Germain was 'to effect a union' with Howe at Albany, the headquarters of the Northern Department of the Continental Army, but he was to press on with it even after receiving a letter from Howe informing him he could expect no significant assistance from the south. Not long afterwards Burgoyne also learned that a separate, diversionary invasion from Lake Ontario towards the Mohawk River Valley had been abandoned. Facing exactly

MAP 11

the sort of war of attrition he had warned against, with no hope of reinforcements and at the end of a tenuous supply line, retreat was the only sane option. After Ticonderoga was abandoned to Burgoyne on 6 July 1776 John Adams wrote to Abigail, 'I presume Gates [who had just taken over the Northern Department] will be so supported that Burgoyne will be obliged to retreat. He will stop at Ticonderoga, I suppose, for they can maintain posts although we cannot. I think we shall never defend a post until we shoot a general'.

If this totally unmilitary, once-mild little lawyer could see the logic of it, Germain in London and Howe in Pennsylvania can be forgiven for assuming the military imperatives of his situation would be obvious to Burgoyne. Perhaps because games of chance were a passion for all their class, they did not perceive he was a *degenerate* gambler, one whose certain response to setbacks was to keep doubling the stakes beyond the point of ruin. He had done it before, with his personal fortune, and now he did it again with the army entrusted to him. There is no questioning his physical bravery, but he lacked the moral courage to admit the failure of his project when the army could still have been salvaged intact. That, indeed, may have been part of the trouble, for when he learned that Howe was sailing south, he had not yet encountered significant military opposition. To withdraw under such circumstances might have opened him to the charge of 'not doing his utmost', for which Admiral John Byng had been shot in 1757 as a sop to an opposition less vicious than the one confronting North's government twenty years later.

There was also the question of momentum, for the campaign opened with the easy capture of Ticonderoga, believed on both sides of the Atlantic to be 'the Gibraltar of the North'. The Rebel garrison abandoned it when the British installed a pair of 12-pounders on the crest of nearby Sugar Loaf Hill, which commanded not only the Ticonderoga promontory but also the works across the lake on Rattle-snake Hill (Mount Independence). The sturdy pontoon bridge between the two was unconscionably left intact, permitting Brigadier-General Simon Fraser, commanding the vanguard, to mount a hot pursuit. In addition to his own 24th, Fraser's force included the grenadiers under Major John Acland, the light infantry under Major Alexander Lindsay, Earl of Balcarres, plus the Ebenezer Jessup's King's Loyal Americans and John Peters' Queen's Loyal Rangers, New Yorkers and New Englanders who had suffered much at the hands of the Rebels. At Hubbardtown select companies of these, in all about 750 men, caught up with a larger force of Massachusetts and New Hampshire Continen-tals, plus Vermonters whose status was always uncertain, under the command of Seth Warner, by now a Continental colonel but still very much his own man. Things were not going well for Fraser until a column of Brunswickers led by Colonel Friedrich von Riedesel came up on the Rebel right flank, after which Warner ordered his men to scatter and meet him at Manchester. Not many did.

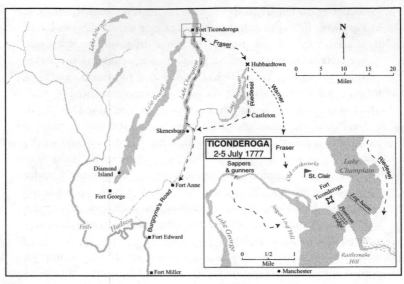

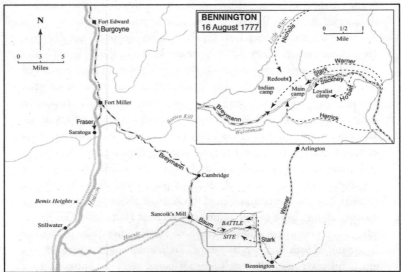

MAP 12

Fraser had much to think about after Riedesel marched off to rejoin Burgoyne, leaving him to cope with 150 wounded and 350 prisoners. The CO of the 24th was dead, Acland was severely wounded and, with thirty bullet holes in his clothing, Balcarres was alive only through the evident grace of God. On the plus side the Loyalists had performed well, but any thought that the training in musketry and skirmishing Fraser had put his men through would provide the answer to combat in the deep woods was dispelled by the rain of fire laid down by what was, after all, only the disorganized rearguard of a retreating army. He returned to Ticonderoga, while to the south Burgoyne captured the Rebel artillery train and most of their stores at Skenesboro, and pursued them as far as ruined Fort Anne, beyond which any advance would interrupt his water-borne supply line. There was an easier alternative, which was to return to Ticonderoga and follow Lake George to the traditional transit point through the site of Fort George – the route later taken by Brigadier-General William Phillips with the artillery – but instead Burgoyne set about constructing a road from Fort Anne to no less ruined Fort Edward.

Corporal Roger Lamb of the 9th recalled, 'the face of the country was . . . so broken with creeks and marshes, that there were no less than forty bridges to construct, one of which was over a morass two miles in extent'. Rebel tree felling and sabotage added to the obstacle, but they did not stay to harass Burgoyne's sappers, which task was left to the clouds of blood-sucking insects that still make a summer walk in this area unforgettable. On 3 August, after completion of this nightmare causeway, Burgoyne received a two week-old letter from Howe in New York congratulating him on the capture of Ticonderoga and announcing his own imminent departure for Pennsylvania. Howe considered it a further success that Burgoyne's expedition had drawn two brigades from Putnam's 4000 in the Hudson Highlands, and that Washington had detached 2500 men under Sullivan to the Northern Department. 'After your arrival in Albany', Howe wrote with feline nonchalance, 'the movements of the enemy will guide yours; . . . Sir Henry Clinton remains in command here, and will act as occurrences may direct'.

Burgoyne's reaction was to throw the dice. His next decision contained an echo of his original extravagant ambition to effect a union on the Connecticut River with the troops Howe's letter specifically told him would *not* be marching to meet him from Newport, Rhode Island. On 4 August he informed an astounded Riedesel that he intended to send 300 Brunswick dragoons under Lieutenant-Colonel Friederich Baum via Manchester to Rockingham, from there to Brattleboro, thence trailing jubilant Loyalists to rejoin the army at Albany (see MAP p. 86), about 200 extremely crooked miles in all, having collected mounts for the troopers, and wagons, cattle and general supplies to provision the army. The unsuitability of the dragoons' high boots and heavy cavalry sabres for whatever forest fighting might interfere with this grandiose plan was to be compensated for by about the same number of Loyalist riflemen and a large party of Native Americans. The crowning touch was that if Baum encountered resistance from Warner's remnant at Manchester, he was to exercise discretion because 'your corps is too valuable to let any considerable loss be hazarded on this occasion'. Riedesel assumed Burgoyne was acting on intelligence he chose not to share with him, and told Baum to expect a triumphal procession.

Which explains why Baum took the regimental band with him, and why Riedesel was later reluctant to send another column under Lieutenant-Colonel Heinrich Breymann after him, but did not think it odd when Burgoyne switched the first objective from Manchester to Bennington at the last moment. It was to be expected that a commander-in-chief would conceal his intentions, especially when among those coming into the camp at Fort Edward, claiming to be Loyalists, there were doubtless many Rebel spies. Burgoyne was indeed acting on information received from Philip Skene, now a major, whose self-interested advice to persist in a line of advance that ran through the settlement he owned may have influenced the general more than was ever admitted. He told Burgoyne there was a large Rebel depot at Bennington, which was true, and that it was lightly guarded, whereas it had become the rendezvous point for nearly 2000 New Hampshire and Massachusetts Militia. Worse, they were under the command of none other than John Stark, who had again been passed over in the appointments of February 1777, and resigned from the Continental Army when men of no experience such as Benjamin Lincoln of Massachusetts and fellow New Hampshireman Enoch Poor were promoted over him. Congress had given Washington the power to promote, and he shares the responsibility for this deliberate slighting of an officer whose combat and leadership credentials exceeded his own. Now, faced with imminent peril, the New Hampshire politicians overcame their own fear of Stark's popularity and appointed him brigadier-general in command of all provincial forces.

Among his last acts as officer commanding the Northern Department, Schuyler thought to bring the surge of New England volunteers under Continental Army control by appointing Lincoln, recently sent to him by Washington, to command them. Fortunately for the Rebel cause, the stout and placid Lincoln did not attempt to insist on this when he met the lean and mean Stark, nor on Schuyler's order for Stark's command to join him at Stillwater. Stark's brief was to defend the borders of New Hampshire, but in addition he could cite Washington's advice that 'an enemy can always act with more vigour and effect when they have nothing to apprehend on their flanks and rear'. Neither he nor Baum knew each other's strength when their scouts clashed around Sancoik's Mill on 14 August, and although the Brunswicker advanced, it was to occupy a defensive position where the Bennington road crossed the Waloomsac River, there to await the arrival of Breymann. Unforgivably, Baum divided his force into four camps, none in supporting range of the other, and failed to post pickets. As a British officer serving with the Loyalists snarled to the Brunswicker surgeon Julius Wasmus:

> I cannot understand how one can entrust so important an expedition to such a man [as Baum], who has no military experience at all, cannot take proper measures, particularly here in the wilderness, and who has no knowledge at all of foreign languages . . . and also despises the counsel of those sent along for guidance, assistance and advice.

Stark, meanwhile, had fallen back to prepare an attack. Many experienced woodsmen had rallied to him, and he sent them to scout and snipe Baum's men continuously. He also received detailed information from locals who pretended to join Peters, only to slip away when they had seen all they wished, who warned him about the approaching relief column. Drenching rain prevented an attack on

15 August, but the gods of war smiled on Stark, for Breymann was another officer out of his depth, who paused frequently to ensure his troops marched with parade-ground dressing. Warner made better time when summoned by Stark from Manchester, where 150–200 Green Mountain Boys had rejoined him after filtering through hills infested with hostile natives and wolves. They were to form the reserve in the skilful plan Stark devised to trap the whole of Baum's force, which was to prove Militia could perform the most intricate battlefield manoeuvres under fire. All it took was to be led by a man capable of infusing them with his fierce determination, as Stark did with the parting words, 'There are the redcoats and they are ours, or Molly Stark sleeps a widow tonight'.

The concept was no less than a double-double envelopment, involving four flanking columns led by New Hampshire/Vermont Militia colonels in addition to the main force under Stark and the reserve under Warner. The wider envelopment was carried out by Moses Nichols to the north and Samuel Herrick to the south, each penetrating along densely wooded tributaries of the Waloomsac. The inner two, sent against the Loyalist camp, were commanded by Thomas Stickney and David Hobart. These were all to engage simultaneously, the signal to be when Nichols' men, who had the longest approach and had to silence Baum's artillery redoubt, opened fire. Stark would then charge the main camp on the banks of the river, and Warner would pass through to deal with Breymann's column. The columns reached their positions simultaneously and achieved complete surprise, despite many of them going into battle roaring drunk.

The Native Americans promptly fled, but the rest of Baum's command put up fierce, if brief resistance. Stark described it as 'the hottest I ever saw in my life. It represented one continued clap of thunder'. The most savage fighting took place at the Loyalist camp, where Peters recognized 'a Rebel captain, Jeremiah Post by name, an old schoolmate and playfellow, and a cousin of my wife'. Both fired at each other and missed, then Post bayoneted him just as he finished reloading. 'Peters, you damned Tory', he said, 'I have got you'. Peters simultaneously fired his musket and killed him, 'though his bayonet was in my body I felt regret at having to destroy him'. The blade deflected by his ribs, Peters was one of only forty Loyalists to escape from the camp, the rest either killed in battle, shot into mass graves after surrender, or led away roped together to be hanged in their communities. Warner's men passed through and savaged Breymann's men, bringing the total Brunswicker loss for the day to 600 men.

A month later Stark's men at last marched into the Continental Army encampment at Stillwater, and out again three days later upon the expiry of their sixty-day enlistment period. On 5 October Congress wrote him a letter of thanks enclosing his commission as a Continental brigadier-general, but he was to be offered no opportunities suited to his talent and played only a minor role in the rest of the war. While fortunate to be in the right place at precisely the right time, facing an opponent who made it easy for him, among the Rebel officers only Morgan was to display anything approaching Stark's tactical skill, or his ability to inspire and control the Militia. He had Oliver Cromwell's gift for war, and that alone may be sufficient explanation why those who ran the war regarded him with abiding distrust.

The loss of 10 per cent of his command brought Burgoyne into unwelcome contact with reality and, in letters to Germain from Saratoga dated 20 August, he complained that Philip Skene (another Bennington survivor) had misled him, and that Loyalist recruitment had fallen far short of expectation. He did not mention how he had wasted the hardcore cadres formed by Jessup and Peters by keeping them in constant and ill-directed action on his flanks, nor that Saint Luc de la Corne's natives, who now departed en masse, had stripped Loyalism of moral justification. Instead he switched emphasis from the operational, for which he could not evade responsibility, to the strategic misconceptions surrounding the campaign, blame for which he could hope to spread more widely. From the overconfidence with which he had launched Baum's expedition, Burgoyne now swung to the other extreme:

> The great bulk of the countryside is undoubtedly with the Congress, in principle and in zeal; and their measures are executed with a secrecy and dispatch that are not to be equalled. Wherever the King's forces point, Militia, to the amount of three or four thousand, assemble in twenty-four hours ... The Hampshire Grants in particular, a country unpeopled and almost unknown in the last war, now abounds in the most active and most

rebellious race in the continent, and hangs like a gathering storm upon my left.

While confirming that he was acting in the knowledge there would be no support from New York, and that the enemy had received a large supply of firearms, artillery and ammunition 'landed from the French ships which got into Boston' – this a shot across the bows of the Lords Howe and Sandwich – he set out to fasten blame for what followed around Germain's neck, the alibi he was to repeat for the rest of his life. 'Had I latitude in my orders, I should think it my duty to wait in this position', he wrote, 'but my orders being positive to "force a junction with Sir William Howe" I apprehend I am not at liberty to remain inactive'.

On the other side, the long wrangle between the wealthy New Yorker Schuyler and the New England politicians came to a head with his replacement by Horatio Gates, an officer the Yankees preferred because of his political views, although even Samuel Adams found him personally unpalatable. Schuyler had shown moral courage in not wasting troops by confronting Burgoyne early, and intelligent anticipation in having rebuilt and garrisoned ruined Fort Stanwix, renamed Schuyler, at the headwater of the Mohawk River, which stopped the advance of St Leger's column advancing from Lake Ontario via Lake Oneida. St Leger lacked siege artillery and only 340 of his 1500 men were regulars. About the same number were Canadians and Loyalists from the Mohawk Valley, but the bulk of his force were Iroquois, who had joined in anticipation of raiding along the valley and became dispirited by inactivity.

They were, however, led by the remarkable Mohawk Sachem Thayendanegea, better known as Joseph Brant, the name on his captain's commission in the regular army, and on the portrait painted of him by George Romney on the occasion of his visit to London in 1775. He showed what they could do at Oriskany, where he ambushed a German Flats Militia column marching to the relief of Fort Schuyler under the command of Nicholas Herkimer, whose brother was serving with St Leger. Herkimer was mortally wounded and the column retreated, but in the meantime the besieged garrison had sortied and destroyed the Indians' camp. When the Iroquois returned from Oriskany they kept going, and St Leger was obliged to abandon the siege. He had tied up 750 New York Continentals in the fort, defeated Herkimer's 800 Militia, and the ensuing panic forced Schuyler to detach Brigadier-General Ebenezer Learned's brigade of Massachusetts Continentals, about 950 men and a quarter of the troops under his command. So exaggerated were the reports of British strength that Schuyler also appointed the newly arrived Arnold in overall command of operations in the area, to rally the frightened settlers. St Leger could not realistically have been expected to achieve more, but his retreat was another element for Burgoyne to add to the melodrama he was writing, with himself in the role of ill-starred hero.

In addition to Arnold, Washington had sent north Daniel Morgan, now colonel of a personally recruited corps of 500 Virginians equipped with long hunting rifles, with which they could consistently hit a man-sized target at 250 yards, four times the effective range of a musket. Morgan and Arnold held each other in high esteem from their shared endurance and heroism during the Québec expedition, but both rapidly became disillusioned with the tactics espoused by Gates, their new commander-in-chief. Although the McCrea incident and his own appointment had stiffened resolve among the New Englanders, and the army at Stillwater now numbered not far short of 10,000 men, Gates intended to do no more than prevent any further British advance along the Hudson by holding a three-bastioned earthwork, which the Polish volunteer and engineer officer Tadeusz Kosciuszko constructed for him at Bemis Heights. This would also protect his right if Burgoyne attempted to outflank the work by hooking inland, to attack from the open, densely wooded western side. Gates was confident his opponent would 'risque all upon one rash stroke', and planned to restore the Continentals' confidence in a tightly controlled engagement, after which the retreating enemy would be nibbled to death by swarming Militia.

Burgoyne sent Phillips with the heavy artillery along the Hudson with Riedesel's Brunswickers in the morning of 29 September, while himself leading the 9th, 20th, 21st and 62nd towards Freeman's Farm. Fraser's 24th, light infantry, grenadiers, Breymann's Jägers and the Loyalists hooked wide to his right, in the expectation of precisely the counterstroke Arnold now launched from what was supposed to be a holding position on a hill wide to the left of the fortifications. Burgoyne's column was met head-on in the clearing by the light infantry element of Arnold's division, Morgan's corps and a regiment of New Hampshire Continentals led by Major Henry Dearborn, who had fought under Stark at Breed's Hill, and under Arnold at Québec. They had the answer to Burgoyne's tactics of swift assaults and aggressively handled artillery, with Dearborn's musketeers providing the rapid fire and bayonets necessary to protect Morgan's slower-loading riflemen, enabling them to concentrate on sniping the British officers and gunners. After routing Burgoyne's advance guard they charged across the clearing, ran into his main force and were scattered, a paradoxically fortunate development for it meant they had recovered the treeline before Fraser appeared on what would have otherwise been their open left flank. Burgoyne's plan may have been to fall back and draw them further into the trap, but his men would have none of it in what became a classic soldier's battle.

Lamb observed that Burgoyne 'shunned no danger; his presence and conduct animated the troops (for they greatly loved the general)'. Arnold also rode wherever the fighting was fiercest, and many years later, despite his intervening treachery, one of his soldiers defiantly recalled, 'He was our fighting general. It was "Come on boys!" t'warnt "Go boys." He was as brave a man as ever lived'. Although Arnold's division included Learned's and Poor's brigades, Gates refused to release them until he rode back to demand them in person, while on the other side Phillips and then Riedesel marched to the sound of the guns, which tipped the balance in favour of the British. Their departure left the road alongside the Hudson virtually open to Gates, who still had two-thirds of his army within the ring of fortifications, but he was indignant at Arnold for spoiling his own plan, and disinclined to take any risks when the overall situation was working so strongly in his favour. Gates was right, but Arnold's desire to restore pride to the Continental Army, and to strip the British of their faith that they would always prevail in the field, spoke to the deeper motivation of men at war.

Both sides came away with heightened respect for their opponents. Burgoyne might declare that possession of the field 'must demonstrate our victory beyond the power of even an American newswriter to

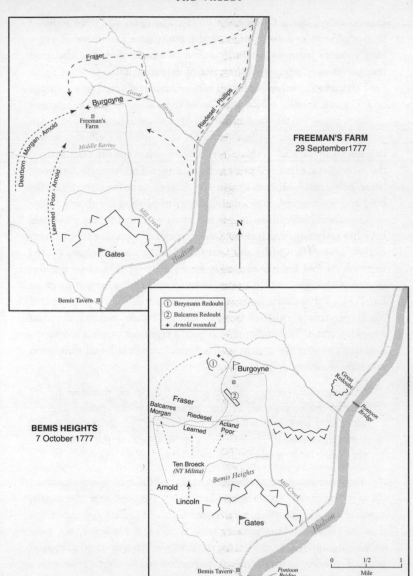

FREEMAN'S FARM
29 September 1777

BEMIS HEIGHTS
7 October 1777

① Breymann Redoubt
② Balcarres Redoubt
✛ *Arnold wounded*

MAP 13

explain away', but his men knew better. The 62nd had been reduced to five officers and sixty men, all the gun teams and three of every four gunners from the central column had been shot, and the guns themselves only salvaged at the price of desperate hand-to-hand fighting. The unattached volunteer Thomas Anburey noted 'the courage and obstinacy with which the Americans fought' and Lieutenant William Digby of the 53rd mourned 'a dear-bought victory if I can give it that name, as we lost many brave men'. John Glover, now a brigadier-general and a reluctantly inactive observer of the battle from the earthworks, expressed pride in both armies. The redcoats, he wrote, 'were bold, intrepid, and fought like heroes, our men were equally bold and courageous, and fought like men, fighting for their all'.

Gates was determined to get rid of Arnold and finally provoked him into resigning, which came close to sparking a mutiny. The officers of Poor's New Hampshire and Learned's Massachusetts brigades voted to thank Arnold for his leadership on 29 September, and to ask him to stay. Although Learned prevailed on his subordinates not to go so far, Poor's submitted a written protest to that effect, despite the bad blood previously existing between their brigade commander and Arnold. Captain Wakefield of Dearborn's regiment penned a description that captures the awe in which Arnold was held by all those who saw him in action:

> Nothing could exceed the bravery of Arnold on this day; he seemed the very genius of war. Infuriated by the conflict and maddened by Gates' refusal to send reinforcements, which he repeatedly called for, and knowing he was meeting the brunt of the battle, he seemed inspired with the fury of a demon.

Burgoyne was granted one more straw to clutch by a message from Clinton, dated 12 September and received the day after the battle, announcing his intention to advance up the Hudson 'in about ten days' to take Fort Montgomery with 2000 men. However, not long afterwards a prisoner released for the purpose brought word the garrison at Ticonderoga had carelessly permitted an enemy surprise attack to seize all the outworks, liberating prisoners and seizing valuable stores. Burgoyne's main logistics base, at Diamond Island on Lake George, had been saved from a similar fate only because an escaped

British prisoner got there ahead of the raiding party. Lake George was Burgoyne's sole line of communications following his decision to abandon the painfully built Skenesboro-Fort Edward causeway, but he was now encumbered by hundreds of sick and wounded, and his decision to fortify the position he held and wait for Clinton was the only option offering at least a chance of avoiding humiliating retreat.

When long-awaited reinforcements from Britain arrived on 24 September 1777, Henry Clinton sailed up the river with 3000 men and made short work of the strong American defences at the southern end of the Hudson Highlands. He landed 1000 men at Verplanck's Point, and the Militia posted there fled to Peekskill with exaggerated reports of his strength. Israel Putnam, whose army was reduced to 1500 men by the detachment of the Connecticut regiments to join Washington and of Glover's men to reinforce Gates, retreated away from the river. This left two works with sixty-seven guns on the western bank to bar passage up the river, both commanded by men also called Clinton. The larger, Fort Montgomery, was on a promontory, covering a log and chain boom behind which were two frigates and several smaller warships of the Continental Navy. It was defended by Continental brigadier-general and governor of New York George Clinton with 200 Militia infantry. The modestly named Fort Clinton, a smaller work barring an attack along the river line, was under the command of his older brother James, of the same rank but with more combat experience, and a garrison of 400 Militia and about 50 Continentals.

Fort Montgomery was stormed by a force of 900 men who had marched around the dominant feature of Bear Mountain, mainly the Loyal Americans regiment and the first battalion of the New York Volunteers under their Colonel Duncan Campbell, officer commanding, with companies of riflemen from the 52nd and 57th, and another of Loyalists raised by the German Captain Andreas Emmerich, oddly known as 'chasseurs'. George Clinton refused a summons to surrender and a massacre ensued after Campbell was killed in the assault, with the governor escaping across the Hudson one step ahead of the bayonets. James Clinton mounted a forward defence in the narrow approach between Hessian Lake and the river, forcing the main British column under Major-General John Vaughn to storm two lines of abatis backed by artillery. But while thus occupied the defenders were

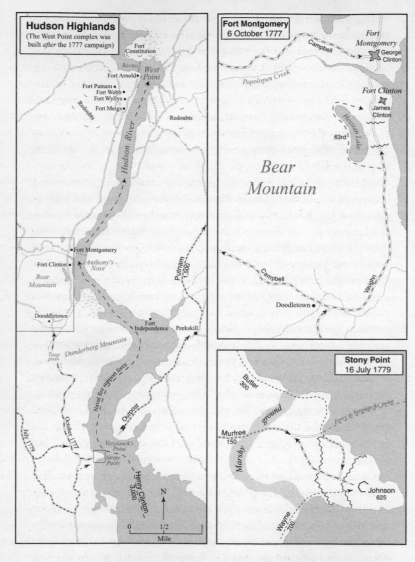

Hudson Highlands
(The West Point complex was built *after* the 1777 campaign)

Fort Constitution
Booms
West Point
Fort Arnold
Fort Putnam
Fort Webb
Fort Wyllys
Fort Meigs
Redoubts
Hudson River
Redoubts
Fort Montgomery
Fort Clinton
Anthony's Nose
Bear Mountain
Dooddletown
Putnam 1,500
Timp pass
Dunderberg Mountain
Fort Independence
Peekskill
Naval fire support force
Outpost
October 1777
July 1779
Verplanck's Point
Stony Point
Henry Clinton 3,000
N
0 1/2 1
Mile

Fort Montgomery
6 October 1777

Campbell
Fort Montgomery
George Clinton
Popolopen Creek
Fort Clinton
James Clinton
Hessian Lake
63rd
Bear Mountain
Campbell
Vaughn
Doodletown

Stony Point
16 July 1779

Butler 300
Murfree 150
Marshy ground
Ferry to Verplanck's Point
Johnson 625
Wayne 700

MAP 14

outflanked around the lake by the 63rd, after which the fort fell easily. James himself was wounded and escaped inland, but in a few hours the Clintons had lost more than 300 men and two substantial works, to men with no artillery whatever. In addition the Continental warships were trapped by contrary winds, and burned to prevent capture when the Royal Navy breached the boom. The debacle continued when the garrison of Fort Constitution, three miles upstream and controlling the river from a low island separated from the mainland by a marsh, abandoned it without further ado, leaving their guns and stores behind.

Clinton sent Vaughn and 1700 men up the river to Esopus and beyond (see MAP p. 129), but although unable to stop this, Putnam and George Clinton had blanket control of the countryside, and all communications with Burgoyne were cut. Henry Clinton was no risk-taker, and he was probably secretly relieved to receive a dispatch from Howe in Philadelphia requiring him to send reinforcements, among them regiments taking part in Vaughn's raid, after which he abandoned even the captured forts. Gates could not know this, however, and when Burgoyne attacked again on the day following the fall of the Hudson forts, Gates falsely concluded the operations were coordinated. In reality Burgoyne's initiative was an empty gesture designed to show that he was 'doing his utmost'. Acland's grenadiers, Riedesel's Brunswickers and Balcarres' light infantry brigades, 1700 men in all under the operational command of Fraser, advanced in echelon from the redoubts built to protect the British right wing. They were met by twice their number of Continentals under the command of Lincoln, whose orders from Gates were to stop the British advance at the Mill Creek line.

Poor's men repulsed a charge by the grenadiers and drove them back to the long enclosure known as the Balcarres Redoubt, leaving Acland shot through both legs on the field. Morgan and Dearborn drove back Balcarres with a flank attack followed by a frontal assault, and mortally wounded Fraser, who felt it his duty to remain still despite two near misses from a sniper he could see taking aim at him from a tree. This was Timothy Murphy, Morgan's best shot and specifically detailed to eliminate the man on the grey horse, which he did with the third shot that tore through Fraser's intestines. Burgoyne also had bullet holes in his clothing and his horse killed under him, and Lamb observed, 'in the service of this campaign, the British officers bled profusely and most honourably'. Modern opinion holds such concepts foolish, but they were valued then, and explain why Burgoyne's men never blamed him for their fate.

The Brunswickers stoically stood firm at the centre, and there it might have ended had Arnold not appeared, in defiance of Gates' orders. He went first to liaise with Morgan, then rode across the front of Learned's cheering men and ordered them to charge across the creek, which they did with a will. At the same time Lincoln's reserve, about 1800 New York Militia under Abraham Ten Broeck, could be seen marching over the crest of Bemis Heights, and Riedesel's men now broke, abandoning the gun line that had dominated the Middle Ravine. Arnold went on to lead an unsuccessful assault on the Balcarres Redoubt, then rode between the two armies to direct further attacks to clear out some log cabins between the two works, and finally hooked around the rear of Breymann's Redoubt, already under strong pressure from Morgan's men. There, resistance collapsed after the unyielding Breymann was killed, but Arnold's luck at last ran out. The shot that broke his 'Québec leg' also killed his horse, which mangled the limb further in its death agony, and although he refused amputation and miraculously escaped gangrene, he was out of the war until May 1778. As we shall see, one of the efforts made by his American contemporaries to resolve the contradiction between how much the revolution owed him with his later apostasy was to make a cult object of that battered leg.

6

TURNING POINT:
'THEY STOOD LIKE SOLDIERS'

'I AM AS WELL CONVINCED, as if I had seen it', Washington wrote of the Northern Department troops, 'that they will not march boldly up to a work nor stand exposed in a plain'. Gates was of the same opinion, and both were proved wrong. The main contemporary source for those seeking to downplay Arnold's role is James Wilkinson, whose memoirs were published when most of those who could have disputed his statements were dead. Intent on turning the war into a morality play, traditional accounts also argue that the brilliant Arnold was a crypto-aristocrat, and that the mediocre Gates, in real life an appalling snob whose career in the British Army had benefited from as good or better social connections than most, was animated by resentment that his lowly birth denied him advancement in Britain. Fortescue rightly dismissed him and Charles Lee as 'a discredit to the country alike of their birth and of their adoption', and whatever disloyalty Gates may have shown to Britain pales beside his constant efforts to undermine Washington, his patron from the time he arrived in Virginia in 1765. A small matter, perhaps, but illustrative of a more general evasion of the question why many who had been in the forefront of the revolution, Arnold chief among them, became disenchanted.

The British abandoned the field and fell back behind the Great Ravine. The following day saw two events that became as iconic for them as Breed's Hill and Washington's crossing of the Delaware for the Americans. First the very pregnant Lady Harriet Acland, who had joined the army to nurse her husband's wounds after Hubbardtown, determined to go to him behind enemy lines, and would not be denied. Secondly, the senior officers gathered on the ramparts of the Great Redoubt to respect Fraser's dying wish to be buried there, and like him felt it was their duty to present a standing target for the American artillerymen, who fired at them with more enthusiasm than skill until they realized what was going on. The beautiful site overlooking the Hudson remains a tourist attraction, as does a bizarre monument to Benedict Arnold's leg, placed there as though in wistful fulfilment of the wish expressed by some of his contemporaries to cut it off and give it honoured burial, prior to hanging the rest of him.

Burgoyne had set out with 3980 British, 3120 German, some 1000 supernumeraries, and about 2000 Loyalist troops. Whether the Loyalists were from north or south of the eventual border with Canada was rather less important at the time than later. British troops left behind to hold Ticonderoga and Diamond Island were approximately balanced by late arriving German reinforcements. At the time of capitulation at Saratoga on 17 October 1777, having left 460 desperately sick and wounded behind, the army numbered 2240 British and 1700 German effectives, about 1800 supernumeraries plus walking sick and wounded, and 480 certifiable Canadians after Jessup, Peters and their few remaining men obtained permission to escape. This they did with an ease that suggests Burgoyne's threat to fight his way out was not as hollow as some believe. But the imbalance of casualties argues he deliberately used up the Germans and the Loyalists while preserving the British component, which he was not now prepared to sacrifice. There was no force between him and Lake Champlain capable of stopping him if he had chosen to abandon his heavy guns and baggage, but he was looking for an 'honourable' solution and found plenty of excuses to dawdle. Finally, he now summoned a council of war to provide one last layer of cover for his decision to seek terms.

Given that opposition politicians were not scrupulous about the sticks they employed to beat the North administration, that they did not pick up this one tells us a great deal about how 'Gentleman Johnny' Burgoyne was perceived by his peers, many of them army officers to whom his motives were transparent. Furthermore, by signing a formal

Convention with Gates he bestowed recognition on the civil power that had appointed him, a matter of crucial importance to both sides. Many British commentators had ceased to refer to the enemy as 'Rebels' and we also shall now use the designation 'Americans', for Arnold's insight was correct. Battles and wars are won and lost in the hearts of men, and from this time onwards the British, at first only Burgoyne's troops but not long afterwards also their political masters in London, accepted that a new nation had come into being in opposition to them.

Lamb recorded an incident that captured the moment, when an Irish private of the 9th called Maguire and an American on the opposite bank waved to each other and then both plunged into the river to embrace in mid stream. They were brothers, who had found different means to better themselves, and one suspects Britain lost and America gained a citizen that day. When the time came to lay down their arms, all were impressed by the bearing of their opponents. 'Their decent behaviour', wrote Digby, 'to us so greatly fallen, merited the utmost approbation and praise'. Riedesel commented, 'not one of them was properly uniformed, but they stood like soldiers, erect with a military bearing . . . as if they wished to do us honour'. Gates, already melted by the odyssey of Lady Harriet, practically fawned on Burgoyne.

Alas, the mood of mutual respect was only local. Keen to puncture the triumphal aura surrounding his old protégé Gates, Washington urged Congress to renege on terms that would have permitted the prisoners to return home under parole. It was a dishonourable deed, but Burgoyne and the British authorities were at least as culpable for quibbling over the details and failing to show the proper humility. In practical terms, although what now became known as the Convention Army was permanently removed from the board, this was to some extent balanced when the deadly Vermonters went home, while Poor's New Hampshire Continentals mutinied a month later, amid growing indications that New England felt it had done enough.

There are many reasons why a general peace did not follow in early 1778, chief among them the impossibility of conducting confidential negotiations with Congress when the only conduit was Benjamin Franklin. His centrality to the process was acknowledged by George III, after receipt of what amounted to a formal French declaration of war in late March 1778, when he wrote letters, here run together, which acknowledged the existence of a separate American nation, although he could not yet bring himself to name it:

> ... it is a joke to think of keeping Pennsylvania for we must form from the army now in America a corps sufficient to attack the French islands ... I think it so desirable to end the war with that country to be enabled with redoubled ardour to avenge the faithless and insolent conduct of France that I think it may be proper to keep open the channel of intercourse with that insidious man.

Nobody disputes Franklin used his privileged position to play both sides off against the middle. The error in historical appreciation has been to assume that 'the middle' was the greater good of the United States. Along with the rest of the American delegation he was raking in commissions on supplies bought with French money, peculations more than tolerated by Vergennes, and had much to lose by an early peace. In 1811 John Adams, trapped between the rock of the reality he observed in Paris, and the hard place of the myth carefully constructed by Franklin, wrote feelingly (my emphasis):

> Had he been an ordinary man, I should never have taken the trouble to expose the turpitude of his intrigues, or to vindicate my reputation against his vilifications and calumnies. But the temple of human nature has two great apartments: the intellectual and the moral. If there is not a mutual friendship and strict alliance between these, degradation to the whole building must be the consequence ... To all those talents and qualities for the foundation of a great and lasting character, which were held up to the view of the whole world by the University of Oxford, the Royal Society of London and the Royal Academy of Sciences in Paris, were added, it is believed, *more artificial modes of diffusing, celebrating and exaggerating his reputation than were ever before or since practiced in favour of any individual.*

In sum, a pioneer PR man whose principal client was himself. His wider interest lay in land speculations in Ohio, inconveniently encumbered by Native Americans, and extensive property in Nova Scotia, even more awkwardly occupied by Highlanders who neither at the time nor since have shown any desire to join the United States.

Also, patently, he wanted revenge for his humiliation before the Privy Council in 1774. As with Samuel Adams, the evidence that Franklin systematically falsified the record is unequivocal, but the following dated 1 February 1778, in reply to a personal letter from an English member of the missionary Moravian sect, shows an illiberal and vengeful streak he was usually careful to conceal. It is also, of course, an example of how information can be imparted 'informally' to a third party, to enhance its credibility in the eyes of the target audience, and illustrates how he and his kind grossly overplayed their hand in the expectation France would win the war for them:

> Instead of honouring and rewarding the ... advisers and promoters of this war, you should disgrace them, with all those who have influenced the nation against America by their malicious writings, and all the ministers and generals who have prosecuted the war with such inhumanity. This would show a national change of disposition and a disapprobation of what had passed. In proposing terms, you should not only grant such as the necessity of your affairs may evidently oblige you to grant, but such additional ones as may show your generosity, and thereby demonstrate your good will. For instance, perhaps you might by your treaty, retain all Canada, Nova Scotia and the Floridas. But if you would have a really friendly, as well as able ally in America, and avoid all occasion of future discord, which will otherwise be continually arising on your American frontiers, you should throw in those countries. And you may call it, if you please, an indemnification for the burning of their towns, which indemnification will, otherwise, be some time or other demanded.

Franklin was in close contact with opposition leaders in London and knew the North administration was desperately anxious to disengage. It was his correspondents who made it impossible for the government to do so without cutting its own political throat. Franklin was either not sufficiently astute to realize, or simply did not care how British perceptions of the American cause would be altered by the alliance he negotiated with France. Thus Chatham, until then a voice calling for appeasement, denounced North's willingness to abandon sovereignty over the colonies as a surrender to 'its ancient and inveterate enemy' in his last speech to the House of Lords in April 1778. The

Americans were now 'the French', and everything was much simpler. 'Let us at least make one effort', Chatham concluded, 'and if we must fall, let us fall like men'. Suiting deeds to words he then collapsed and was borne away to his deathbed.

North made a belated effort to get around Franklin by sending a peace commission headed by Frederick Howard, Earl of Carlisle, to treat with Congress, which arrived in Philadelphia just as whatever negotiating leverage it might have possessed was thrown away by the evacuation of the city. The key man on the commission was William Eden, Carlisle's friend since school days, who would not have been included unless well-oiled secret negotiations were contemplated. Further cover may have been provided unwittingly by another member, who was sent home after making clumsily overt attempts to bribe the congressional committee. This may have been a stratagem designed to distract attention from Eden, for the man thus discredited had fought a duel with Germain in 1770. Indeed, the Carlisle Commission included so many men known to be hostile to the North administration that one is compelled to wonder whether, beyond the more evident fall-back purpose of demonstrating the intransigence of the Americans, another intended secondary benefit may not have been to discredit the parliamentary opposition.

On the other side of the English Channel, although Germantown and Saratoga may have persuaded Vergennes that the money he was paying the Americans was not entirely wasted, small-scale battles in places about which he knew little and cared less cannot have been of more than 'circumstantial' significance in his decision to go to war. Just as 'the French' means something other than the French people to the British, what they call 'the Anglo-Saxons' are not specifically the British and the Americans, but the random variables that have obstructed the emergence of an ordered world in which all roads lead to Paris, as once they did to the Rome whose linguistic and cultural successor they consider France to be. The cultural gulf is illuminated by the philosophic dichotomy, alien to English-speakers, between the terms 'circumstantial' and 'conjunctural'. 'Conjunctural' are those events that deep thinkers, by definition French, identify as the manifestations of great historical currents, while those not central to the grand design are 'circumstantial'. Thus their naval strategy, in which the 'conjunctural' maintenance of a fleet in being took precedence over the 'circumstantial' battles annoyingly sought by the British. Vergennes' aim was to force the Royal Navy to concentrate in home waters, thus unable to protect British interests in the Mediterranean, the Caribbean and the Indian Ocean. Keeping the war going in North America served to stretch the Royal Navy further, particularly by tying down scarce frigates on blockade duty to the detriment of their primary function as the eyes of the fleet.

What began now was a war for empire against Britain by France, later joined by Spain, in which the United States was a very junior partner. The Americans had won the political struggle for independence, something recognized by the terms of the French alliance, which bound the United States not to accept even 'tacit' recognition by Britain unless forming part of a general peace treaty. It is amusing how passionately men like Patrick 'Give me liberty or give me death' Henry embraced the prospect of absolutist France invading Britain, without considering what the likely fate of their fractious little republic would have been once the Bourbons eliminated the British presence in the Americas. Washington was alert to this, and wrote to warn that, treaty or no, a Canada won with the help of France would become French again. 'It is a maxim founded on the universal experience of mankind', he wrote, 'that no nation is to be trusted further than it is bound by its interest; and no prudent statesman or politician will venture to depart from it'.

Within the confines of the land war in North America, Saratoga marks game, set and match in one war – the struggle to subdue New England by force. In the middle colonies it also partially offset the moral effect of Washington's defeats and the fall of Philadelphia, although by the time news of the Convention filtered south it was already clear there was no silent majority of Loyalists ready to spring to life. The king never had believed there was. 'The regaining [of] their affection is an idle idea', he wrote before Saratoga, 'it must be the convincing them that it is their interest to submit, and then they will dread further broils'. The Howes still adamantly refused to obey requests to tighten the blockade and to make punitive coastal raids, but with their alternative approach now revealed to have been built on sand, both asked to be relieved. William Howe tried to blame his failure on lack of support from London, but Germain refuted this in Parliament by detailing the enormous effort made to provide all Howe had requested. He also convincingly demonstrated that Howe had been given an unprecedentedly free hand, and that his secretive command style had contributed significantly to the Saratoga disaster. Even Germain's most vicious critics felt obliged to change the subject.

Five years later Franklin pronounced that there never was a bad peace or a good war, yet the terms he accepted behind the back of the French in late 1782 were not greatly different from the British offer he revealed to them in order to cement the alliance for war in early 1778. The commercial ties between America and Britain, once linked to the cession of Canada and Florida, were already on their way to prewar levels before peace was declared, with the former still firmly in British hands and the latter recovered by Spain. Along with many other 'patriots' Franklin had done very well out of the intervening years but the people whose interests he claimed to represent paid a heavy price, and the only reason they did not suffer more was that the British never wholeheartedly adopted a policy of counterterrorism. The rebellion, obviously, would have been drowned in blood by a more ruthless colonial power, but equally obviously Franklin and his ilk counted on the British being inhibited from winning the game by a self-denying concern about how it should be played. It was a nearly fatal miscalculation.

While Franklin played his games, Washington's army came close to falling apart during the winter following Saratoga. The inspiring legend of true-hearted patriots bravely bearing hardship at Valley Forge during the winter of 1777–78 was largely an invention of the mid nineteenth-century Romantic Era. Only a small number of those who had nowhere else to go remained with Washington, and his army actually suffered even more during the following, truly dreadful winter at Morristown, New Jersey. What was remarkable about Valley Forge was that nothing whatever was done for the soldiers, not even payment of the pittance they were entitled to in devalued Continental paper money. In Joseph Martin's opinion, 'had there fallen deep snows . . . or even heavy and long rainstorms, the whole army must inevitably have perished'. Their deprivation was made more galling by reports of the redcoats, snug in Philadelphia, partying down. Christopher

Marshall, a civilian who had abandoned the city rather than remain under British rule, sourly noted:

> . . . our enemies revelling in balls, attended with every degree of luxury and excess in the City, rioting and wantoning, using our houses, utensils, and furniture; . . . add to this their frequent excursions . . . destroying and burning what they please, pillaging, plundering men and women, stealing boys above ten years old, deflowering virgins, driving into the City for their use [a mouth-watering list of farm products] upon our horses . . . Oh, Americans, where is now your virtue? Oh, Washington, where is your courage?

Martin and his fellows were not prepared to starve 'in the midst of a plentiful country', and no fencing timber, unattended animal or carelessly secured cellar was safe from them. Six months later, when Thomas Anburey and other members of the captive Convention Army passed through, the locals were still indignant about this, and wanted to know why Howe had not attacked when Washington's army was his for the taking. Although armies of this era did not campaign in winter, on this occasion it must also have seemed there was little point in venturing out to assail an army in an advanced state of decomposition. Peebles recorded:

> . . . deserters coming in frequently and in parties – twelve ser-geants and one corporal of their artillery came in today who say that their army at Valley Forge are in great distress for want of clothing, shoes, etc. – and yesterday some country men brought in one of their Militia Cols. prisoner, and some people from the Jerseys brought in a Committee-man – well done my lads keep it up.

Added to which the contrast between Gates' victory at Saratoga and Washington's failure to defend Philadelphia gave rise to some of the most venomous intrigue and backbiting of the war on the American side, stirred up by none other than James Wilkinson. Somehow he set the Gates and Washington factions at each other's throats while convincing Congress he himself was trustworthy. He was promoted to brigadier-general, prompting something so close to mutiny among the senior officers that Congress hastily promised them pensions (half-pay), a provision they had long been demanding, for giving up other opportunities to make money in the service of their country. Congress also appointed Wilkinson Secretary to the new Board of War, but by now Gates had woken up to his game and would not work with him. Wilkinson was forced to resign, in a letter so abusive of his erstwhile patron that it was, alas, destroyed. In July 1779 he was appointed clothier-general, from which post he was evicted by a threat to audit the accounts in March 1781. He never lost his ability to manipulate politicians and did further harm to his country for another thirty years. Happily, however, he now passes from our story.

On Christmas Day Johann 'Baron de' Kalb, who had returned to America in 1777 to demand, and receive, the rank of major-general promised him by Deane in Paris, reported to his French patron, 'the quartermasters-general provide quarters for the commander-in-chief and for themselves, but for nobody else . . . The very numerous assistant quartermasters are for the most part men of no military education whatever, in many cases ordinary hucksters, but always colonels'. This was in marked contrast to the increasing professionalism of the infantry officer cadres, as Ewald noted on 2 December 1777:

> For the love of justice and in praise of this nation, I must admit that when we examine a haversack of the enemy, which contained only two shirts, we also found the most excellent military books translated into their language . . . Moreover, several among their officers had designed excellent small handbooks and distributed them in the army.

Howe was not deceived by the flood of enemy deserters. Like Washington, he did not believe they could be trusted in combat against their old comrades, and the Maryland and Pennsylvania regiments formed from deserters were sent to garrison Jamaica in 1778. At the same time the genuinely Loyalist units were animated by a visceral hatred that forced him to face the incompatibility between military effectiveness and reconciliation. Long before Howe finally sailed for England in May 1778 it had become apparent that the Loyalists, even commanded by regular army officers and combined with British regiments, were bent on revenge. In March 1778 an expedition under Mawhood, the officer defeated at Princeton, was sent to clear the banks of the Delaware in the vicinity of Salem (see MAP 5), and after engagements with local Militia were followed by the murder of civilians and wounded prisoners at Hancock's and Quinton's Bridges, Lieutenant-Colonel John Simcoe, recruiter and commander of the Queen's American Rangers, reported with studied understatement that 'some very unfortunate circumstances happened here ... events like these are the real miseries of war'.

British regulars now operating under the looser rules of irregular warfare were not backward in adopting the same methods. Wayne's men had taken no prisoners at Germantown in retaliation for Paoli, and the light infantry wanted revenge. In early May at Hatboro, in conjunction with troops from the 16th and 17th Light Dragoons, they surprised a large band of Militia under the command of John Lacey, who reported 'some were butchered in a manner the most brutal savages could not equal, even while living some were thrown into the buckwheat straw and the straw set on fire, the clothes were burnt on others, and scarcely one without a dozen wounds with bayonets and cutlassess'. A Hessian officer confirmed nine wounded prisoners were thrown into the fire, the traditional punishment for incendiaries, and it should be noted that Lacey himself once complained about the 'villainous actions' of his own men. Men confronted with evidence of enemy brutality do not pause to consider who started the spiral into uncontrolled savagery, and are less inclined to exercise restraint.

As a general rule mounted men did not take prisoners, because to do so would slow them down. The role of the light infantry was also to move fast and strike hard, but in an echo of the dispensation traditionally enjoyed by the knightly class, their ruthlessness garnered more opprobrium. A British line officer harrumphed that the light infantry were 'for the most part young and insolent puppies, whose worthlessness was apparently their recommendation to a service which placed them in the post of danger, and in a way of becoming food for powder, their most appropriate destination next to that of the gallows'. Another component of the British forces that now came to greater prominence was the Highlanders, in particularly the 71st, which grew to three full battalions during the course of the war. During the Saratoga campaign Captain John Money observed that Highlanders made the best irregulars, 'if well trained for the occasion, as they are a hardy, nimble and intelligent people', and so they proved.

An element of self-selection was also at work – hard men tend to gravitate towards units where a kill or be killed ethic prevails. The grenadiers, like the light infantry also selected from the line regiments, were no less ruthless. To get slightly ahead of our narrative, after the British Army had returned to the New York islands, and during the course of a large-scale foraging operation along the west bank of the Hudson, Cornwallis detached 'No-Flint' Grey to repeat his Paoli exploit against the New Jersey Militia at Tappan in the night of 28 September 1778. The Militia got wind of this and decamped, but did not inform a nearby regiment of Continental dragoons, Virginians under the command of Lieutenant-Colonel George Baylor, who were consequently surprised and slaughtered by men under orders to show no mercy. Lieutenant-Colonel Charles Stuart of the 26th dissapprovingly commented:

> General Grey had the good fortune to surround their cantonment before they were alarmed, by which means sixty were killed, including a lieutenant-colonel [not so, Baylor survived a bayonet thrust through the lungs] and a major, and fifty taken, most of whom were wretchedly wounded with bayonets. As they were in their beds and fired not a shot in opposition, the credit that might have been due to the corps that effected the surprise is entirely buried in the barbarity of their behaviour.

To economize on any further tut-tutting, human sensibility recognizes the difference between a refusal to give quarter on the battlefield and the cold-blooded killing of those whose surrender has been accepted. In the matter of the treatment given to enemy non-walking wounded when medical and transport resources were limited, few would quibble over a *coup de grâce* given to a desperately injured man where the only alternative was to leave him to die of exposure or, literally, to the wolves. It was also within the well-understood rules of war that the lives of those who refused an offer to capitulate on terms were forfeit to those obliged to subdue them by force. Irregular warfare opened up a number of additionally sanctioned horrors by blurring the line between combatant and civilian, but a distinction can still be

made between reprisals aimed at discouraging civilians from har-
bouring guerrilla combatants, and wholesale devastation designed to
depopulate a given area. At a time when men, women and even children were executed for property crimes, the readiness of Americans
to hang each other in the midst of a war for the possession of a
continent is not remarkable. Soldiers might view hanging as a relatively
merciful release, if less honourable than death by firing squad, for
military punishments included flogging to death and 'breaking on the
wheel', in which a heinous offender would have all his bones smashed
with iron bars.

Acts of nauseating sadism were common whenever Native and
African Americans were involved, and it is fair to hold those claiming
to be members of the Christian community to a higher standard than
those they denounced as 'savages'. The cause of independence for
whites meant only continuing servitude and oppression for the other
races, and created a blood-guilt that has troubled American society
ever since. The not-so-fine distinction between the two was that Afri-
cans were regarded as backward human beings in the North, and as
valuable property in the South, in either case granted greater consideration than the Natives, who were generally regarded as vermin infesting
otherwise desirable real estate. Added to which, acts of resistance by
the 'property' were generally limited to running away, whereas the
'vermin' had sharp teeth. Ewald recorded a fascinating conversation
with the son of an English gunsmith, brought up among the Iroquois,
who gloated that in Major John Butler's raid on the Wyoming Valley
(on which more later), 'two whole brigades were massacred, of which
the greater part were scalped half-dead, and in such misery lost their
lives'. Ewald asked if he, also, had taken scalps:

'Oh, yes!' – whereat a wild laugh expressed in his features his
delight at the recollection. 'In the same affair I worked so hard
with my tomahawk and scalping knife that my arms were bloody
above the elbows ... He who lives with the Indians and wants
to enjoy their friendship must conform to them in all respects,
but then one can depend upon these good people. They are
indeed good, sincere people'. 'But cannot Colonel (sic) Butler
prevent this cruelty?' 'No, not in the least. If he dares to do this,
and meddles with our customs and laws, he would be deserted

instantly by these people. Indeed, they would soon become his enemy and certainly murder him'.

Tempting though it is to put a reverse spin on American propaganda, the more humane treatment of the other races by the British confers no greater claim to righteousness, for it was based on no higher moral purpose than tactical advantage during and after the war. As noted earlier, the only difference between the southern American and West Indian British slavocracies was opportunity, and it is questionable whether William Wilberforce would have prevailed against the slave trade in 1807, or the abolitionists against the institution itself in 1833, had the colonies become part of a Union of Great Britain and America. The Southern planters would have formed a blocking majority in Parliament with their West Indian peers and the Liverpool and Bristol slavers. The jury will have to remain out on whether or not the Native Americans might have received fairer treatment within such a Union, as they did in Canada, but it seems unlikely. To cite only a few examples: the governor of South Carolina invaded the lands of the Cherokee during the French and Indian War, while they were serving the British cause in the capture of Fort Duquesne/Pitt; the violent jurisdictional conflict between Pennsylvania and Connecticut that left the frontier 'Paxton Boys' unpunished for their massacre of Christian Conestoga and Delaware farmers in 1763; and, not least, the gift of smallpox-infected blankets to the Seneca during Pontiac's Rebellion by General Jeffrey Amherst, commander-in-chief in America until 1763, and titular head of the British Army thereafter.

Thus the background to a war that now went the way civil wars usually do if prolonged. Since it was the Americans who insisted on terms amounting to unconditional British surrender as a precondition for peace talks, one might have expected they would now make one more concerted effort to provide some military justification for their presumption. They did not, and although the number of long-term enlistees peaked at about 35,000 in late 1778, this corresponds more closely to growing economic hardship than to popular enthusiasm. The most patriotic probably shared the views of Martin, who compared himself to 'a loyal and faithful husband, with a light-heeled wanton of a wife. But I forgive her and hope she will do better in future'. The only offensive activity contemplated was another invasion of Canada, which foundered on the indifference of the New Englanders, while Washington sent Sullivan to Massachusetts to prepare for an assault on Newport in combination with the French. Both sides knew they were coming, and that the Spanish would throw their hat in the ring eventually, but as Don Higginbotham dryly puts it, 'this would not be the last time that American diplomats would equate the interests of their country with those of the world'. Their conceit led to diplomatic rebuffs in Madrid and elsewhere in Europe, and strained even Vergennes' patience. Yet they still expected France to win the war for them, as though by divine right, and had no answers to the strategy adopted by the British to deal with the changed circumstances.

The first step was to abandon Philadelphia in order to free troops for deployment elsewhere. Although appointed commander-in-chief in March, Clinton did not formally take over from Howe in Philadelphia until May. He found himself faced with the same conundrum that had kept the British Army in Boston through the winter of 1775–6 – insufficient shipping to evacuate the army, its stores and the thousands of civilian Loyalists who could not be left behind. The latter, their personal effects, the sick and the women camp followers were given the first priority on the convoy that sailed on 18 June 1779, simultaneously with the departure overland of about 15,000 men, and a column of 1500 wagons and artillery stretching twelve miles. More than 10 per cent fell out during the march, the majority of them Hessians who had seen how well the German immigrant population lived in Pennsylvania, and who vanished into it like water to a sponge. However this was not a demoralized army, as it proved at the most durably controversial battle of the war (see MAP 15).

It was the last occasion when American arms might have won the war unaided. If Clinton's army were defeated so soon after Saratoga, North's administration would have fallen and the opposition would have scuttled. Nearly half the British troops were committed to the defence of the lumbering wagon train, whereas the Americans could march at twice their pace, and could choose when and where to attack. Washington had 15,300 men under his command, all except 800 of them Continentals. These were at last drilled to something approaching European standards thanks to the efforts of the Prussian volunteer

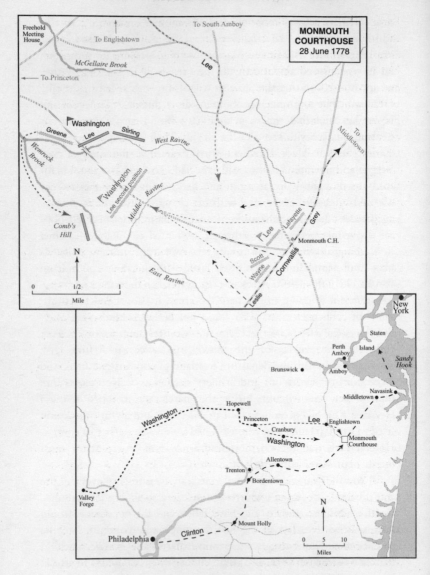

MONMOUTH
COURTHOUSE
28 June 1778

MAP 15

Baron Friederich von Steuben, and if Ewald had remarked upon it, the improvement in the quality of his junior officers cannot have escaped the notice of their commander-in-chief. Washington therefore had the means and opportunity to win renown for American arms and for himself, but instead continued to seek the cover of councils of war, which he summoned on 17 and 24 June, and once again divided his army in the face of the enemy. He later made every effort to focus attention on tactics, and hence on the doubly convenient scapegoat Charles Lee, but it was above all a half-hearted performance at the strategic and operational levels. Since Washington was far from being timid, the most likely explanation is he judged the certain risk to his political aspirations of a possible defeat or yet another inconclusive engagement outweighed the military advantage he might gain by forthrightly committing his whole force to battle.

Washington detached Morgan's 600 riflemen and 2100 mixed New Jersey Continentals and Militia to harass the British column. Although Morgan did not, the New Jersey brigade joined Lee at Englishtown, where he took it under his personal command. Three other brigades under the command of the young Marquis de La Fayette, Wayne and the Virginian Charles Scott brought Lee's division to 6100 men, while Washington retained 8500 men in two divisions commanded by Stirling and Greene. Lee was to pin the British rearguard with a flank attack from the north, while Washington closed in from the west. Unfortunately the rearguard was under the command of the hyper-aggressive Cornwallis, and the 8000-plus men under his command included the light infantry and the Queen's American Rangers, now brigaded with them, also the British and Hessian grenadiers, the Guards battalion and twelve line regiments including two battalions of the Royal Highlanders. Poor Lee did his best to follow orders, but Scott's brigade deployed incorrectly and found its fire masked by Wayne's, while La Fayette's very mixed brigade of Yankees, Marylanders, Pennsylvanians and New Yorkers began to retreat before it had become fully engaged. Outflanked on both sides and counter-attacked by some of the best infantry in the world, Lee did very well to extract his division, but that was not the way it looked to Washington when he rode forward through crowds of men in flight.

It is no more easy to stop a charge than it is to turn fleeing men around, and after driving in the second position occupied by Lee's division (where Washington won many hearts by abandoning his Olympian composure to ride among the men cursing and threatening like a drill sergeant), the grenadiers and the Highlanders led an over-pursuit into a line of artillery backed by the rest of the Continental Army along the broad West Ravine of the Wemrock Brook. When they were slow to retreat from this exposed position, Greene smartly marched his division to a hill overlooking the East Ravine and opened a brisk fire on their left flank. In seven years of service, this was the sole occasion when Joseph Martin recorded a possible 'kill', although his description explains why such claims were always problematical in the black powder era:

> I singled out a [Highlander] and took my aim directly between his shoulders (they were divested of their packs), he was a good mark, being a broad-shouldered fellow; what became of him I know not, the fire and the smoke hid him from my sight; one thing I know, that is, I took as deliberate aim at him as ever I did any game in my life. But after all, I hope I did not kill him, although I intended to at the time.

Nineteenth-century American chroniclers created an uplifting legend about one Molly Pitcher, symbol of righteous womanhood, acting as the loader for a gun after her husband was killed. This was Mary Hays, a real heroine who did indeed form part of a gun crew during the battle, whom Martin remembered somewhat differently:

> A cannon shot from the enemy passed directly between her legs without doing any other damage than carrying away all the lower part of her petticoat – looking at it with apparent unconcern, she observed, that it was lucky it did not pass a little higher, for in that case it would have carried away something else, and ended her and her occupation.

Under a blazing sun, the battle tapered off in mutual exhaustion. The British recorded 60 and the Americans 37 dead of heatstroke among about 360 casualties on either side. Officer casualties were also equally heavy on both sides, the most senior being Lieutenant Colonel Henry Monckton, killed within yards of Wayne's brigade at the centre of the final American line when leading his grenadiers in a last charge. Thousands of men and dozens of cannon blasted away at each other, often at very close range, during the better part of a whole summer day, to inflict a total of only 450 wounds. To lead by example was to increase the chances of injury exponentially, and the Monmouth casualty figures confirm Continental line officers were now as fully prepared to pay this price as their British counterparts. This in turn argues that Washington may have greatly underestimated the opportunity presented to him.

Although Clinton formed his army for battle at Navasink, with his back to the beaches off which Lord Howe's ships were waiting to transport the army, his hope that Washington might abandon prudence was dashed. The embarkation that followed might have been less leisurely had Clinton been aware that a French fleet of twelve line of battle ships under Rear Admiral Charles Théodat, Comte d'Estaing, had recently sailed past on the way to the Philadelphia, and was to appear off Sandy Hook a week later. Some of the more interesting 'what ifs' of this war are concentrated in this short campaign, for if Estaing had arrived a week earlier he would have trapped Howe's convoy in the Delaware, and if he had known about Clinton's intentions he might have risked the sand bars to prevent the evacuation, and forced him to march overland to Amboy. Even if he did not attack him again on the march, Washington could have assaulted or besieged Perth Amboy, and another Saratoga might still have been achieved.

With apologies for not introducing La Fayette properly upon first mention, let us now consider the meteoric career of this young nobleman, who was promoted to major-general and given the divisional vacancy created by the carefully orchestrated disgrace of Lee. Arnold, newly returned to the army and the obvious choice, was appointed to administrative duties in Philadelphia. If we allow that he may not have been fully fit after his long convalescence, among those serving with Washington's army there still remained Brigadier-Generals Glover and Poor – not to mention Morgan, who was still only a colonel – all proven combat leaders crowned with laurels stretching from Boston and Québec, through Trenton and Princeton, to Freeman's Farm and Bemis Heights. It was militarily unconscionable to insult these veterans by promoting above them a twenty-one year old French volunteer who had joined the army in mid 1777, and whose only battle experience was to get himself shot in the leg when riding around with no specific duties at the Brandywine. Nor can it be excused on diplomatic grounds, for La Fayette was in bad odour with the French court, and the over-promotion of a notorious dilettante merely deepened the contempt in which career French officers were already inclined to hold their rustic allies. His sole qualifications were his class, and an open admiration for Washington bordering on idolatry. When, after this, we find men of the calibre of Morgan resigning because of alleged ill health, the traditional explanation is that they were disillusioned with Congress. It is far more likely they were disenchanted by the partiality shown by Washington to what Lee sourly called his 'earwigs', the handsome and ambitious young men of his personal entourage.

The first Franco-American combined operation came as a wake-up call to those who thought their new allies would sacrifice themselves for them. Although he would shortly dispatch 5000 men under Grant to attack the French West Indies, and a further 4700 to East and West Florida in anticipation of war with Spain, at this time Clinton had about 28,000 men on Manhattan, the Bronx Peninsula, Long Island and Staten Island. Washington marched to White Plains, the armies thus returning to more or less exactly the positions they occupied in October 1776, but could make no move against Clinton. Instead he detached 3000 men under La Fayette and Greene to join Sullivan at Providence, Rhode Island, towards which Estaing's fleet also sailed. Their target was the British outpost at Newport, in most respects a far better port than New York and with a no less Loyalist population, but held only by 3000 men under the command of Sir Major-General Robert Pigot, (see MAP 16). La Fayette found himself obliged to ride to Boston to hasten the arrival of 6000 Massachusetts Militia under the command of John Hancock, at last able to wear his handsome uniform without provoking undue mirth. The fly in the ointment was that Sullivan, a back-country lawyer whose military career had so far been ignominious, was the overall officer commanding.

Upon arrival, Estaing was astounded to find Sullivan considered himself empowered to give him orders, and that instead of hovering offshore to prevent any relief arriving from New York, he was expected

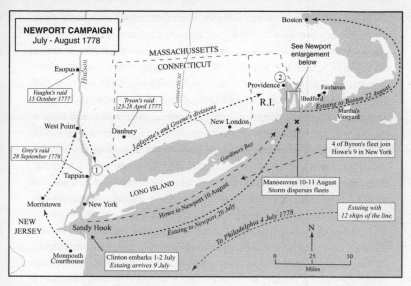

NEWPORT CAMPAIGN
July - August 1778

MASSACHUSSETTS
CONNECTICUT

Boston

See Newport
enlargement
below

Esopus

*Vaughn's raid
15 October 1777*

Hudson

*Tryon's raid
23-28 April 1777*

Providence

Fairhaven

R.I.

Bedford

Estaing to Boston 22 August

Martha's
Vineyard

West Point

Lafayette's and Greene's divisions

Danbury

New London

New York

*Grey's raid
28 September 1778*

Gardiners Bay

4 of Byron's fleet join
Howe's 9 in New York

Tappan

LONG ISLAND

Manoeuvres 10-11 August
Storm disperses fleets

Morristown

New York

Howe to Newport 10 August

Estaing to Newport 20 July

Sandy Hook

Estaing to Newport 20 July

Estaing with
12 ships of the line

NEW
JERSEY

To Philadelphia 4 July 1778

N

Monmouth
Courthouse

Clinton embarks 1-2 July
Estaing arrives 9 July

0   25   50
Miles

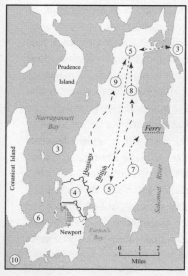

Prudence
Island

Narragansett
Bay

Ferry

Conanicut Island

Hessians

British

Saconnet River

Newport

Easton's
Bay

0   1   2
Miles

1   Washington's army arrives at White Plains 16 July.

2   Sullivan's 1000 Continentals joined by 3000 under
    Lafayette & Greene, 6000 Militia under Hancock.

3   Estaing sails past Newport, lands sick on Conanicut.
    Sullivan masses his forces at Tiverton.

4   British garrison of 3000 under Pigot behind double
    line of earthworks, frigates scuttled to block harbour.

5   Sullivan crosses 9 August, a day earlier than agreed,
    begins siegeworks on eastern side of Newport.

6   10 August - Estaing warned that Howe is approaching,
    recovers troops and puts out to sea.

7   20/21 August - French straggle back, Estaing departs
    to refit in Boston. Massachusetts Militia go home.

8   28 August - Pigot sorties, drives Continentals to their
    works at Butt's Hill ⑤, driven back to Quaker Hill.

9   29 August - Hessians stopped at Turkey Hill by Glover's
    Massachusetts Continentals, orderly evacuation follows.

10 30 August - Clinton arrives with 4000 reinforcements.

MAP 16

to mount an amphibious assault. He agreed, at what price to his pride we can only speculate, but Sullivan jumped the gun and crossed a day early, driving the British garrison behind two lines of earthworks that could only be taken by a formal siege. Estaing had taken the precaution of keeping a copy of the plan, explaining with an exquisite irony that he had done so, 'because anything made by yourself is too precious a keepsake'. He was relieved of the necessity of telling Sullivan that he would not be risking his ships in an artillery duel with the British shore batteries by the appearance of Lord Howe's fleet from New York, equal in number but of considerably less firepower than his own. Retrieving the men he had landed on Conanicut Island, he sailed out, if not to do battle, at least to go through the motions prescribed by current French naval orthodoxy. Knowing the British would always seek the windward gauge, the French had decided to make a virtue of leeward necessity and use the greater elevation it gave their broadsides to fire chain and bar shot at maximum range, in order to damage their opponents' masts, sails and rigging. Once crippled, they could then be hammered from bow or stern until they surrendered, or boarded at will.

That, at least, was the theory. A violent storm prevented a fleet engagement, and although several single-ship actions took place, none was lost by either side. All, however, were sufficiently damaged to make the thoughts of both admirals, particularly Estaing on his dismasted flagship, turn to repair yards. He put in at Newport only long enough to inform an apoplectic Sullivan that, *désolé*, he must sail to Boston to refit. Among the remarks in the written reply – another precious keepsake – was that his actions 'stain the honour of France, are contrary to the interests of His Most Christian Majesty, are most pernicious to the prosperity of the United States, and an outrageous offence upon the alliance between the two nations'. Indignant at being thus abandoned, Hancock's Militia now abandoned the Continentals in turn. As these 4000 men retreated from their siegeworks, Sir Pigot's 3000 sortied and chased them to the north of the island, until Glover's brigade upheld the honour of Massachusetts by checking the pursuit so sternly that no further attempt was made to interfere with them, as next they rendered their now traditional boat-handling service to their comrades in the evacuation of the island.

A day later Clinton arrived with 5000 men from New York, found nothing to do and sailed on to pay a distant visit to Boston before returning to New York. On the way back a task force under Grey raided the privateer ports of Bedford and Fairhaven, burning some seventy ships, and the island of Martha's Vineyard, where he destroyed the whaling fleet, and carried away hundreds of cattle and thousands of sheep. Meanwhile La Fayette found it necessary to warn his American colleagues that he would challenge the next one who insulted his country to a duel, no light threat from one schooled in the use of pistol and épée from childhood, and Estaing found that as well as being charged several times the going rate for everything, his men could not venture into Boston without fear of assault by armed mobs. The young hereditary knight of Saint Sauveur was killed while trying to prevent the sacking of a bakery the French had set up ashore, for which the House of Delegates undertook to make amends by erecting a monument over his grave – which they did the next time they were allied with France, in 1917.

7

NORTHERN ENDGAME

WE SHALL FOLLOW the continuing tribulations of Estaing in later chapters, turning now to consider the many and messy ways in which the war in the north and northwest grumbled on, not merely until the formal peace treaty of 1783 but well beyond. The most active front was the old-new one that flared up because the Americans used the military slack cut for them by the French alliance to seek a final solution to the problem of the hostile Native Americans in the area, hereafter the 'Indians' of contemporary usage. If there is anything praiseworthy in the Anglo-American treatment of the indigenous peoples of North America, I regret it has escaped my notice. It was genocidal from the beginning, and while one can accept that warrior cultures must live or die by battle, there is no excuse or mitigation for the fate of Indians who abandoned traditional ways and became Christian farmers wishing only to live in peace, who became the preferred targets for the rapists, arsonists and scalp-hunters of the frontier. Both sides routinely committed stomach-churning atrocities during campaigns usually portrayed as glorious first steps towards the achievement of Manifest Destiny.

The first was an expedition not mounted in the name of the United States at all. It was a secret freebooting expedition funded by Virginia in order to peg out its particular claim to an empire reaching from the Atlantic to the Mississippi River. Nobody knew where the headwaters of the Mississippi lay, and the common belief was that it originated in the Great Lakes. It was so obviously crucial to the development of the North American hinterland that the first state to lay claim to

MAP 17

the eastern bank (the western being in the hands of the Spanish) would
be in a strong negotiating position vis-à-vis the rest postwar. The East–
West highway was the Ohio River, along which in April-June 1778
parties of Kentucky frontiersmen journeyed in ignorance of their
eventual destination. Gathered on an island above the Ohio Falls (site
of present-day Louisville), they were joined by a young Virginia Militia
captain called George Rogers Clark, who put an armed guard on their
boats and informed them they were to advance a further 200 miles
along the Ohio to plant the flag of Virginia on the Mississippi. Surprisingly few resented the trick.

The French settlers at Kaskasia, Cahokia and Vincennes were not inclined to resist Clark's pretensions, and when news of the Franco-American alliance reached them some even served under him. But so did others in the small force assembled by the lieutenant-governor of Canada, Henry Hamilton, falsely branded 'Hair-Buyer' by Franklin and the object of particular hatred to the rulers of Virginia, whose own bounty for Indian scalps was so generous that men dug up cemeteries to obtain them. Hamilton occupied Vincennes in December after an epic winter march from Fort Miami, but he became a prisoner after it was retaken on 24 February following a rapid counterattack by Clark from Kaskasia. Hamilton was sent to Williamsburg, Virginia, under a heavy armed guard to keep him from being lynched, where he was kept chained in a windowless and intentionally unsanitary cell by Thomas Jefferson until Washington protested, and then paroled. Clark's fabled ability to win over the Indians was really limited to tribes such as the Kaskasia, Kickapoo, Fox and Sauk, whose contact with white men had so far been limited. He did not even try to win back the Shawnee, implacable enemies of the revolution since the treacherous murder of peace-seeking Chief Cornstalk by Pennsylvanian frontiersmen in 1777, nor the majority of the Delaware tribe, nor the Mingo, Miami, Wyandot, and least of all the fearsome Seneca, who all drew supplies and arms from the British, and who prevented Clark from ever mounting the assault on Fort Detroit that was intended to crown his campaign.

To say the war parties that ravaged the Ohio and Kentucky territories for the duration of the war and beyond were ever 'led' by white men is to misunderstand the nature of Indian warfare. As we saw during the Burgoyne campaign, the Indians were unamenable to discipline, undependable in battle and perfectly capable of turning against their paymasters over matters the latter might regard as trifling. A later age was to argue the Indians did not know right from wrong, to which frontiersmen dryly riposted the test was to wrong them, and see what ensued. There were those like the Anglo-Iroquois interviewed by Ewald, and the infamous Simon Girty, son of an Irish immigrant captured by the Seneca in 1756, who were assimilated and commanded a following by outstanding boldness and cruelty, but British Army officers exercised only a tenuous control over their wild allies. Thus, despite having six light artillery pieces that gave him considerable

LEFT The Better Part –
Captain Joseph Brant
(Thayendanegea)

BELOW Lady Harriet Acland
goes to her wounded
husband

Failure to Overawe – Breed's Hill

Total War Advocate – Henry Lee   People's War Advocate – Horatio Gates

'Discredit to the country alike of their birth and of their adoption'?

ABOVE 'Expect nothing but complaints' – Sir Henry Clinton

LEFT Intelligently Indolent – Sir William Howe

BRIGADIER GEN.L ARNOLD.

Talented Turncoat – Benedict Arnold

Stage Strutter – John Burgoyne

A Gift for War – fierce John Stark in old age

Teacher's Pet – Gilbert du Motier, Marquis de La Fayette

practical authority, Virginia Loyalist Captain Henry Bird was unable to save fellow Virginian Captain Ruddles and his men after they surrendered their fort to him in mid 1780, nor to prevent the Indians of the raid he was 'leading' from carrying off the refugees who had sought refuge there. This may have been a factor in his decision not to attack Lexington, cutting short the largest British-'led' raid ever mounted in the area.

How much authority even Girty exercised is difficult to assess, but in October 1779 he was a member of the party that captured a delegation sent by Virginia to New Orleans, returning along the Ohio with some of the British prisoners from Vincennes, and a chest containing coin valued by Clark at two million livres, half the amount of the annual French subsidy to the United States and, if it reached their hands, enough for the British to finance the low-intensity war in the West for a number of years. Clark's attempts to retaliate fell on the deserted Miami village of Piqua and Shawnee Chillicothe in 1780, and the latter again (at a new location) in 1782, but with Forts Detroit, Miami and St Joseph under the competent administration of the Loyalist New Yorker Colonel Arent Schuyler De Peyster, this affected the tribesmen not in the slightest. From the Virginian perspective, therefore, Clark's expedition was an unmitigated disaster.

Nor did things go well for others when they thought to fly their flag along the Ohio. When Colonel Archibald Lochry and his Pennsylvania Militia were ambushed by Brant and Girty in August 1781, about a third fell in battle, another third killed at leisure and the remainder permitted to escape. When Girty sneered at him for this, Brant gave the final touch to what was already a startlingly sinister face by laying his cheek open with a sabre. If Girty was not involved in the defeat inflicted on a large force of Virginia Continentals and Militia under the command of Washington's friend Colonel William Crawford at Sandusky River in June 1782, he was gloatingly present at the subsequent hideously prolonged death of the unfortunate colonel. It is too neat to attribute this to revenge for the massacre at Gnadenhutten (see Introduction), for Girty himself had been menacing the Moravian Delawares for months, while many warrior societies, worldwide, have honoured prominent enemy captives by torturing and eating them. The one battle honour definitely attributable to Girty came two months later at Blue Licks, where he was the architect of a rare successful ambush of about 200 Kentucky frontiersmen, including the legendary Daniel Boone, in which seventy were killed and the rest routed.

Although some believe the British might have achieved greater things with larger subsidies, it is difficult to see what more they could have obtained from such anarchic allies. As it was, they waged what proved to be a highly cost-effective proxy war against the Americans along the Ohio Valley until 1795, when they gave up the forts as part of the true final settlement. The same can also be said of their involvement with the Iroquois Confederation in what is today western New York. It was ironic they should now become the last hope of the Iroquois, since royal administrators had done little to prevent white settlers from gradually driving the component tribes of the Confederation from their ancestral lands – the Tuscarora, for example, from as far as South Carolina – into their last ditch northwestern corral. It is yet more so that the most Loyalist colony of all was to become the 'Empire State' as the result of this war, and that when Americans in British service drove Connecticut settlers out of the Wyoming Valley and German Flats, they spared the postwar Pennsylvania and New York oligarchies further embarrassment along the lines pioneered by Ethan Allen in Vermont. Along the Erie Canal, which was to make New York the commercial capital of the United States, only the musical Indian names remain to remind us that this was once the site of a proto-nation, with well-established and prosperous farming communities and many of the trappings of white man's civilization, which went down fighting tenaciously against overwhelming odds.

Another book would be necessary to do justice to the complex interweave of personal, political, sectional and racial rivalries that characterized the war on the New York/Pennsylvania frontier. The 'British' forces were almost exclusively New York frontier Loyalists who had been driven out of the Mohawk Valley early in the war, in many cases being obliged to leave their relatives behind. Arnold used them as hostages during his operations against St Leger's column during the Saratoga campaign, and several future forays by the Loyalists had the primary objective of rescuing their families. Although the modern euphemism 'ethnic cleansing' applies particularly to the actions taken by the Americans against the Iroquois, it was of a piece with the dispossession of the Loyalists, particularly the estate of Sir William Johnson, prewar king of the Mohawk Valley, and one must also wonder why the Connecticut settlers were left exposed to reprisals in 1778–79. Ohio land speculation by prominent Pennsylvanians and Virginians was a significant factor in their revolutionary motivation and conduct of the war, and the interests of the intermarried (and interfeuding) Clinton, Livingston, Schuyler, Van Cortlandt, Van Schaik and Van Rennsselaer families were no less influential in shaping the war for control of the western projection of New York state.

The most important Loyalist leaders were the variously related Sir John Johnson, who recruited the regiment known as the King's Royals or Johnson's Greens, Guy Johnson, Joseph Brant, and the father and son team of John and Walter Butler, who recruited Butler's Rangers. The latter were not related to the five Butler brothers who served in various capacities in the Continental Army, of whom Zebulon, William and Richard feature in our story, and who with Sullivan and Clinton made the struggle among the whites in this area virtually an Irish-American civil war.* In July 1778 John Butler led his Rangers, Johnson's Greens and an equal number of Iroquois from Oswego in a raid on the Wyoming Valley, and at Wyalusing defeated a large Militia force under the command of Zebulon Butler, the prewar leader of the Connecticut settlers (see MAP p. 138). This was the battle of annihilation recounted with such ghoulish relish by Ewald's Anglo-Iroquois warrior, after which the settler women and children fled into the wilderness, where many also perished. At the same time Brant, operating from his base at Unadilla, sacked Andrustown and then must have literally run down the upper Delaware Valley to raid the New Jersey frontier settlement of Minisink two days later. As he had at Oriskany, he then ambushed a relief column on 22 July, sending waves of panic along the Hudson Valley.

In September John Butler and Brant joined forces at Unadilla and raided German Flats in force. The settlers received warning and took shelter in Forts Dayton and Stanwix, but when they emerged their livelihoods were gone and they joined the growing stream of refugees to Schenectady and Albany, where camp diseases completed their misery.

* The reader may find it advantageous to visit these gentlemen in Appendix A.

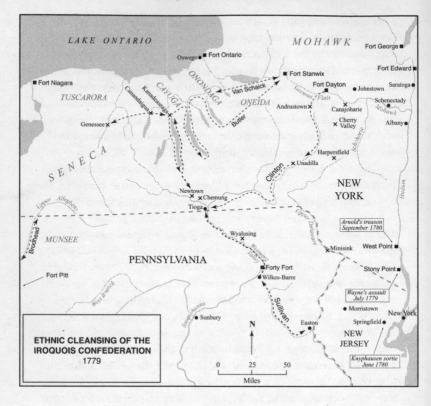

MAP 18

Continentals and Militia guided by Oneidas struck back at Unadilla in October, only to find it abandoned. From their new base at Chemung, Walter Butler and Brant mounted a devastating raid in November on the culpably unprepared New Yorker settlement in Cherry Valley, where many noncombatants were slaughtered and Butler took hostages to secure the release of his mother, aunt and other Loyalist womenfolk imprisoned in Albany.

With the coastal situation settling into a stalemate only the French could resolve, crushing the Iroquois was something Washington felt was within the capability of the shrinking forces under his command. When Gates cited his age as a reason not to lead the punitive expedition, Washington decided to give Sullivan another chance and nominated him to lead the main force of 2500 New Jersey, New Hampshire (Poor's brigade) and Pennsylvania Continentals from Easton, on the Pennsylvania-New Jersey border. James Clinton would march from Fort Dayton in the Mohawk Valley with 1500 New York Continentals, to meet him at Tioga, where the upper tributaries of the Susquehanna join. Operational ambivalence dogged the expedition from the start, for although military common sense indicated a force this large should have attacked the logistical heart of Iroquois resistance at Forts Niagara and Ontario, Washington's orders were the 'total destruction and devastation' of their settlements, and 'the capture of as many prisoners of every age and sex as possible' for hostages. The operation was to be preceded by a diversionary raid into Onondaga country by 500 men under Colonel Van Schaick out of Fort Stanwix. A separate expedition of 600 Pennsylvanians under Colonel Daniel Brodhead was to march north from Fort Pitt, again with orders to devastate all in its path, with only the secondary mission of attacking Fort Niagara if it could effect a union with Sullivan's column at the largest (128 longhouses) Seneca town of Genessee.

The Butlers and Brant had some 500 Loyalists and as many Indians with which to oppose Sullivan's 4000, but after the Continental Army occupied their base at Chemung, they tried to ambush the vanguard at Newtown. This was Poor's brigade, and its own advance guard of three companies from Morgan's rifle brigade combined, as at Bemis Heights, with Dearborn's New Hampshiremen, detected the trap and dispersed the enemy with little loss on either side. Afterwards, New Jersey Lieutenant William Barton recorded his satisfaction at defeating the 'savages', and that he skinned two of the dead 'from their hips down for boot legs; one pair for the Major and the other for myself'. It was the savages' turn when they ambushed a 26-man patrol near Genessee, led by Lieutenant Thomas Boyd, who was unfortunate enough to be one of two survivors. The other, a famous Oneida marksman, was butchered for the pot immediately, but Boyd was tortured to death after interrogation by the Butlers. Possibly because the remaining sixty-five miles to Fort Niagara offered no waterway for his supply boats, but also because it was Seneca country, Sullivan turned back after burning Genessee, just as to the south Brodhead limited his activities to the despoliation of the generally inoffensive Munsee.

Sullivan evidently regarded the Cayuga and Onondaga as less daunting, for after destroying the towns of Canandaigua and Kanadeaseaga at their head, he divided his command into three groups to march along both banks of the two largest finger lakes. Two columns marched south, rejoined at the end of Lake Seneca and returned to the Wyoming Valley, without a single hostage but proudly reporting the destruction of forty townships, 160,000 bushels of standing corn and the uprooting of countless orchards. William Butler led a separate raid that scoured both banks of Lake Cayuga before returning to Fort Stanwix. Apparently oblivious to the deeper contradiction, Boatner concludes 'the irony is that although Sullivan destroyed the Iroquois civilization he did not eliminate their savagery'. After one of the most bitter winters ever recorded, the Oneida paid a terrible price when their erstwhile confederates descended on them from Fort Ontario, and the survivors fled to Schenectady. There they became the saddest refugees of all, spiteful assaults by white trash their reward for being the only one of the six Iroquois Confederation tribes to side with the Americans.

Lacking the early warning system the Oneida had previously provided, and having infuriated and united the remaining Iroquois tribes in a manner never before achieved, during 1780–81 the Americans were driven back further than Burgoyne and St Leger had managed in 1777. The Champlain–Hudson front flared back into life in March 1780, when a Mohawk raiding party captured the American supply depot and boatyard at Skenesboro. This was followed by a major Loyalist incursion in May led by Sir John Johnson, who took Crown Point before marching around Ticonderoga to raid south as far as Johnstown, the capital of what had once been his father's fief, where before burning the town they freed families held hostage by Governor George Clinton. Further south Brant was also back in action, sacking Harpersfield on 2 April and then racing down the Delaware to hit Minisink again two days later. In early August he struck at Canajoharie, then joined Johnson's second 1780 raid, out of Oswego, which ravaged the Schoharie Valley in mid October, destroyed one group of pursuing Militia and fought another to a standstill, before withdrawing with an immense amount of plunder. Governor Clinton reported 'the inhabitants in consequence of their apprehension of danger, are removing from the northern parts of the state', and that a 'moderate computation' of material losses during 1780 included 200 dwellings burned and 150,000 bushels of wheat, virtually the same results as those proudly claimed by Sullivan in 1779.

The heightened tempo of British-supported operations out of Canada reflects Germain's success in finally provoking Carleton to resign, and his replacement in mid 1778 by the most no-nonsense general the British were to employ in America during the war. This was the Swiss Sir Frederick Haldimand, an officer with enormous American military experience, who but for his nationality would have succeeded Gage by seniority in 1775. Instead he was recalled for 'consultations', making way for Howe with the results we have seen. After the Saratoga debacle most of the 7–8000 regulars in Canada were German, making Haldimand's linguistic limitations an asset, while lack of fluency in his adoptive language no doubt contributed to an un-English emphasis on deeds over words. There is evidence of great subtlety in his 1780 strategy, for he sent two small parties of (British) regulars through Lake Champlain, the first of which, unopposed in advance and unharried in retreat, struck the New Yorker settlement of Royalton (see MAP p. 86). Given the record of the Vermont Militia against other incursions, this strongly suggests the tacit cooperation of Ethan Allen, who was also engaged in driving out the New Yorkers, and with whom Haldimand was in secret correspondence.

Haldimand's second group of regulars drove south from Fort George to within twelve miles of Schenectady, focusing New Yorker eyes very firmly to the north, while at the heart of the state Benedict Arnold, commander of the complex of forts at West Point (see MAP p. 106), was in secret dealings to deliver it to Clinton. Haldimand may have been privy to this plot, for in September he reported to Germain that his strategy of concentric attacks was designed (my emphasis) 'to divide the strength that may be brought against Sir Henry Clinton, or *to favour any operations his present situation may induce him to carry on . . .*' However this may have been no more than an educated guess, based on Clinton's puzzling evacuation of the Newport outpost in late 1778. For what purpose must have seemed apparent in late May 1779, when he sent an expedition to recover Stony Point, abandoned at Howe's insistence in 1777. The expedition also took Fort La Fayette, built by the Americans on Verplanck's Point opposite, between them commanding King's Ferry, an important but not indispensable link between western New York and Connecticut. These remained in British hands during 1780, but before then had been the scene of a rare Continental Army success.

Washington himself scouted Stony Point, and on 15 July sent Wayne's new light infantry brigade on a wide inland hook from Fort Montgomery. The operation that took place in the early hours of 16 July was a 'no flint' bayonet assault, with the exception of the small group under the command of Major Hardy Murfree which made a noisy frontal feint to draw a sortie by the garrison, mainly the 17th under its Lieutenant-Colonel Henry Johnson. The principal force under Wayne himself waded across the marshy approaches to the fort from the south, while Richard Butler led a secondary charge from the north, and they cut off the sortie while storming the central keep. British losses were 20 killed and 74 wounded but, most unusually in the normally merciless sequel to such desperate engagements, 472 men were able to surrender and 58 escaped. Commodore Sir George Collier, recalled abruptly from blockade duty off New London, observed, 'the Rebels made the attack with a bravery they never before exhibited, and they showed at this moment a generosity and clemency which during the course of the rebellion had no parallel'. This did not stop him sinking the galley bearing the guns and other loot from the fort as it rowed towards West Point, thereby depriving Wayne and his men of a tidy sum under rules newly instituted by Washington governing prize money. On 19 August the Virginian 'Light Horse Harry' Lee prevailed on Washington to let him mount a similar raid on Paulus Hook, a British outpost across the river from lower Manhattan. It was a somewhat more qualified success, but still another much-needed boost to Continental Army morale.

Neither outpost could be retained by the Americans, and when the British returned to Stony Point they turned it into a formidable fortress, the defensive works serving to disguise that it was also being prepared to act as an advanced staging post for an assault on West Point, fifteen miles upriver. Only when placed in the context of this preparation and Haldimand's operations out of Canada does it become apparent why Clinton encouraged Arnold to seek the post of commandant of what Washington now called 'the key to America'. Clinton's adjutant-general Major John André disobeyed his instructions and went ashore from a ship in the Hudson with civilian clothes over his uniform. He regarded this as something of a lark, but after he was captured returning from a rendezvous with Arnold, with documents incriminating for both found in his boot, he was convicted and hanged as a spy. Wounded pride, frustrated ambition and financial considerations all played a part in Arnold's decision, but we should not discount the reasons he gave in the call he made for recruits to join his 'Legion'. In it he expressed outrage that Congress, 'with sovereign contempt of the people of America, studiously neglected to take their collective sentiments of the British proposals of peace', and had allied with 'the enemy of the Protestant Faith'.

In a memorandum to Clinton and Germain, Arnold wrote scathingly about the American leaders. 'Money will go further than arms in America', he wrote, and suggested an offer of land, acreage according to rank, would lead to the wholesale defection of the Continental Army. His objection was not to people making money out of the war – something he was not, to put it mildly, in a position to criticize – but to the meanness of the cheating and money-grubbing he had observed among his compatriots. He may not yet have been fully aware how ruinously corrupt his new paymasters were, but one gets the impression he shared their view that it was different if gentlemen did it. In fact military administration on both sides in this conflict was equally riddled with duplications and contradictions, and wide open to extensive fraud. This was the result of an historic resistance to the concept of a professional army, itself only one aspect of a general distrust of governmental efficiency as a generator of uncontrollable power, which remains profoundly implanted in the Anglo-American psyche.

Even if Arnold had delivered West Point successfully, whatever advantage might have been obtained was certain to have been dithered away by Sir Henry Clinton. More to his taste was the ponderous sortie made by Knyphausen, who crossed into New Jersey from Staten Island in June with 6000 men. The operation was based on intelligence 'that

Washington's army was very discontented [and] that many of them wished to have an opportunity given them of coming in to join the royal army'. When the second part of this assessment proved false, Knyphausen ordered the pointless burning of Springfield and withdrew, although he was opposed by no more than 1000 men under Nathanael Greene. The first part, on the other hand, was all too true. After their humiliation at Newport there had been small mutinies over pay and conditions in the Continental Army contingents in Rhode Island during the winter and spring of 1778–9, and there were similar expressions of discontent during 1779 at West Point and as far away as Charlottesville, Virginia. The Massachusetts Continentals 'downed tools' during 1780 at Lancaster, Pennsylvania, and at Fort Stanwix, contributing to the abandonment in 1781 of the work that had stopped St Leger in 1777. However Knyphausen's sortie came in response to a more serious act of armed protest in May 1780 by the two Connecticut Line regiments at Basking Ridge, New Jersey, in which Joseph Martin was a participant:

> For several days after we rejoined the army, we got a little musty bread, and a little beef, about every other day, but this lasted only a short time, then we got nothing at all. The men were now exasperated beyond endurance; they saw no alternative but to starve to death, or break up the army, give all up and go home. This was a hard matter for the soldiers to think upon; they were truly patriotic; they loved their country, and they had already suffered every thing short of death in its cause; and now, after such extreme hardships to give up all, was too much; but to starve to death was also too much.

Although the protest came close to violence, once the commissariat provided rations it subsided, although the ease with which this was accomplished confirmed the soldiers' suspicions that they were being cheated by their own officers. There were to be many further mutinies by Continentals, and even some among the generally better cared for Militia, but contrary to Clinton's wishful thinking none was in any way pro-British. During the most serious, when 2400 Pennsylvanians complete with artillery set out towards Philadelphia after someone imprudently issued them with rum to celebrate the 1781 New Year, the mutineers arrested two emissaries sent by Clinton to encourage them to defect and handed them over to the civil authorities for hanging. Congress, with no right to tax, could offer nothing but paper money, the purchasing power of which by then was less than 1 per cent of its face value, but Governor Joseph Reed of Pennsylvania was able to pacify them with a little hard cash and the promise of a lot more. Needless to say, such promises were never kept.

Martin was not even paid in paper money after August 1777, but recalled one payment in coin before the march to Virginia in 1781, an exception to the rule made possible by the French, who provided Washington with the means to pay his army for what proved to be the final campaign of the war. Before that the American commander-in-chief was caught in a vicious circle of congressional demands for action, to encourage the individual states to pay the money they owed, without which he could not keep together an army large or dependable enough to undertake any significant military initiative. He was fortunate in his opponent. At a time when Washington was in despair because of the mutinous state of his army, Clinton wrote to Eden, 'for God's sake send us money, men, and provisions, or expect nothing but complaints. Send out another admiral or let me go home'. Rear Admiral Marriott Arbuthnot, Lord Howe's successor and the incumbent Clinton wanted rid of, was indeed a thorn in his side, but in his study of the effect of logistics on the war Arthur Bowler concluded the British Army was never seriously hampered by lack of resources. Logistics were the excuse for, not the cause of, Clinton's inactivity. Vice Admiral Sir George Rodney, in New York at this time, contrasted him very unfavourably with Arnold in a dispatch to Germain:

> . . . you must not expect an end of the American war till you can find a general of active spirit, and who hates the Americans from principle. Such a man with the sword of war and justice on his side will do wonders, for in this war I am convinced the sword should cut deep . . . Believe me, my Lord, this man Arnold, with whom I have had many conferences, will do more towards suppressing the rebellion than all our generals put together [but jealousy], unless commands from home signifies His Majesty's pleasure, will prevent [him] being employed to advantage. He certainly may be trusted, as the Americans never forgive, and the Congress to a man are his personal enemies.

Arnold was not alone in believing that more than just steady wages must be offered to recruit a decisive number of Americans. Major Patrick Ferguson, seconded by Clinton from the 71st to recruit another Loyalist Legion, also proposed offering every man a farm. Trapped by their own rhetorical contrast between pure-hearted American patriots and dastardly British mercenaries, the Foundation Mythologists made an unnecessary meal of this – people do not suspend individual self-interest simply because they are involved in collective enterprises. Two months before Arnold's defection, in a presentation of officer corps grievances to Congress, the prewar revolutionary firebrand and now Major-General John McDougall violently rejected an appeal to idealism by Samuel Adams. 'I have explicitly told Mr Adams that our Army no longer consider themselves fighting the battles of Republics in Principle', he wrote, 'but for Empire and Liberty to a people whose object is property, and that the army expect some of that property which the citizen seeks, and which the army protects for him'.

All those involved in recruiting and leading the new Loyalist units, particularly at this late stage of the war when many of the new recruits were deserters from the Continental Army, were well aware this must lead to greater ruthlessness in the field. Upon the conclusion of his ill-starred mission, Lord Carlisle wrote: 'Beat General Washington, drive away Monsieur d'Estaing, and we should have friends enough in this country; but in our present condition the only friends we have, or are likely to have, are those who are absolutely ruined for us, and in such distress I leave you to judge what possible use they can be to us'. However it was precisely this element of desperation, repellent to those like Carlisle who hoped for reconciliation, which made the Loyalists so attractive to the hard-liners in London. Having seen the enemy let off the hook time and again, the field officers in America were understandably of the same mind, and this also contributed to increased harshness at the cutting edge. Ferguson argued this was appropriate, urging Clinton to consider that it was now 'necessary to exert a degree of severity which would not have been justifiable at the beginning'.

In the final analysis, although the king and Germain talked freely about the need to make the Americans suffer, the means proposed by Arnold and warmly supported by Rodney were far too radical to be entertained by men devoted to the maintenance of the status quo at home, in particular in Ireland, where concessions offered to win over the Americans had already led to demands for a larger piece of the Great British pie. They were also inhibited by the thought that anyone they might appoint to replace Clinton might whine less but would have better political connections. Accordingly they could only cajole, and found that getting Clinton to obey orders with which he was uncomfortable was akin to pushing a wet noodle. In addition, for as long as the conflict was regarded as a rebellion, and not a declared war, recent legal precedents were not such as to encourage an army officer to take drastic action. The soldiers who fired on the Boston mob in 1770 had been put on trial for their lives, and there had been other examples in Britain of the same happening to officers who acted to quell disturbances without a magistrate, and even of magistrates for having authorized the use of deadly force. For as long as his superiors chose not take the responsibility on their shoulders in formal written orders, Clinton was wise to refrain from outright counter-terrorism.

It was also one thing to will beastliness at a distance, another altogether to take responsibility for administering it at close range, and to sanction the wholesale programme of reprisals the Loyalists were only too keen to embark upon, in a cause most on the ground regarded as ultimately unwinnable. Another consideration that must have weighed on Clinton was the certainty that, should the government fall, the parliamentary opposition would make a scapegoat of him if he acted in the spirit rather than the letter of his orders. Finally, unlike Haldimand, he was acutely aware that the manner in which he waged the war would condition the eventual peace settlement. Shy's review of the irregular warfare waged on the periphery of the British strongholds in New York and New Jersey concludes the only reason the conflict in the North did not follow the example of the South was British restraint, and that although Clinton's unwillingness to embark upon a programme of counterterrorism owed something to gentlemanly fastidiousness, he was also constrained by a conviction that it would permanently poison relations between the two countries.

Attitudes on the other side were not so well defined. It had never been in the interests of those directing the American war effort to inhibit the terrorist tactics of the vigilante groups, but the signature American deference to the forms of legality, along the lines of 'give him a fair trial, then take him out and hang him', was already much in evidence. Oddly, Militia Colonel Charles Lynch of Virginia, who gave his name to 'Lynch Law', seems never to have ordered anyone executed. However, in 1782 the Virginia Assembly did issue a special dispensation to hold him harmless for other sentences imposed by his informal court, so evidently not all his victims were the Loyalists he thought them to be. At the other extreme, in December 1779 after the local sheriff arrested a group of men who returned to Hackensack after completing a three-year enlistment with the Loyalist New Jersey Volunteers, Anthony Wayne, the local Continental Army commander, persuaded him to release them. Wayne, whose tight control over his men at Stony Point we have already remarked, shrewdly argued that a clear demonstration of a willingness to forgive would subvert morale among Americans serving the British cause far more effectively than continued persecution. He was certainly correct, but as we have seen not merely each state, but at times even each county was by this time waging the war as it saw fit, and no coherent overall policy for the sensible handling of repentant Loyalists ever emerged.

Joseph Martin, who believed 'it was impossible to commit murder with Refugees', received his only wound of the war, a hack in the shin from the sword of the commander of a group of 'Refugee-cowboy plunderers', who was, 'when we were boys, one of my most familiar playmates, was with me, a messmate, in the campaign of 1776, had enlisted during the war in 1777, but sometime before this [1781], had deserted to the enemy, having been coaxed off by an old harridan, to whose daughter he had taken a fancy; the old hag of a mother, living in the vicinity of the British, easily inveigled him away'. Recognized in turn, he believed his old comrade ordered his men not to fire on him as he ran away. There is a particular poignancy in this anecdote, and a reminder of the millions of personal histories soured by the calculations of 'great' men.

We cannot close this chapter on the prickly stalemate that developed in the North without considering Massachusetts' last independent military effort, a tragi-comedy no less imperialistic in intent than the efforts of Virginia and Pennsylvania, and an American naval disaster on a scale not to be repeated until Pearl Harbor. This took place at Penobscot Bay in the large, and largely uninhabited, territory that was to become the state of Maine in 1820, but which at this time was part of the charter granted to the Massachusetts Bay Colony. A minor subtext of the need to invent an ideological justification for treason, which gave birth to the Foundation Myth, was the practical legal problem of enforcing land rights awarded by the very authority the Americans had declared illegitimate. Massachusetts' claim to the Maine territory was revocable, and threatened by the settlements made in the north by the British, originally to provide a buffer for the colonies against the French in Québec. In addition the most important ports for the Royal Navy in North America were Halifax and Saint John, Nova Scotia, from which they were able to conduct a damaging blockade of the Massachusetts and New Hampshire coasts, and in particular to deny the Yankees access to their traditionally lucrative fishing grounds off Newfoundland.

In June 1779, 650 men of the 74th and part of the 82nd, both newly formed Highland regiments, and fifty Royal Artillerymen and Engineers, with Colonel Francis MacLean the officer commanding, landed on the Bagaduce Peninsula in Penobscot Bay, halfway between Nova Scotia and New Hampshire's extension to the sea. The purpose of the expedition was to provide a forward defence for a colony to be called New Ireland, to be populated with disaffected Americans of that national origin, to provide a secure port from which to ship timber to the Halifax shipyards, and to create a base for fast privateers to plug the leaks in the blockade of New England. MacLean issued a proclamation promising free access to their traditional fishing grounds under the protection of the Royal Navy to those who took an oath of allegiance. Although the locals had been very badly treated by Massachusetts, most of them prudently adopted a wait and see attitude. There was no doubt the authorities in Boston would react violently to this challenge to their authority and to their own imperial hopes, which encompassed Nova Scotia, and MacLean devoted himself to clearing the forest around the highest point, where he built a log fort. To protect the harbour, where he retained three sloops of war and four transports under Captain Henry Mowat, he built batteries at sea

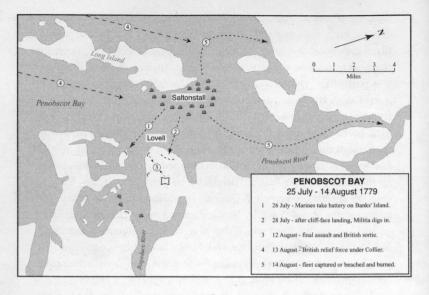

PENOBSCOT BAY
25 July - 14 August 1779

1   26 July - Marines take battery on Banks' Island.

2   28 July - after cliff-face landing, Militia digs in.

3   12 August - final assault and British sortie.

4   13 August - British relief force under Collier.

5   14 August - fleet captured or beached and burned.

MAP 19

level on the western side of the peninsula, and another to provide a crossfire on an island close offshore.

The General Court, Massachusetts' collective executive, prepared its response without even informing Congress or Washington. Militia General William Howard declared 'if but ten Continental soldiers are concerned, the Continent will take all the honour'. Anxious to strike before MacLean had time to prepare his defences fully, they assembled a fleet of 18 warships, ranging from the flagship *Warren* (32 guns) to the schooner *Rover* (10), and 21 transport sloops and schooners, including practically the whole of the Massachusetts privateer fleet, plus the only one flying the flag of New Hampshire. The *Warren* and two others were officially part of the Continental Navy, as was the naval commander Commodore Dudley Saltonstall. The commander of the land force, an ill-assorted collection of 900 boys, old men and Stockbridge (Mohican) Indians, was the politician and Militia Brigadier-General Solomon Lovell, who was also in joint command of the expedition. In command of the artillery was Militia Lieutenant-Colonel Paul Revere, he of the iconic midnight ride in April 1775, who in common with Saltonstall, indeed with all politicians, was powerfully possessed of the philosophy that it mattered not who won or lost but how you placed the blame. This began to pile up after the fleet arrived off Bagaduce on 25 July, to find that MacLean's preparations posed operational questions to which neither of the inexperienced joint commanders had any answers.

While the transports anchored two miles away off Long Island, Saltonstall's warships sailed across the mouth of the harbour firing their broadsides, to which Mowat's sloops and the shore batteries responded briskly, neither side managing to damage the other. Lovell's first attempt at a landing was turned back by a small group of soldiers, who killed the first of the Mohicans. On 26 July the 225 Marines from the warships took the island battery, but Saltonstall was not prepared to 'risk my shipping in that damned hole', although the *Warren* alone carried more and much heavier (18 and 12-pounders) guns than all the British artillery afloat or ashore. Both sides formed exaggerated estimates of the other's strength, the Americans with less reason because they received information from locals who had been inside the British works. But the main reason why the place was not taken is that each of the joint commanders wanted the other to take all the risks, in Saltonstall's case probably compounded by his privateer's instinct to avoid battle unless the outcome was assured.

After another two failed attempts by Lovell to land the Militia at the same point, where some steep bluffs overlooked the bay, MacLean reasoned his opponent must surely try something different, withdrew the small force posted there and sent it to cover the neck of the peninsula, where there was a hill that overlooked the four-foot walls of his little fort. He was therefore taken by surprise when the next effort scaled the self-same cliffs, and was ready to surrender if called upon when he was further, and most agreeably, surprised to see the Americans dig in along the crest. Two weeks of unconscionable dithering followed until, on the 12th, having previously worked around the peninsula to force the evacuation of one of the batteries at the mouth of the Bagaduce, Lovell sent skirmishers up the hill towards the fort. The plan was to draw a sortie, which would then be pounced upon by his reserves, but when the Highlanders obliged the whole force took flight. That evening a council of war narrowly divided in favour of one more attempt, hopefully this time concerted. Those against were Saltonstall and half the naval officers, who were nervous about being trapped by the Royal Navy, plus Revere, who had shown his lack of enthusiasm for the whole enterprise by staying on board while his guns went ashore. The doubters had reason to worry, for Commodore Sir George Collier, fresh from sinking Wayne's loot-laden galley at Stony Point, had sailed from New York on 3 August with *Raisonable* (64) and five frigates. News of unknown sails approaching the mouth of the bay reached Salstonstall and Lovell early next morning when they were, at last, about to launch the combined assault that could have taken the fort at any time during the preceding weeks. The operation was cancelled and the land force hastily re-embarked.

Wind and tide now doomed the expedition. Collier's squadron came in on a southerly breeze and a flood tide, and although the sloops and schooners which made up the bulk of the Massachusetts armada could point into the wind better than the square-rigged British ships, the breeze did not reach them until after their escape routes were closed off. To add to their woes, MacLean captured the island battery, where Revere's heavy guns had been abandoned and inadequately spiked, and turned them around to fire at the milling invasion fleet, which was also attacked by Mowat's sloops. In the ensuing panic the transports and supply ships took the shortest route to run aground, where the Militia abandoned their officers and broke up into small parties to make their way south. The warships might have held the narrows at the mouth of the Penobscot River, but they fled upstream and were beached, burned or blown up. Seven more supply ships had arrived during the siege, making the final tally forty-six vessels. Added to the destruction of the Connecticut fleet at Bedford and Fairhaven a year earlier, this debacle effectively ended New England's leading role in the naval war, at the same time declining motivation was eroding its once dominant contribution on land.

As though to confirm the opinion in which they were held by their compatriots, the Yankees now sought to pass the cost of this fiasco to 'the Continent' they had taken such pains to exclude from the expedition. Having solemnly acquitted Lovell and the other senior Militia officers of incompetence and, in the case of Revere, of commandeering his ship's boats to salvage his personal possessions before evacuating the soldiers on board, they concluded the fault was exclusively Saltonstall's. Documents were altered to show he had been in sole command, therefore the expedition had, after all, been undertaken under Continental auspices and was a legitimate charge to the general account. They claimed seven million dollars, and Congress generously awarded them two – to be paid some day. The cowardice and bad faith shown by every 'patriot' involved in this affair makes it easy to understand why the British authorities remained so confident the American cause would implode without much effort on their part. They maintained a strong base at Penobscot for the duration of the war, but the mass defection of Irish-Americans never materialized and it was abandoned in 1783.

The broad conclusion to be drawn from the northern and northwestern fronts during the latter part of the war is that the Americans squandered the moral effect of the victory at Saratoga, and were hopelessly unprepared for the qualitative change in warfare that came about once the British abandoned their illusions about reconciliation. After the French made it plain they would not support another invasion of Canada, the strategic argument in favour of continuing the war evaporated and Americans near the frontier of settlement paid an appalling price as the British and their Loyalist and Indian allies began to give greater substance to their premature demonization by American propagandists. These, safe from harm in Paris, Philadelphia, Boston, Charlottesville and all the other places where patriots of the word gathered, continued to make money while denouncing the British for prolonging the war. The manner in which Americans were now voting with their purses and their feet shows that few believed in them anymore.

8

OPENING SHOTS: THE SOUTH

THE MOST EMETIC CONTRIBUTIONS to the Foundation Myth are attempts to sanitize the war in the South, when it was a vicious struggle for supremacy undisguised by ideology fought mainly among Americans, won by the insurgents despite, with one notable exception, being defeated whenever they attempted to take on the relatively few non-American regulars in the field. Setting a tragic precedent for the centuries to follow, poor whites fought each other when they should have united to overthrow the promoters of the rebellion, the wealthy coastal slavocrats who oppressed them all equally. As they were to do again eighty years later, men fought for the maintenance of a pseudo-aristocratic social structure that kept their own standard of living depressed in the name of a freedom to live only slightly better than animals, which nobody wished to take from them.

Hindsight permits us to see the South was lost in 1776, when the Loyalists in the Carolinas were left unsupported for three years after an ambitious British plan to restore royal authority ended with a ludicrous failure to take a small, half-finished fort that dominated the main entrance to the port of Charleston, the wealthiest city in North America. This was an expedition of 1200 men under the command of Clinton, sent south by Howe from Boston in January to rendezvous off Wilmington, at the mouth of the Cape Fear River, with a force under Cornwallis sailing directly from Dublin. Clinton was also supposed to combine with a strike force of North Carolina Loyalists, some 1700 Scottish Highlanders including the husband of the Jacobite heroine Flora MacDonald, led by officers sent by Gage from Boston in 1775. On 27 February this invaluable resource was wasted, and the Loyalist cause in North Carolina crippled, when the Highlanders succumbed to atavism and launched a wild charge with drums hammering and bagpipes howling against North Carolina Militia across Moore's Creek Bridge, twenty miles north of Wilmington. Reconnaissance would have revealed the Militia dug in and waiting with two pieces of artillery, and that the planking had been removed from the bridge. Fifty were killed, 850 captured and the insurgents then systematically drove the Highlanders from the coastal areas of North Carolina. Although the commander of the victorious army was the eponymous James Moore, Richard Caswell raced to Hillsboro to take the credit, and as a result was elected governor 1776–80.

Some of the elders among the Highlanders in both Carolinas, like those on Canada's Prince Edward Island, were men who had followed the doomed standard of Charles Edward Stuart in the rebellion of 1745–6, while others had taken part in the 'Regulator' rebellions of 1768–71 against . . . taxation without representation. Many had sworn oaths of fealty to the crown at the end of these rebellions and, unusually in America, felt bound by them. However a large group of Regulators migrated across the Blue Ridge Mountains to avoid doing so, and to get away from the authority of the coastal elite. These became the 'Over Mountain Men' who dealt the Loyalists the most stinging defeat of the war at King's Mountain in October 1780. Even more than in the North, it is unwise to generalize about who was loyal, to what, and the reasons for it. Every man made up his own mind, and having done so was perfectly willing to kill friends or relatives who decided otherwise. Most non-Southerners were appalled to find themselves involved in a struggle undisguised by either the brittle veneer of honour and glory, or emollient pap about religion and virtue. The South's contribution to the euphemistic vocabulary with which the whole American enterprise has been wrapped since the beginning was 'Liberty and Property', the property being the slaves to whom liberty must forever be denied.

When the Clinton-Cornwallis juncture finally occurred in May the game was already over in North Carolina, and all they could do was land 900 men south of Wilmington to destroy the settlement of Brunswick, which included the plantation of Brigadier-General Robert

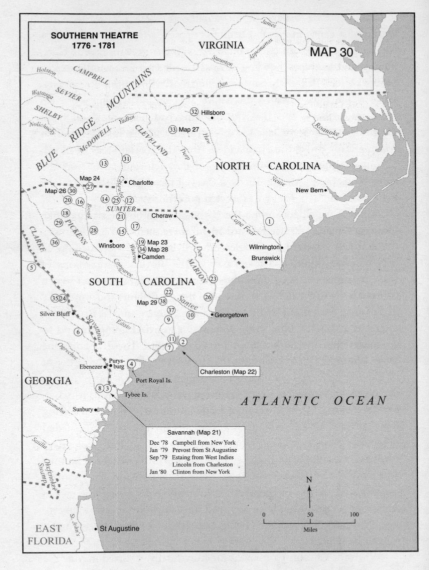

SOUTHERN THEATRE
1776 - 1781

VIRGINIA

MAP 30

NORTH CAROLINA

SOUTH CAROLINA

GEORGIA

EAST FLORIDA

ATLANTIC OCEAN

Charleston (Map 22)

Savannah (Map 21)

Dec '78   Campbell from New York
Jan '79   Prevost from St Augustine
Sep '79   Estaing from West Indies
          Lincoln from Charleston
Jan '80   Clinton from New York

N

0   50   100
Miles

MAP 20

156

1. Moore's Creek 27 February '76	Highlanders defeated.
2. Sullivan Island 28 June '76	William Moultrie defeats Henry Clinton's expedition.
3. Savannah 29 December '78	Archibald Campbell defeats Richard Howe.
4. Beaufort 3 February '79	Moultrie defeats Major Gardiner.
5. Kettle Creek 14 February '79	Andrew Pickens/Elijah Clarke defeat James Boyd.
6. Briar Creek 3 March '79	James Prevost defeats John Ashe/Pickens
7. Stono Ferry 20 June '79	John Maitland defeats Benjamin Lincoln.
8. Siege of Savannah 9 October '79	Augustine Prevost defeats Comte d'Estaing/Lincoln.
9. Monck's Corner 14 April '80	Banastre Tarleton defeats Isaac Huger.
10. Lenud's Ferry 6 May '80	Tarleton defeats Anthony White.
11. Siege of Charleston 12 May '80	Lincoln surrenders to Clinton.
12. Waxhaws 29 May '80	Tarleton defeats Abraham Buford.
13. Ramsauer's Mill 20 June '80	Francis Locke defeats John Moore.
14. Williamson's Plantation 12 July '80	William Bratton defeats, kills Christian Huck.
15. Rocky Mount 30 July '80	George Turnbull drives off Thomas Sumter.
16. Thicketty Fort 30 July '80	Surrendered to Isaac Shelby/Charles McDowell.
17. Hanging Rock 6 August '80	Sumter defeats John Carden.
18. Cedar Springs 8 August '80	Clarke/Shelby drive off James Dunlap
19. Camden 16 August '80	Charles Cornwallis defeats Horatio Gates.
20. Musgrove's Mill 17 August '80	Clarke/Shelby defeat Alexander Innes.
21. Fishing Creek 18 August '80	Tarleton defeats Sumter.
22. Great Savannah 20 August '80	Francis Marion liberates Camden prisoners.
23. Blue Savannah 4 September '80	Marion defeats Micajah Ganey.
24. Siege of Augusta 18 September '80	Thomas Brown/John Cruger defeat Clarke.
25. Wahab's Plantation 21 September '80	William Davie defeats George Hanger.
26. Black Mingo Creek 29 September '80	Marion defeats John Ball's 'King's Friends'.
27. King's Mountain 7 October '80	Arthur Campbell *et al.* defeat, kill Patrick Ferguson.
28. Fishdam Ford 9 November '80	James Wemyss captured raiding Sumter's camp.
29. Blackstock's Farm 20 November '80	Tarleton defeated, Sumter severely wounded.
30. Cowpens 17 January '81	Daniel Morgan defeats Tarleton.
31. Torrence's Tavern 1 February '81	Tarleton shatters North Carolina Militia.
32. Haw River 25 February '81	Harry Lee massacres John Pyle's Loyalists.
33. Guilford Courthouse 15 March '81	Cornwallis's Phyrric victory over Nathanael Greene.
34. Hobkirk's Hill 25 April '81	Lord Rawdon defeats Greene.
35. Siege of Augusta 5 June '81	Brown surrenders to Lee.
36. Siege of Ninety-Six 19 June '81	Cruger holds off Greene, relieved by Rawdon.
37. Quinby Bridge 17 July '81	John Coates drives off Sumter/Marion/Lee.
38. Eutaw Springs 8 September '81	Alexander Stewart defeats Greene.

Howe, the foremost figure in the prewar organization of the North Carolina Militia. Torn between heeding the pleas of the ousted governors of Virginia and South Carolina, Clinton now chose the latter as offering a greater chance of arousing the mass of oppressed Loyalists the governors believed would rise up decisively once the regulars won a symbolic victory. This, Clinton decided, would be to take Sullivan Island, which controlled one side of the entrance to Charleston harbour and was defended by a small fort under the command of Militia Colonel William Moultrie, whose brother John was the fiercely Loyalist lieutenant-governor of East Florida. The successful defence of this fort has a good claim to being the most important American victory of the war, for it left Charleston open to become the principal port serving the rebellion until 1780, and the fabulously wealthy 'Rice Kings' undisturbed to extend their hegemony. The most prominent were the intermarried Drayton, Laurens, Lowndes, Manigault, Middleton, Pinckney and Rutledge families, who may fairly be compared to the robber barons of medieval England.

Clinton uncharacteristically failed to order prior reconnaissance and after the 2200-man assault force was landed on Long Island, he found the channel dividing it from Sullivan Island was not fordable. He persisted in the error instead of re-embarking, and this left the reduction of the fort to the Royal Navy under Commodore Peter Parker. A complex of sand bars and shallows known as The Bar obliged him to row over the guns separately from his larger ships to permit them to reach the anchorage known as Five Fathom Hole, and then to await a favourable wind before anchoring closer to the fort than any sane officer would have done against a respected opponent. In addition the fort was constructed of several walls of spongy palmetto logs filled with sand and clay, which simply absorbed the 7000 cannon-balls fired into them. Hope that the American gunners would flee from this weight of fire proved unfounded, thanks largely to the exemplary leadership of Moultrie. A surgeon on board one of Parker's ships commented that American return fire 'was slow, but decisive indeed; they were cool, and took care not to fire except their guns were exceedingly well directed'.

With 31 guns against 260, and expending about one-seventh the amount of powder, Moultrie's gunners nearly sank Parker's flagship

Bristol (50), a splinter tearing away the commodore's breeches to leave 'his posteriors quite bare', severely damaged the other 50-gun ship and drove the frigate *Actaeon* aground, where she was burned to prevent capture. The bomb-ketch *Thunder*, which could have wrecked the interior of the fort, was anchored too far out and consequently employed excessive powder charges in her heavy mortars, cracking her reinforced deck and taking her out of the action early. The surgeon concluded 'this will not be believed when it is first reported in England. I can scarcely believe what I myself saw that day'. The expedition limped north to rejoin Howe in time for the assault on Long Island, and the next time the Royal Navy came to Charleston was in 1780, when it completed the same evolution without significant loss. It was by then under the command of the widely disesteemed Arbuthnot, suggesting that the missing ingredient on the second occasion must have been the officer whose name, but not his indomitable spirit, remained attached to the fort.

One does not have to be possessed of an unduly levelling spirit to rejoice that the overweening arrogance of the Rice Kings was shattered before the war ended. Possibly one should never think of the human cost of stately homes, but it is impossible not to do so when viewing the Georgian mansions of old Charleston. Pathetically few African American voices speak to us across the great divide, one of the few being the runaway slave and preacher David George, who founded the first African American Baptist church at Silver Bluff, South Carolina. When the British took Savannah and marched on Augusta in early 1779, the enlightened slave owner who had encouraged George fled, and the little congregation took refuge in the city, thence eventually to Halifax. George recalled that before he escaped from servitude he was 'whipped many a time on my naked skin till the blood has run down over my waistband; but the greatest grief I then had was to see them whip my mother, and to hear her, on her knees, begging for mercy'. The likely fate of George's congregation had it not sought British protection was demonstrated in March 1776 when a party of forty whites and thirty Catawba Indians, authorized by the Georgia Council of Safety, exterminated a peaceful community of 200 African Americans on Tybee Island, lest their example encourage slaves to run away.

Nemesis for the Rice Kings was assured when the Americans persisted in the war and the Howes asked to be relieved. Clinton's formal orders from London dated 8 March 1778 instructed him to rely mainly on the navy and the Loyalists to continue the war. By land he was to send 7000 regulars as well as the bulk of the Loyalists to recover Georgia, the Carolinas and eventually Virginia, while the rest of the colonies were to be reduced by blockade and coastal raids. Clinton, who was to cling to his property investments in New York for the rest of the war, judged that after detaching Grant with 5000 men to the West Indies and nearly as many, mainly 'turned' Continental Army prisoners, to Florida, he could only spare 3500 men, one-third of them Loyalist regulars, to recover Georgia. They were, however, commanded by the able Lieutenant-Colonel Archibald Campbell, at last exchanged and anxious to repay the indignities he had endured in captivity. With two battalions each from his own 71st Highlanders, the Hessians, the New York Volunteers and the New Jersey Volunteers, he arrived off Tybee Island just before Christmas 1778.

With accurate intelligence and guides provided by local African Americans, Campbell's light infantry vanguard took Savannah after routing a force of John Elbert's Georgia Militia and Isaac Huger's South Carolina Continentals, under the overall command of Robert Howe, now a major-general and officer commanding the Southern Department. Campbell's report to Germain expressed his hope 'of being the first British officer to rend a star and a stripe from the flag of Congress', to conclude, 'if I am successful it will rest with my Sovereign to decide its merits and consequences'. Thereby hangs a tale. Although given command of eight battalions and also appointed acting governor of Georgia, Campbell had been refused the local rank of brigadier-general and was obliged to issue the usual proclamation in the name of the senior naval officer, Commodore Hyde Parker, who shortly departed for the West Indies. Clinton was a detail man, and the denial of commensurate rank to the officer entrusted with initiating the new strategy was certainly deliberate. Like all weak people, his overriding concern was to discourage those possessing the self-confidence he lacked.

The second string of Germain's plan was to activate the Indian threat on the frontier, but the Cherokee and Creek had suffered severe defeats early in the war, and as warriors do not appear to have been in the same league as the Seneca and Mohawk, possibly because their backs were not yet against the wall. Nor was there a Southern equivalent to the Johnson/Brant combination in the North, nor Loyalist leaders like the Butlers who might have operated with the Indians to give them greater combat effectiveness and operational direction. The one man who might have done so was the Yorkshireman Thomas Brown, who only arrived in Georgia in late 1774 and less than a year later was the victim of brutal public torture by the Augusta 'Sons of Liberty'. First felled by a blow that cracked his skull and left him with headaches for the rest of his life, he was then scalped and his legs coated with tar so hot he lost two toes. Although Brown was demonized by the historians of the revolution, it should be noted that when he was the commander of the Augusta garrison in 1780–81 he did not take revenge on those who had assaulted him in 1775. That he hanged a number of parole-breakers is undeniable, but his main claim to Foundation Myth infamy lay in his role as chief liaison officer between the British and the Indians. Even at the end of the war, when East Florida was traded to Spain in exchange for the Bahamas, Brown brokered a deal between the Spanish and the Indians, which after his departure was kept alive by his able Creek-Scots associate Alexander McGillivray and frustrated Manifest Destiny for a generation.

Overall, however, the policy was misconceived, for it completed the alienation of the frontier settlers who had rejected the rebellion in 1775 precisely because it would leave them exposed to Indian attacks. They were won over, and given a stake in the revolution, when North Carolina negotiated the Transylvania Purchase (see MAP p. 10) from the Indians, resulting in a flood of new 'Over Mountain' settlers who in the eyes of the British were not merely squatters on Indian lands, but trespassers on lands granted by royal charter to John Carteret, Lord Granville. However, although royal officials had pandered to the coastal planters at the expense of the interests of the smallholders of the interior, the behaviour of the slavocrats after 1775 made the prewar administration seem a model of even-handedness, creating the preconditions for a rebellion within the rebellion that might have been turned to decisive British advantage. The opportunity was aborted by Clinton's refusal to commit the necessary resources to Germain's southern strategy, which in turn forced local commanders to rely far too soon and too much on local troops. While the northern Loyalists were belatedly being sorted into a regular American Establishment of five regiments and a second tier of Provincial units, most of the highly motivated Loyalists of Georgia and the Carolinas were not even supplied with the uniforms that would have made them feel valued, and would have saved some from the noose.

The force Clinton sent to take Savannah was self-evidently inadequate to do much more, even when joined by 900 men under the command of Brigadier-General Augustine Prevost, the elderly Swiss in command of British forces in East Florida, who took over from Campbell on 15 January. His little army consisted of two battalions of the Royal Americans (60th), who were mainly non-Americans and decidedly unregal, plus Brown's King's Rangers and the South Carolina Royalists. Campbell's first opinion of the Rangers was that they were 'a mere rabble of undisciplined freebooters', yet he entrusted Brown with leading a march on Augusta, which fell on 29 January. This encouraged 700 Loyalists, mainly from the district around the settlement known as Ninety-Six, to gather under the command of James Boyd and march to join him. Less than half of them escaped to join Campbell after they were ambushed at Kettle Creek by about half their number under the command of Elijah Clarke and Andrew Pickens, but the seventy prisoners taken were condemned to death for 'high treason'. In fact only five were hanged in the presence of the rest, who were then pardoned and released on parole.

Most titles of rank for the commanders of irregular forces will be omitted, not least because the great Southern tradition that anyone of standing in the community is a colonel was already well established. Rank mattered among the Continentals, for often the officers so distinguished had no other claim to lead, but among the partisans an officer commanded a following because of a good record in the field, and led by force of personality. Once formally constituted provincial authority collapsed, the men who waged guerrilla warfare against and for the British are best regarded as warlords. Some on both sides were criminals taking advantage of the situation, and when captured these would be hanged, as they would have been in peacetime. Others were the victims of false accusations and the settling of personal scores, but overall the principal reason men were killed after surrendering was because the irregulars lacked the safe areas and resources to hold them securely, and had to choose between letting them go or making sure they would do not further harm by the only other means available.

On the other side the British retained only captured Continentals, many of whom donned the red coat and were sent to garrison the West Indies, and released the Militia on parole. This led to the summary hanging of men later taken in arms who were believed, not always correctly, to be oath-breakers, and a spiral of reprisals and counterreprisals that demonstrated just how much restraint was exercised by both sides in the North to avoid the same outcome. A clear illustration of this came late in the war, when the French monarch intervened personally to prevent Washington executing a British officer captured at Yorktown, after Loyalist irregulars hanged a prisoner in retaliation for the murder of one of their own. The charge of 'high treason' for which the five scapegoats were hanged at Kettle Creek also begged an important question. Were the traitors those who forcibly imposed a new order after 1775, or those who rose up against their oppressors when the British returned? All were guilty of capital offences according to one side or the other.

Following the loss of Savannah, Howe was replaced by Benjamin Lincoln, whom last we saw nominally in command at Bemis Heights. He marched the main force of Continentals from Charleston to Purysburg, facing Prevost at Ebenezer across the marshes of the lower Savannah. Looking for a way around the impasse, Prevost sent 200 men of the 60th under Major Gardiner to seize Port Royal Island. William Moultrie rallied the Militia at Beaufort, and in an unusual reversal of form attacked from the open against a British position in the woods. Both sides began to withdraw at the same time, but Moultrie checked his retreat in time to claim victory, and this served to swell Lincoln's ranks with volunteers, enabling him to send a column of 1500 Continentals under Brigadier-General John Ashe to join Elbert and the remaining Georgians facing Augusta, where they were also joined by Pickens' men after Kettle Creek.

Their fate was sealed when one of their raiding parties hacked to pieces one Sergeant MacAlister, whom Campbell had posted to guard the house of a captured American officer against Loyalist reprisals.

The 71st swore vengeance and took it after Campbell, due for well-earned leave, handed over command to Prevost's son James during the retreat from Augusta. Before leaving, Campbell had suggested Prevost might turn on his pursuers at Briar Creek, which he duly did to inflict a crushing defeat from which the Georgia Continentals and Militia never recovered. A ferocious attack by the Highlanders overcame the numerical disparity, with many preferring to drown in the rice swamps rather than face their bayonets. Two hundred were killed and Elbert was among the 170 captured, presumably by other regiments, with the majority of the survivors dispersing to their homes.

Lincoln was stung into marching north, and Prevost waited until he was committed before crossing the river to advance on Charleston. President John Rutledge and the older members of the governing council proposed offering to drop out of the war, whether to buy time or in all sincerity is hard to know, but they were fiercely denounced by the younger members, which was to colour their reaction to the next time the city was threatened. Charleston would have fallen to a bold thrust, but the man who might have administered it was on his way home and Prevost was content with forcing Lincoln to pull back from Georgia. He withdrew most of his army by boat along the coast, leaving a rearguard of 800 Hessians and Highlanders under Lieutenant-Colonel John Maitland, Campbell's successor in command of the 71st, to inflict a costly defeat on twice their number under Lincoln and Pickens at Stono Ferry. This was an unnecessary assault on fieldworks Maitland was about to abandon, and proportional American officer losses were comparable to those of the British at Breed's Hill. The failure of a flank move by Moultrie to negotiate the marshes was a contributory cause, and salt was rubbed in his wounds when Maitland now occupied Port Royal without opposition.

At this point the Comte d'Estaing, after further disappointments in the West Indies following his sojourn in Boston, judged he could spare the Americans a further short period of assistance before returning to France, and in September 1779 sailed to Savannah with 32 warships escorting 50 transports carrying 4000 troops. His mood sweetened by the capture of British ships carrying Prevost's successor and £30,000 to pay the British garrison, Estaing disembarked on Tybee Island. The only 'Americans' to greet him before the hastily constructed defences of Savannah were a Legion (mixed cavalry and infantry) of 300–400 men, mainly British deserters, under the command of the Polish Count Kazimierz Pulaski, a source of greater terror to civilians than it was to the enemy. Estaing summoned Prevost to surrender 'to the arms of the King of France' and gave him twenty-four hours to think about it, which were put to good use by Maitland's Highlanders, Cruger's New Yorkers and Brown's Rangers, recalled from Port Royal, Sunbury and Ebenezer, who got into Savannah just before Lincoln arrived from Charleston on the 16th with 600 Continentals and 750 Militia.

Although the easy-going Lincoln was an improvement on the abrasive Sullivan, relations were strained from the start by dissatisfaction about the wording of Estaing's summons to surrender, and by Moultrie's proposal that the French should make an immediate assault. Although a full investment was impossible because the river approaches were denied by sunken blockships and Hutchinson's Island was held by the British (according to the contemporary French map on which MAP 21 is based, in fact by Indian auxiliaries), Moultrie's proposal was rejected in favour of a formal siege, and work began on the zigzag approach trenches (saps) familiar to the French and British, but an arcane mystery to the impatient Americans. The outcome, a foregone conclusion given time, was thwarted by the mosquitoes, which descended on the French fleet and, in combination with the scurvy already rife among sailors who had been eighteen months at sea, carried them off in dozens every day. Under pressure from his captains, and informed by his engineers they needed another ten days to batter the place into submission, Estaing decided to mount an assault after all, at dawn on 9 October.

Huger's South Carolina Continentals were assigned the task of keeping the defenders' attention fixed on the saps in the southeast by making a credible feint against the redoubt held by Cruger, before the main attack went in along a ridge from the southwest blocked by the Spring Hill Redoubt, held by Brown and Maitland, the latter dying of malaria. Unfortunately Huger's men did not even venture into musket range, and another feint by French General Dillon from the west got lost in Yamacraw Swamp, arriving late into hot fire from an artillery redoubt manned by sailors, and enfiladed by warships in the river.

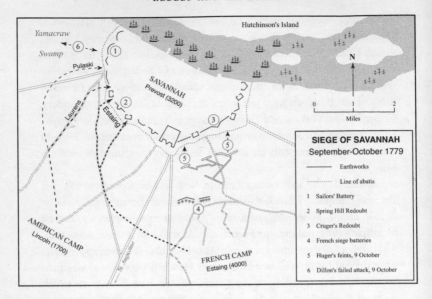

MAP 21

The main, French, assault was beaten back with heavy loss and Estaing himself was wounded, while the flanking attack by another column of South Carolina Continentals and the socially elite Charleston Militia led by John Laurens (son of Henry, the richest merchant in Charleston and twice President of the Continental Congress) clawed its way to the ramparts before falling back. Sergeant William Jasper, already a folk hero for waving the American flag from the walls of Fort Sullivan in 1776, was killed doing the same on the Spring Hill Redoubt. On the left Pulaski collected more dubious glory and a mortal wound when charging an unbroken line of *abatis*, his troopers sensibly choosing not to follow him. The attackers suffered about 1000 casualties, two-thirds of them French, among them twelve year-old Henri Cristophe, future king of independent Haiti.

Estaing re-embarked his men and sailed to Charleston, while Lincoln's men returned by land, bearing tales of Gallic arrogance and treachery to explain their failure. What followed along the waterfront made the riots in Boston pale by comparison. Returning soldiers joined with the usual riffraff to mount assaults on the French ships, and had to be repelled by cannon fire, with dozens killed and wounded. Trying to retrieve something from the wreck Estaing ceded four frigates to the Americans before sending the troops back to Martinique and glumly sailing back to France. Somehow it seems inevitable that a violent storm scattered the fleet, which limped back in varying states of disrepair. One is compelled to wonder if the animosity towards the United States of the Gaullist ex-President Valéry Giscard d'Estaing may not be rooted in the insolence and ingratitude piled upon chronic bad luck experienced by his ancestor.

Strange things had meanwhile been happening further north. News that Estaing's fleet had sailed north from the West Indies caused Clinton to order the evacuation of Newport to over insure New York, and to postpone a planned expedition to the south, leaving Savannah to be saved by the mosquitoes while making the French a gift of an ice-free port where they could impose their will on the Loyalist inhabitants without offending their allies. His response to Germain's urgings that he should obey orders was to submit a request that he be relieved and Cornwallis appointed in his place, with the result that when the earl returned from England at the end of 1779 he had every reason to believe he would soon activate a 'dormant commission' as commander-in-chief, which had been burning a hole in his pocket since his last return, newly promoted to lieutenant-general, in April 1778.

Whether Germain was more at fault than Clinton for creating this command ambivalence, with its self-evident potential for catastrophe, is hotly debated. The case against Germain was set out by Fortescue, who alleged Clinton was required to make one army do the work of two, the whole dependent on command of the sea. But this was the consequence of his refusal to accept that strategy is the prerogative of politicians, rodents though they may be, and that a soldier's first duty is to obey. As clearly as anyone expressed themselves in those wordy times, Germain instructed Clinton to 'Americanize' the war and to shift the operational centre of gravity south, leaving the north to be strangled by naval blockade and coastal raids.

This was unquestionably the best option after France entered the war. The cash crops of the rebellion were all produced in Virginia and the Carolinas, they were the grand avenue for contraband of every description, and their revolutionary leadership was the least popularly based. In addition, concentration in the South could respond quickly to any Franco-Spanish threat to the West Indies, which were considerably more valuable than Canada and the northern colonies put together. The dispersal of forces Fortescue blamed on Germain was not a consequence of conflicting orders from London, rather these were irritated replies to Clinton's demands for more of everything and ever-changing excuses for not doing what he was told. Like William Howe, he abused the operational freedom properly enjoyed by a commander-in-chief in a time of slow and uncertain communications to subvert a strategy with which he did not agree, but to which he never proposed an alternative tailored to the resources at his disposal.

The stronger indictment of Germain is that he, in turn, refused to accept the political judgement of Lord North and the king in denying his wish to replace the politically neutral Clinton with Cornwallis, a protégé of the opposition grandee Rockingham. However aggravating he found Clinton, Germain should have known that to try to work around him by direct correspondence with Cornwallis was a recipe for disaster. But before convicting him we must revisit the extenuating circumstances of the system within which they all operated. It is not even slightly remarkable that a polity capable of dithering its way isolated and unprepared into an unwinnable war should have mismanaged its prosecution. Against which the Franco-American alliance never achieved its aim of dictating terms to the British, and indeed never really took the military initiative away from them. If it had been politically possible to admit the colonies were irretrievably lost in 1777, operations in North America could have been overtly defended as the exercise in loss limitation outlined in the confidential orders issued to Clinton. However it was not, and it became necessary to pretend that recovery was still possible in order to encourage the Loyalists, to keep domestic opinion in Britain on-side, and to put pressure on the American elite. The French and the Americans were made to pay a ruinous price for continuing the war, while the Royal Navy gradually reasserted the oceanic dominance upon which every vital British interest depended. Not many would call that losing.

It went wrong because the level-headed recognition that the war in the North was lost did not survive the easy successes in Georgia, and Germain lost the plot upon persuading himself the verdict of 1777 might yet be reversed. The first casualty was the principle of concentration. Leaving Knyphausen in New York with 10,000 effectives and another 6000 sick, Clinton sailed with 8700 in ninety transports on 26 December, just before ice closed the harbour, escorted by Arbuthnot with ten warships. The troops included the light infantry corps, two British and three Hessian grenadier battalions, the 7th, the 23rd (which included the newly promoted Sergeant Roger Lamb, who had escaped from the captive Convention Army against the orders of his officers and was judged an 'honourable deserter'), the 33rd and the 63rd, reinforcements for the 71st and the Hessian and Loyalist units already in Savannah, and two new Loyalist formations that feature prominently in the following pages.

The first was the British Legion, a mixed dragoon and infantry unit originally formed from Scots colonists in Philadelphia by the youthful Lieutenant-Colonel William, Baron Cathcart, and completed in New York with local recruits. It was now commanded by another young man, Lieutenant-Colonel Banastre Tarleton, whom we saw last capturing Charles Lee at Basking Ridge in 1776, a rare individual who never bothered to disguise that he loved risking and dealing in death. The other was the Loyal American Volunteers, some 150 New York Rangers including the diarist Lieutenant Anthony Allaire, adjutant during this campaign to the recruiter and leader of the unit, Major Patrick Ferguson of the 71st. Ferguson was the inventor of an accurate, fast-firing and dependable breech-loading rifle, a concept not accepted by any army until the mid nineteenth century. The Volunteers were in their second incarnation and no longer equipped with this weapon, because after Ferguson's right arm was crippled while skirmishing for Knyphausen's column at the Brandywine, Howe disbanded the unit and stored the rifles, on the grounds that he had approved neither. Ferguson believed he had the opportunity to snipe Washington on that occasion, but declined because 'it was not pleasant to fire at the back of an unoffending individual who was acquitting himself very coolly of his duty, so I let him alone'. Nice, but there is no corroboration Washington was out among the skirmishers in front of Chad's Ford, nor any reason for him to have been there. However the anecdote does explain why Ferguson refused, after one experience, to cooperate further with Tarleton.

Clinton's armada ran into a series of severe winter storms, which dispersed it so thoroughly that one of the Hessian transports ended up in England, two others packed with artillery went down, and nearly all the horses had to be put down after suffering broken legs. Ewald recorded a particularly horrifying moment when a ship with Hessian grenadiers came 'so close to ours that had a big wave not flung us a great distance away both ships would have collided and sunk, for no ship could help herself, since all sails were lowered with steering tied down'. The survivors regrouped and limped into Savannah at the end of January, where Clinton disembarked his now horseless troopers and 1400 infantry to march to Augusta, picking up mounts on the way, in the hope of drawing Lincoln's garrison out of Charleston. The rest of the army surely shared their commander-in-chief's 'no small dread' as the fleet crept along the coast until safely disembarked on 11–12 February at North Edisto Inlet, thirty miles southwest of Charleston, as yet another tempest lashed the coast (see MAP 22).

The advance was led by Ewald's Jägers and the 33rd, Cornwallis's own regiment, both under the command of Lieutenant-Colonel James Webster, an officer singled out for praise by every important memoirist of this campaign. At the crossing between John's and James Islands Ewald rode forward to parley with the Americans, hoping to discover something of their dispositions, while they in turn disingenuously warned him the river was swarming with alligators. Lincoln believed Clinton would not be able to bring his artillery across the marshy terrain and chose not to defend any of the crossings, but he had overlooked the significance of Stono Inlet, along which the army's guns and heavy supplies were rowed from the fleet offshore. The British advance was harassed only by cavalry of the late Pulaski's Legion commanded by the hereditary knight Pierre-François Vernier, and in the light of his later fate it should be noted his troopers were merciless when they ambushed British foraging parties.

The failure to contest Clinton's advance on land was matched by the astonishing decision taken by the American Commodore Abraham Whipple not to employ his eight frigates – which included the four acquired from Estaing, admitted even by the British to be the best

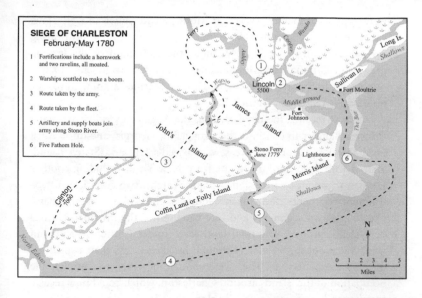

SIEGE OF CHARLESTON
February–May 1780

1   Fortifications include a hornwork and two ravelins, all moated.

2   Warships scuttled to make a boom.

3   Route taken by the army.

4   Route taken by the fleet.

5   Artillery and supply boats join army along Stono River.

6   Five Fathom Hole.

MAP 22

built ships of their type in the world – to defend The Bar. Instead he withdrew them to the inner harbour, where he scuttled five to make a boom of their masts, behind which he anchored the other three. Unhindered, Arbuthnot brought three ships of the line and four frigates across The Bar, rearmed them and sailed under fire from the heavy guns of Fort Moultrie to anchor in the middle harbour. Ewald, normally critical of his employers, was moved to comment:

> Only an English fleet can execute such a masterpiece. It appeared, too, as if all the heavens wished to enhance their brilliant performance, for it was the most beautiful weather in the world, with hardly any wind; the manoeuvre was carried out only with the aid of the flood tide.

The passage of the natural and man-made obstacles in the Charleston estuary illustrates how the Royal Navy routinely performed extremely demanding tasks, even under a commander like the generally disesteemed Arbuthnot, and how acutely aware of this its opponents were. Not all of them, however, as Moultrie had shown in 1776. Now, while he was in Charleston doing nothing important, the fort bearing his name performed miserably under the command of the leading prewar revolutionary Charles Pinckney, who later surrendered it without a fight to a party of sailors and Royal Marines accompanied, for no obvious reason, by Patrick Ferguson.

Clinton recalled the regulars from the Augusta expedition, leaving Brown's Rangers to continue the struggle for Georgia, and on 16 April Lord Rawdon, whom last we saw at Breed's Hill and Staten Island, arrived with 2500 reinforcements from New York, including another Hessian regiment and the 42nd (Black Watch), two American Establishment regiments, the Queen's Rangers, the Volunteers of Ireland (Rawdon's own regiment) and one battalion of the Provincial Prince of Wales Regiment. The total land force under Clinton's command was now about 12,500 men, although he alleged less than two-thirds of them were effectives. They were enough, however, to complete the occupation of the islands around Charleston, which could now receive supplies and reinforcements only along the Wando and Cooper Rivers.

Rather than bringing more men into the bag, as happened during the night of 8 April when 750 Virginia Continentals in eleven small craft joined the garrison, Lincoln would have been better advised to evacuate the city while he still had the chance, but as a northerner commanding exclusively southern troops, his authority was tenuous. On the 15th Rutledge and the older members of the governing council, who might have given Lincoln the political cover to try and save his army, decamped after a few houses were set on fire by heated shot (promptly halted by Clinton, on grounds that it was 'impolitic and inhuman to burn a town you mean to occupy'). Before going they delegated authority, one suspects with malice aforethought, to the young radicals led by John Gadsden who had denounced them as cowards in 1779.

Lincoln summoned a council of war on 25 April to which he was unwise enough to invite Gadsden, who arrived accompanied by enraged citizens who demanded the army should remain, on pain of destroying its boats and opening the gates to the enemy. By this stage it was extremely unlikely, for the reasons we shall consider next, that any substantial part of the army could have escaped the trap, and the incident is only mentioned to highlight the sequel. As usual bravado proved fragile, and after Clinton lifted his prohibition on heated shot during the night of 10–11 May, Gadsden and the members of the council begged Lincoln to accept whatever terms he could get. These pointedly did not include the honours of war, normally conceded only to a garrison that had put up a spirited defence. On 12 May after losing 89 killed and 150 wounded, Lincoln led out six other generals and 290 lower-ranking officers, 2275 Continentals and 800 Militia to stack their arms in the British camp, and to surrender his sword to Clinton. Two thousand and ninety-five invalids swelled the total to 5466 officers and men. The British lost 268 killed and wounded, 50 of them in an explosion that destroyed most of the captured materiel in the evening of 12 May, plus 27 casualties among the Royal Navy's 5000, and had dealt the American cause the most severe blow it had suffered since New York, four years earlier.

Nor was that the sum of the debacle. A month earlier Clinton had dispatched a mixed force of infantry and cavalry under Webster to attack a force of 400 Continental cavalry and about the same number of Militia infantry under Isaac Huger at Monck's Corner, a vital position at the navigable headwaters of the Cooper River. These included Vernier's troopers and four other regiments under the command of George Washington's long-serving cousin William. He had clashed twice with Tarleton during his march from the Savannah, easily outriding a force only partially mounted on requisitioned farm horses and mules. This may have contributed to an inexcusable failure to post pickets, with the result that when Webster sent Tarleton's Legion and Ferguson's riflemen racing ahead of his column, they were able to take the Americans by surprise during the night of 13–14 April.

Huger's dispositions were flawed, with his cavalry and infantry divided by a stream, but the decisive factor was Tarleton's hell-for-leather attack, in which only three men were wounded and five horses killed. Vernier tried to offer resistance, but he was hacked down along with thirteen of his men when belatedly asking for quarter, to die hours later cursing the Legion troopers who came to jeer at him. The rest fled, leaving 19 wounded among the 93 captured, plus 400 fully equipped horses and 50 wagons of supplies, which permitted Tarleton to bring his Legion back to full fighting strength. If the attack showed

Tarleton at his best, the aftermath also revealed severe ill discipline among his men, some of whom raided the nearby plantation owned by Sir John Colleton, a prominent Loyalist, and terrorized the ladies of the household. Ferguson intervened and wanted the dragoons shot on the spot, but instead they were sent back to Webster, who had them flogged. Ten days later, after Cornwallis had taken over the job of screening the besieged city, he ordered Tarleton to raid towards the Santee River with the concluding words:

> I must recommend it to you in the strongest manner to use your utmost endeavours to prevent the troops under your command from committing irregularities, and I am convinced that my recommendation will have weight, when I assure you that such conduct will be highly agreeable to the commander in chief.

This explains why the Legion behaved with unusual restraint following their next battle, on 6 May against Continental cavalry and infantry recently arrived from Virginia under the command of Colonels Anthony White and Abraham Buford. They were joined by Washington and other survivors of Monck's Corner, but unaccountably Tarleton's ability to drive men and horses beyond their normal limits was again underestimated. Once more the Americans were caught divided by a river and White's troopers were routed, with 41 killed or wounded and 67 captured. Tarleton lost 2 men and 4 horses in action, plus 20 horses dead of exhaustion, but these were made good from the ones the enemy left behind when, as Tarleton observed with grim humour, 'Colonels White, Washington, and Jamieson, with some officers and men, availed themselves of their swimming, to take their escape, while many who wished to follow their example perished in the river'. Buford's 450 infantry and his supply wagons had, however, crossed safely, as had President Rutledge and his entourage, whom Tarleton had hoped to capture. The much-defeated Isaac Huger became area commander upon the fall of Charleston, and ordered the sole remaining Continental Army presence in South Carolina to withdraw from the province in order to join a new army forming at Hillsboro, North Carolina.

Despite the preceding years of terrorism and extortion by 'patriots', despite Kettle Creek and the Sergeant MacAlister incident, American historians generally blame Tarleton's next victory for allegedly setting the tone for what followed. In fact the war that developed following the fall of Charleston resembled a brawl in an old Western film, in which one man hits another and this is the cue for everyone else to smash a chair over his neighbour's head. In addition to the engagements marked in MAP 20 (see p. 156) there were 176 smaller ambushes and raids, with one or two dead, houses burned, slaves stolen and livestock run off. Nonetheless Tarleton's reputation, for good and ill, was finally made by the pursuit and brutal destruction of Buford's Continentals on 29 May. They had a ten-day lead and Cornwallis had little hope his cavalry commander could catch up with them before they made good their escape. Tarleton set out on 27 May with 170 cavalry, including a 40-man detachment of the 17th Dragoons whose scarlet jackets stood out among the green of the Legion, 100 mounted infantry and one 3-pounder, and drove them 105 miles in fifty-four hours. Leaving behind the gun and a trail of men and horses prostrate or dead of heatstroke, he still had 200 with him when he caught up with Buford at Waxhaw's Creek, on the border between the two Carolinas.

Rutledge and his party made use of their fine horses to flee, but after sending 100 men ahead with the artillery and supply wagons, Buford turned to fight with the rest. On receipt of a demand for surrender from Tarleton, in which he claimed to have 700 men, Buford replied, 'Sir, I reject your proposals, and shall defend myself to the last extremity'. Bearing in mind our earlier review of contemporary rules of war, this could only be interpreted as an invitation to battle without quarter. Added to which he was a cavalryman with no experience of handling infantry, and committed the appalling blunder of forming his men in a single line along a road running through an open wood, compounded by ordering them to hold their fire until the cavalry were at point-blank range. Tarleton was not one to hesitate when offered such an opportunity. He sent the red-coated dragoons with a few of his own men to keep the enemy's attention to the front and most of his mounted infantry to attack the American left flank, while he led 'thirty chosen horse and some infantry' in a hook around their right flank. The Virginians were obviously first-class troops, for they stood their ground and held their fire as ordered, but they were hopelessly betrayed by their deployment. The first and only volley dropped 31 horses, including Tarleton's, but most of the Legion's 19 killed or wounded must have come in the hand-to-hand battle that followed, with the Virginians desperately swinging their unloaded muskets at the men riding them down. In Tarleton's words 'slaughter was commenced' and although not normally given to making excuses he offered an explanation:

> The loss of officers and men was great on the part of the Americans, owing to the dragoons so effectually breaking the infantry, and to a report among the cavalry that they had lost their commanding officer, which stimulated the soldiers to a vindictive asperity not easily restrained.

Whether because of this, or wild fury after three hellish days of pursuit, Tarleton's men went berserk. Were it not for the telltale casualty ratio one might be inclined to view American propaganda about this episode in the same light as the Paoli and Tappan 'massacres', but with 113 dead and 150 of 203 prisoners wounded, many repeatedly (not including those escorting the wagons and artillery, who later surrendered safely), the account written many years later by Dr Robert Brownfield, surgeon to Buford's regiment, is entirely credible:

> ... for fifteen minutes after every man was prostrate they went over the ground plunging their bayonets into every one that exhibited any signs of life, and in some instances, where several had fallen over the other, these monsters were seen to throw off on the point of the bayonet the uppermost, to come at those below.

Buford fled, to claim he had shown the white flag as soon as his line was broken, only to have its bearer cut down. This was believed and aroused the Americans to transports of hatred against Tarleton, although the time to surrender is emphatically not when the enemy, having endured your fire, is at your throat. One who certainly did not try to surrender was Captain John Stokes, who suffered the loss of his right hand and a blow that split his skull while fighting on horseback. Even when helpless on the ground he twice refused offers of quarter, and received no less than four bayonet thrusts intended to finish him off. Rather than sheep savaged by wolves, it seems the Virginians were brave men who fought to the death, as their commander had said they would – and as he did not. He now disappears from our story, eventually to lay the foundations for Kentucky's tradition of horse-rearing. However we cannot leave him without commenting on the historically resonant fact that his namesake grandson was a notable cavalry leader for the Confederacy for the duration of the next civil war, while his brother's great-grandson John Buford died of typhoid in 1863, six months after his cavalry brigade had laid the basis for the Union victory at Gettysburg.

9

PARTISAN WAR

AFTER THE FALL of Charleston and Waxhaws the campaign in the South was on a knife edge. The leaders of South Carolina felt abandoned by the rest of the United States and were faced with the unpalatable choice between continued resistance and the expropriation of their lands and 'property', or reaching an accommodation with the resurgent British. As to the first, James Duane of New York reported to Philip Schuyler in May 1780 that he and a number of other Congressmen had discussed the possibility of seeking a 'ten-colony' settlement with Britain. Many northern politicians were delighted to see their haughty southern colleagues humiliated, and some even predicted the political schizophrenia that must follow from a union of slave states with free. The high level of Loyalist/separatist sentiment in the Carolinas and Georgia was also disconcerting, and from Pennsylvania to the north no state would agree to send troops to an area where they might find themselves bereft of popular support. The Rice Kings could expect some assistance from their peers in Virginia, Maryland and Delaware, but everything hinged on proving that a dependable will to resist the British existed in South Carolina, which in turn depended on whether the back-country men hated the British or the coastal oligarchy more.

On the British side, following Waxhaws the Loyalist regiments fanned out to occupy a perimeter from Georgetown on the coast up the Pee Dee River to Cheraw, west to camps at Rocky Mount and Hanging Rock to the north of the town of Camden, then southwest past Winsboro to Ninety-Six and Augusta. The Prince of Wales Regiment was entrusted with Hanging Rock, the New York Volunteer battalions under Turnbull and Cruger were assigned to Rocky Mount and Ninety-Six respectively, while Brown's Rangers and the South Carolina Royalists under Lieutenant-Colonel Alexander Innes held Georgia. Clinton appointed Ferguson Inspector of Militia, and entrusted him with the task of recruiting and training volunteers in the strongly Loyalist district around Ninety-Six. Lord Rawdon was posted to the Waxhaws district with his Volunteers of Ireland, mainly Scotch-Irish deserters from the Continental Army, in the hope that they would attract recruits among their fellows in the region, whom Allaire considered 'the most violent Rebels I ever saw'. Instead desertion soared and Rawdon judged it necessary to pull back to Camden before the entire regiment melted away.

Clinton made these dispositions shortly before returning to New York on 5 June 1780 with the bulk of the non-American regulars (alas for historians, including Ewald), leaving Cornwallis with only 4000, preponderantly Loyalists, to complete the reconquest of the Carolinas. Relations between the two generals had been strained since 19 March, when a letter arrived from Germain rejecting Clinton's request to be relieved because the king 'was too well satisfied with your conduct to wish to see the command of his forces in any other hands'. Cornwallis declared that if he was not to have command he did not wish to share responsibility, and petulantly refused to meet with Clinton unless ordered to do so. The flurry of appointments and orders issued by Clinton before departure were intended to show his subordinate who was the boss, which lamentable display of immaturity was crowned by the most disastrous of all the ill-considered proclamations made by the British during this war. The Militia captured at Charleston had been freed on parole, and the surrender of others throughout South Carolina accepted on the same lenient terms, but now Clinton announced that all must swear an oath of fealty, and would be regarded as rebels should they refuse to serve the king's cause. This clumsy attempt to turn acquiescence into collaboration gave men like Andrew Pickens, who had given his parole and retired to his farm, no choice but to resume hostilities when his Loyalist neighbours tried to administer the oath, and finding him gone burned his home. In conjunction with the below-minimum force Clinton left behind, the proclamation might have been designed to set Cornwallis up for failure, and so to discredit Germain's southern strategy.

The ensuing irregular war was extremely complex and we cannot here devote more than cursory attention to it, other than to summarize the broad lines of activity. The first of the South Carolinian guerrilla leaders to make his presence felt was Thomas 'Gamecock' Sumter, appointed senior Militia officer by Rutledge, who was to operate thereafter as though determined to prove that South Carolina could go it alone. His band initially drew heavily on the 'violent rebels' of Waxhaws and, oddly, on the Catawba Indians from much the same area, who had no reason to fight alongside those determined to take away from them the little land they still occupied. The appearance of Sumter's force along the North Carolina border between the Catawba and Pee Dee Rivers forced Rawdon to evacuate the garrison from Cheraw, another Rebel hotspot, and prompted a mutiny by two regiments recruited from South Carolinians who had taken Clinton's oath, and who now joined the Gamecock. Even mythologists flinch from dealing fairly with a man who left so many corpses dangling from trees that they became known as 'Sumter's fruit', but he took on the British at their moment of greatest success, and Cornwallis rated him the most troublesome of the guerrilla leaders.

Among the other irregular commanders we have met Francis Marion and Elijah Clarke, whose main areas of operation were the lower Pee Dee and the Georgia border respectively. Andrew Pickens, who recruited in the area between the Saluda and Broad Rivers, did not renounce his parole until September 1780, and unlike the others devoted himself primarily to reactivating the formal Militia system with an eye to collaborating with the Continental Army when it returned. Markedly less celebrated was Benjamin Cleveland, who terrorized the upper Yadkin territory in North Carolina in conjunction with his polar opposite, the refined Joseph Winston, both the sons of immigrants from Yorkshire. Cleveland was a psychopath who liked to hang men unbound, leaving their hands free to prolong the death agony, and on at least one occasion made a prisoner cut his own ears off to escape the noose.

Finally there were those who raided into South Carolina from bases in the Blue Ridge Mountains. Among the most active were the brothers Charles and James McDowell, the only ones we can safely say were Scotch-Irish, whose catchment area was on the eastern flanks of the mountains. Isaac Shelby and John Sevier were properly 'Over Mountain' and illustrate how unwise it is to generalize about ethnic origins, for the former was the son of a Welsh immigrant and the latter of a French ne'er-do-well in flight from his debtors. Their subsequent history is also illuminating as to motivation, for Sevier was later the leader of the state of Franklin, which declared its independence from North Carolina in 1787, and then the first governor of Tennessee. At the time of Sevier's first secession, bloodshed was prevented by Evan Shelby, Isaac's father, who lived to see his son become the first governor of Kentucky. They were fighting for a deeper independence than the Foundation Myth accommodates.

With the exception of Pickens they all had only a small core of constant companions and would assemble larger bodies of men for particular enterprises. Afterwards the men would disperse, taking as much or as little part in the war as their particular circumstances dictated. A representative clash took place at Ramsauer's Mill in North Carolina on 20 June 1780, when John Moore assembled about 1700 Loyalists from the area between the Broad and Catawba Rivers in premature anticipation of a British advance into the territory. They were set upon by a smaller force under the nominal command of Francis Locke and after a remarkably bloody free-for-all with 150 casualties on either side, the majority of those engaged on both sides went home. Fifty miles to the south another engagement diluted some of the terror Tarleton's men now inspired, when a detachment of fifty Legion dragoons and New York Volunteers plus several hundred local Loyalists under Legion Captain Christian Huck got much the worst of an encounter with a war band led by William Bratton at Williamson's Plantation. Huck and most of his dragoons were killed and only fifteen New Yorkers returned to Rocky Mount, along with a mere dozen of the locals.

Cornwallis was furious about Moore's premature rising, and confessed to 'great uneasiness' at Huck's defeat. His peace of mind was further disturbed by a flurry of activity between 30 July and 8 August, which began when Shelby and Charles McDowell combined to bring together about 600 men, who forced the surrender of the Loyalist outpost of Thicketty Fort. On the same day Sumter, with about the same number of men, made an unsuccessful assault on Rocky Mount. Turnbull had taken the precaution of fortifying some log cabins, but only survived thanks to a providential downpour, which extinguished an attempt to burn him out. Tarleton commented 'the repulse [Sumter] had sustained did not discourage him, or injure his cause: the loss of men was easily supplied, and his reputation for activity and courage was fully established by his late enterprising conduct'.

Sumter had better luck a week later across the river at Hanging Rock, where Major John Carden of the Prince of Wales Loyalists was alerted when another partisan group destroyed a detachment of the North Carolina Provincials a few miles away, taking 60 horses, 100 muskets and no prisoners. Sumter attacked clumsily but in overwhelming numbers and Carden's regiment was all but destroyed, as was a troop of Tarleton's Legion that arrived in mid battle, before the survivors formed a square and beat off further attacks. The partisans then succumbed to premature looting, the bane of every military commander's life, and got into the rum. Unable to stir what were soon his staggeringly merry men to further action, Sumter withdrew burdened with loot and buoyed up by the knowledge his South Carolinians had succeeded where the Continentals had failed, and beaten the British Legion at its own game.

Disregarded by Cornwallis as something foisted on him by Clinton, the Loyalist force built up around Ferguson's American Volunteers shared neither the Legion's success nor its evil reputation. Ferguson trained them in infantry tactics better suited for warfare in the northern woods than for the conditions prevailing in South Carolina, where the enemy was not only mounted but knew the terrain better, with the result bitterly recorded by Allaire:

> . . . there is not a regiment or detachment of His Majesty's service, that ever went through the fatigues, or suffered so much, as our detachment. In the first place we were separated from all the army, acting with the Militia; we never lay two nights in one place, frequently making forced marches of twenty and thirty miles in one night; skirmishing very often; the greatest part of our time without rum or wheat flour.

Worst of all, they were never able to close with the enemy, always arriving to find camps abandoned, smoke curling tantalisingly from the cooking fires, with stay-behind snipers taking their toll before riding away. Although Ferguson recruited mainly from the strongly Loyalist area around Ninety-Six district, where men were raised to the saddle, he employed only 150 of them as mounted infantry. Led by John Dunlap, a local man, this small vanguard caught up with the combined forces of Clarke and Shelby at Cedar Springs on 8 August and unhesitatingly attacked despite being outnumbered four to one. Clarke received sabre cuts to the head and shoulders, but Dunlap was forced to retreat after losing 30 men killed and 50 captured. By the time Ferguson arrived, the partisans and their prisoners were gone.

All these engagements were writing on the wall, but from the north came a challenge very much more suited to the British Army and to the combative tastes of Cornwallis, eager to abandon the administrative burdens of Charleston for the field. His opponent was Horatio Gates, who delivered up the Continental Army in the South as though working from a script written by his opponent. Or, to take a more cynical view, to one written by George Washington, who could have imposed Nathanael Greene, his own candidate, but agreed with suspicious readiness when Congress appointed the Hero of Saratoga to redeem a theatre of war that had already curtailed the military careers of officers Washington considered far more able than Gates. In defence of Congress it must be said that Gates was the only Continental major-general who professed faith in the Militia, a prerequisite for operations in the South when the Continental Army could spare only a nucleus of regulars for the task.

The army Gates took over on 25 July amounted to about 1400 men, what was left of Delaware's sole Continental regiment and seven of Maryland's eight, sent south under the command of Major-General Johann Kalb in April to relieve the siege of Charleston, plus 130 survivors of Pulaski's Legion, now commanded by Charles, Marquis de Rouerie, alias 'Armand'. Kalb continued to advance after learning of Lincoln's surrender, but lack of support from the North Carolina authorities led to soaring desertion and forced him to halt at Deep River, midway between Hillsboro and Cheraw. The most detailed account of the campaign was written by the Marylander Otho Williams,

Kalb's adjutant and not precisely an unbiased witness, but he did not need to gild the lily of the succession of blunders that followed.

Putting too much reliance on Sumter's assurance that thousands of men would join him in the Waxhaws district, Gates marched directly towards it across inhospitable terrain rather than making a sweep through Salisbury to Charlotte, as recommended by Kalb and Williams. Gates also dismissed offers of light cavalry support from Francis Marion, William Washington and Anthony White, all of them Continental officers, declaring South Carolina was not good cavalry country. Just across the border the army was joined by 2100 well fed and furnished North Carolina Militia under the command of Richard Caswell, until recently governor of North Carolina on the strength of the speed of his ride from Moore's Creek. The Continentals were furious to observe the opulent baggage train of the man who had left them to starve, and there was not even social contact between the two halves of the army as it marched south. Finally 700 Virginia Militia under Edward Stevens joined within a few miles of Rawdon's base at Camden.

Gates intended to recreate Bemis Heights a few miles north of Camden, to draw Cornwallis away from Charleston and so expose his line of communications to attack by Sumter and Marion. He was undone because Cornwallis reacted instantly upon receipt of Rawdon's report that the Continental Army had returned in force and made a forced march to Camden, arriving in the evening of 13 August with four companies of light infantry, his own 33rd, three companies of the 23rd and five of the 71st. Rawdon had about 800 men in the Volunteers of Ireland, British Legion and two regiments of North Carolina volunteers, giving Cornwallis 2240 men with which to oppose what Gates supposed were 7000 men under his command. On the eve of battle Williams made a hasty count and reported only 3050, less than three quarters of the true figure, but Gates was unfazed, airily replying 'there are enough for our purpose'. He had earlier detached 100 Marylanders and 300 North Carolina Militia with two guns to join Sumter in attacks on the British line of communications, which were supposed to pin his opponent in Camden. The attacks were duly delivered on 15 August at Wateree Ferry, opposite Camden, where Sumter captured convoys coming from Charleston and Ninety-Six, taking 50–60 wagons and large herds of cattle and sheep and raising the number of prisoners

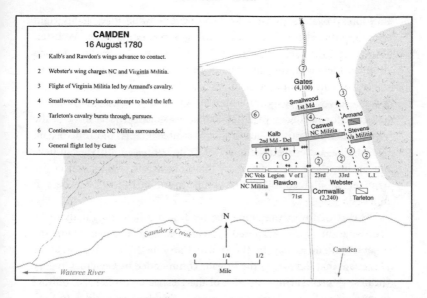

MAP 23

with his column to about 100. That night Gates marched confidently south and was stupefied when a clash between Armand's and Tarleton's troopers at a passage between two marshes six and a half miles north of Camden revealed Cornwallis had sortied to find him.

Upon seeing Gates advance to meet him Cornwallis must have thought Christmas had come early in 1780. Believing he faced nearly double the actual number opposite him, he would nonetheless have attacked even if Gates had done the sensible thing and made a stand on the high ground to the north of the chokepoint between the marshes. By marching into it, the Americans were forced to advance three or four deep in an extremely clumsy formation, with the Virginia Militia deployed in front of the North Carolinians (whose line extended further than it has been possible to show in MAP 23), while the gap was perfectly spaced for the proper deployment of the British. As a bonus, Gates had not even tried to integrate the components of his army and deployed the Continentals on one side of the road running through the battlefield and the Militia on the other. Cornwallis ordered

Rawdon's Loyalists to face the Continentals while loading his right wing opposite the Militia with the British regiments under Webster. When the light infantry advanced with a cheer the Virginia Militia dropped their weapons and ran from the field, followed by most of the North Carolinians and led by Armand's troopers, who paused only to loot Caswell's baggage train on their way back to Hillsboro. Williams had gone forward with volunteers to act as skirmishers in front of the Virginians and testified not a shot was fired before the rout began. 'He who has never seen the effect of panic upon a multitude can have but an imperfect idea of such a thing', he wrote. 'Like electricity it operates simultaneously – like sympathy, it is irresistible where it touches'.

The 23rd, advancing along the road, had a harder fight than the rest. Sergeant Lamb tempered his comments on the panic with the observation 'in justice to the North Carolina Militia, it should be remarked, that the part of the brigade commanded by General Gregory [nearest the reassuring presence of the Delaware regiment] acquitted themselves well, and kept the field while they had a cartridge to fire'. Brigadier-General William Smallwood had joined the flight, so Williams took command of the reserve 1st Maryland Brigade and wheeled it to support the left wing. However the damage was irretrievable and most of those who stood and fought were trapped against the marshes as the light infantry and the 33rd wrapped around them, with Kalb mortally wounded as he led his men against the Loyalists to their front, and further into the trap. Williams himself escaped and recorded his quiet satisfaction in joining the looting of Caswell's personal liquor store. But he could not tarry, for this was the only battle of the war followed by a relentless cavalry pursuit, with Tarleton's men harrying the fleeing Militia for twenty miles before themselves falling on the baggage train with glad cries.

British losses were only 68 killed and 256 wounded, whereas barely 700 men rejoined the American colours in Hillsboro over the following months. Gates, who got there before anyone else, was ruined. As he had with Charles Lee, Alexander Hamilton applied the stiletto on behalf of his chief: 'One hundred and eighty miles in three days and a half! It does admirable credit to the activity of a man at his time of life. But it disgraces the general and the soldier'. On the other side, although we can allow for a considerable amount of wisdom after the event, Lamb may have had the many setbacks preceding Camden in mind when he wrote:

> Such was the issue of this campaign. The minds of the Americans were totally alienated from the British government, and to keep them under subjection when conquered was an enormous expense to the parent country. The struggle had almost exhausted the resources of America; but the cause of Great Britain had not in the least point been forwarded.

This was not an attitude shared by the dashing Tarleton, no sooner returned from the pursuit of Gates' broken army than sent after Sumter with a detachment of the light infantry in place of the Legion foot, who were exhausted after a hard battle with the Marylanders. Although Sumter's column was slowed by the captured wagons, livestock and prisoners, by now he had more than 800 men and the two guns sent him by Gates and may have succumbed to complacency. In the course of yet another fanatical pursuit Tarleton's command was whittled down to 100 dragoons and 60 mounted light infantry, but when he came upon Sumter's camp at Fishing Creek on 18 August he charged without hesitation. It was almost as complete a rout as Camden, with 150 partisans killed, the entire contingent of Continentals captured, 100 British prisoners freed and the wagons and livestock lost at Wateree Ferry recovered. Sumter himself only just escaped a four man detail sent by Tarleton specifically to kill him, but as before had little difficulty in rallying the survivors and attracting new recruits to make up his losses.

Fishing Creek was balanced by a shattering British defeat on the 17th at Musgrove's Mill, where Clarke and Shelby ambushed Alexander Innes, marching from Ninety-Six to join Ferguson with 400 New York and New Jersey infantry and 100 of his mounted South Carolina Royalists. Innes was crippled and most of the other officers killed or wounded, but the most disheartening aspect of the defeat was that when the Loyalists charged with the bayonet, the talisman of British military superiority, Clarke met them with a furious countercharge that scattered them. The Loyalists lost 63 killed and 70 missing, and came away with 90 wounded, nearly 50 per cent casualties against only 4 partisans killed and 7 wounded from a force considerably smaller than their own. Clarke and Shelby were planning to follow this up with an attack on Ninety-Six when they received news of the disaster at Camden. What happened to the men captured at Musgrove's Mill is a question probably best left unanswered, for their captors retreated so fast that Ferguson's mounted infantry could not catch up with them, which could not have been done with prisoners in tow. Clarke quickly regrouped and returned to the Georgia border area, but Shelby devoted himself to the slow process of convincing the sceptical Over Mountain Men, who cared only a little more for the fate of the South Carolina Piedmont than they did for the coastal elite they called the 'Tidewater Rats', that Ferguson also posed a threat to their interests.

Some of the rats under reference now abandoned the Continental ship with outstanding shamelessness. Cornwallis announced the estates of all insurgents would be 'sequestered', not quite the confiscation and redistribution that would have affirmed British rule, but sufficient to convince the wealthy it was time to reach an accommodation. They published a statement in the Charleston *Royal South Carolina Gazette* congratulating Cornwallis on his victory and referring to those still fighting as 'the contemptible remains of that expiring faction'. The statement also expressed what remains the great unspoken truth of the revolution, namely that Americans had enjoyed a higher degree of civil and political liberty under British rule than they had enjoyed since 1775. For this the signatories, including one of the Huger brothers, a Pinckney and a Manigault, lost their estates in 1782. William Moultrie refused to sign, saying he would rather be considered a man of honour than of property, but he was unusual at a time when even captured Continental officers were signing up for the British Army.

Sumter the Gamecock and Marion the Swamp Fox both owned modest plantations near Eutaw Springs on the lower Santee, which were to be laid waste during 1780 as a result (not, as in myth and film, the cause) of their continued resistance. They were the mirror images of Tarleton and Major James Wemyss, whom we shall see in action shortly – men not born to power but with a taste for it, seeking social promotion through military prowess. All were to be denied the acceptance they sought because they did not observe the forms of civilized behaviour so dear to their social superiors. They tortured prisoners, hanged fence-sitters, abused parole and flags of truce, and shot their own men when they failed to live up to the harsh standards they set. Parson Weems, Washington's hagiographer and inventor of the cherry tree myth, gave Marion the same treatment and the South its very own Robin Hood, although Sumter was the better candidate. Marion was almost dwarfishly small and had seriously malformed legs, not the stuff of legend but a tribute to the strength of a personality capable of overcoming these handicaps as well as all the operational difficulties of waging irregular warfare deeper in the heart of enemy territory than anyone else.

Marion made his presence felt immediately after Camden at Great Savannah, Sumter's abandoned plantation (now submerged along with his own under Lake Marion), where he wiped out the British escort and freed 147 Continentals on their way to Charleston. After a rapid ride east to the Little Pee Dee, on 4 September he routed a larger force of local Loyalists led by a man with the charming name of Micajah Ganey at a plantation confusingly called Blue Savannah. His attention now powerfully drawn to an area in his rear he had hoped would remain quiet, Cornwallis detached Wemyss with 200 men of the 63rd, which along with the 40th rivalled Fraser's Highlanders (71st) as a source of British officers with a taste for irregular warfare, for no apparent reason other than that the vehemently anti-American General James Grant, MP, himself a hard-bitten Scot, was or had been colonel of both. Wemyss in fact deserves his place in the American rogue's gallery, unlike Tarleton whose main claim to obloquy seems not to have been the swaggering ruthlessness he shared with every light cavalryman in history, but the unsettling good looks displayed in the homoerotic portrait Reynolds painted of him, which made him doubly offensive to the fabricators of the Foundation Myth.

Wemyss, on the other hand, was an individual similar in spirit to Benjamin Cleveland. He mounted his soldiers on horses taken from the farms of Rebel sympathizers in the High Hills at the junction of the Wateree with the Santee and rode south to Fort Watson, then east to Kingstree and finally to Georgetown, collecting a small army of about 400 Loyalists. Marion could not oppose such a force and fled along the Little Pee Dee, leaving a frustrated Wemyss to burn homesteads and hang suspected parole breakers along the Great Pee Dee Valley as far as Cheraw. Wemyss was aware he was acting as a recruiter for Marion, but in his report to Cornwallis he came close to enunciating an almost modern concept of the need to dry up the water in which the partisan fish swam. He did not succeed, however, for as soon as he left Marion returned and in an audacious night attack on 29 September scattered a group of prominent 'King's Friends' under the command of the Rice King John Ball at Black Mingo swamp, not twenty miles from Georgetown. To jump slightly ahead, Wemyss's American career ended on 9 November when he was so severely wounded in a surprise attack on Sumter's camp at Fishdam Ford that he was left behind under a flag of truce. Sumter, who had once again escaped a squad detailed to assassinate him, returned and found in Wemyss's pocket a list of places burned and men hanged along the Pee Dee two months earlier. Sumter read it, then dropped it in the campfire without a word, an act of professional courtesy from one executioner to another.

In late September Cornwallis marched the whole army into North Carolina to set up a new base at the village of Charlotte. Tarleton was ill with yellow fever and in his absence the British Legion was commanded by his dissolute friend George Hanger, who although an aristocratic Englishman had come to America as a captain in the Hessian Jägers. Hanger lost sixty men when his camp at Wahab's Plantation was surprised on 21 September, and where his opponent William Davie, a Yorkshire-born survivor of Pulaski's Legion, previously Sumter's subordinate and now leading a band of his own, gave orders that no prisoners were to be taken. Five days later Davie dealt Hanger another blow at Charlotte, where Cornwallis felt compelled to ride forward and urge the dragoons on with the exhortation, 'Legion, remember you have everything to lose, but nothing to gain'. Who knows whether this odd, but poignantly accurate choice of words did not prey on the minds of these men, far from home and seeing their numbers whittled down in ceaseless small-scale engagements. For whatever reason, even after Tarleton's return the cavalry of the British Legion was never the same again.

To the south the indefatigable Clarke mounted a rash attack on Augusta with about 600 men in mid September. Brown held out in a fortified house until a relief column led by Cruger arrived from Ninety-Six and dispersed Clarke's men, after which retribution was visited on the back-country Georgia insurgents by Brown's Creek allies, while thirteen prominent parole-breakers were hanged in Augusta. This promoted Brown into the top rank of American demonology even though the senior officer present was Cruger, who sent patrols as far as the Saluda River to burn out those who had joined Clarke, and jocularly promised they would be 'roughly handled, some very probably suspended for their good deeds'. It may have been this razzia that provoked Pickens into renouncing his parole. Beyond the Saluda the pursuit of Clarke was taken up by Ferguson, which led directly to the South's equivalent of Bennington, in which men with little personal stake in the broader conflict struck an annihilating blow against the British, and in the process laid the political basis for the emergence of two new states.

The on-line discussion of the King's Mountain battle indicates I am not alone in finding this battlefield peculiarly haunted. The only other place where I have felt the same as on that wooded ridge on the border between the Carolinas is on a bare hill in Montana, overlooking the Little Big Horn amid the lonely white markers showing where George Armstrong Custer's men paid the ultimate price for their commander's audacity in 1876. The only similar marker on King's Mountain records the death of Ferguson, the only nonimmigrant present, whose body was mutilated and urinated upon at the time, a crude reply to the insulting proclamation he issued 'To the Inhabitants of North Carolina' when he reached the Broad River on 1 October:

Gentlemen: Unless you wish to be eat up by an inundation of barbarians, who have begun by murdering an unarmed son before an aged father, and afterwards lopped off his arms, and who by their shocking cruelties and irregularities, give the best proof of their cowardice and want of discipline; I say, if you wish to be pinioned, robbed, and murdered, and see your wives and daughters, in four days, abused by the dregs of mankind – in short, if you wish or deserve to live and bear the name of men, grasp your arms in a moment and run to camp. The Backwater men have crossed the mountains; McDowell, Hampton, Shelby and Cleveland are at their head, so that you know what you have to depend upon. If you choose to be pissed upon forever and ever by a set of mongrels, say so at once and let your women turn

their backs upon you, and look out for real men to protect them.
Pat Ferguson, Major, 71st Regiment

He was mistaken about the English-born Andrew Hampton, who
was not one of the war party leaders, and he was also, fatally, unaware
that Shelby's efforts to unite the fractious Over Mountain Men had
at last been crowned with success. On 25 September Shelby's own 240
men and 160 led by the McDowells were joined at Sycamore Shoals
on the Watauga by the giant Virginian frontiersman William Campbell
with 200 men from the Holston Valley and Sevier with 240 from the
Nolichuky. Campbell, who was married to the sister of Patrick Henry
and would no doubt have featured prominently in Virginia politics
had he survived the war, was elected the overall commander because
none of the North Carolinians would accept subordination to another.
However the true architect of Ferguson's downfall was Isaac Shelby,
and the host he had assembled crossed the mountains to a reunion
five days later with 350 men under Cleveland and Winston at Quaker
Meadows on the upper Catawba. It was news of this gathering and of
one of Cleveland's acts of inventive sadism that prompted Ferguson's
proclamation, after which he marched to Gilbert Town at the urging
of Colonel Ambrose Mills, the senior North Carolina officer, who
promised a strong turnout from the downtrodden local Loyalists.

There was no such response, and after two deserters from Sevier's
band informed him of the numbers approaching, Ferguson began to
retreat along the Broad River in the direction of Cornwallis at Charlotte. His pursuers were joined along the way by thirty of Clarke's
Georgia partisans including the bestial Patrick Carr, and twenty men
from the South Fork of the Catawba led by William Chronicle. At
Cowpens, a place where cattle were fattened before being herded to
the coast, the column was joined by two mutually hostile factions
from Sumter's band, which was at that time camped near Gilbert
Town. Sumter himself was of the opinion that Ferguson was for the
North Carolinians to deal with, he having quite enough on his hands
with the whole British Army occupying his AO, but 100 men followed
Edward Lacey, who had fought alongside Bratton at Williamson's
Plantation, while sixty others followed James Williams under the
impression they were riding to raid around Ninety-Six. Realizing

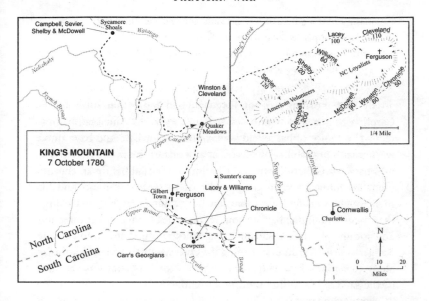

MAP 24

Ferguson might make good his escape to Charlotte only the best horsemen, a little more than 900 men, continued the chase and found their quarry at bay on King's Mountain (see MAP above).

Ferguson's last letter to Cornwallis, dated 6 October, reported that Sumter and Clarke had joined his pursuers and that although 'I should hope for success against them myself; but numbers compared, that must be doubtful'. He said he was 'on my march towards you' and asked for 'three of four hundred good soldiers, part dragoons' to 'finish the business'. Despite this he chose to make a stand on a long bare ridge surrounded by trees and boulders that provided perfect cover for the attackers who closed in around him during the afternoon of 7 October. The Over Mountain Men were concentrated against the narrowest and highest part of the ridge, held by Ferguson's Rangers, and one Loyalist described the impression they left on him, glimpsed between half-closed lids as he pretended to be dead:

> ... they were the most powerful looking men he ever beheld ... tall, raw-boned, and sinewy, with long matted hair ... he could

plainly observe their faces and eyes; and to him those bold, brave
riflemen appeared like so many devils from the infernal regions,
so full of excitement were they as they darted like enraged lions
up the mountain.

By that morning's count Ferguson had more than 1000 North
Carolina Militia and slightly fewer than 100 of his American Volunteers. His choice of battlefield is inexplicable, for he could have stood
with greater probability of success at any one of the many river crossings between Gilbert Town and Charlotte. As usual before an engagement he donned a vivid chequered coat to set an example, and his
men fought well for more than an hour. But every bayonet charge
they made had to pull back to counter an attack from another direction
and meanwhile their assailants' long rifles whittled them down. The
Rangers were overrun first, freeing the Over Mountain Men to advance
along the spine of the ridge, and finally, after Ferguson was shot out
of the saddle, the Militia tried to surrender.

For anyone wishing to know the difference between hard men and
the merely vicious, King's Mountain offers a clear contrast. The sort
of men likely to follow a Cleveland or a Carr saw an opponent's
surrender simply as an opportunity to shoot more and easier targets
and it took heroic efforts by Campbell, Shelby and Sevier, at risk to
their own lives, to halt the massacre of men who had ceased trying
to defend themselves. Dozens of men fired into Ferguson's corpse,
testimony to the passionate hatred inspired by one who had expressed
the desire to 'march my army over the mountains, hang their leaders
and lay their country waste with fire and sword'. Amid the horror,
men on both sides were struck by the tragedy of two brothers joined
in death, one pierced by the bayonet of the other as he shot him.
There were 157 Loyalist dead, with a high proportion of head shots,
and 63 mortally wounded. They had killed 28, including Chronicle
and Williams, and wounded a further 68, mainly with the bayonet.

Nearly 700 prisoners were marched away rapidly in anticipation
of a swift reaction from Cornwallis, but with Tarleton ill there was
nobody to whom he could entrust such a mission. Just north of Gilbert
Town the back-country men prevailed on Campbell and the other
Over Mountain leaders to allow what Allaire rightly called an 'infamous

mock jury' to try the North Carolina Loyalists for their lives. Thirty men were condemned to death, inevitably including Mills and other senior officers, but after nine had strangled slowly to death Shelby proposed a stop to the proceedings, which was agreed over the objections of those who shared Patrick Carr's view that 'every tree in the wilderness [should bear] such fruit as that'. Had the issue gone the other way there is little doubt the men they slaughtered in hot blood and hanged in cold would have wished to do the same to them, but it seems the Over Mountain Men left their hatred on the battlefield and had no stomach for the murder of men who no longer posed a threat.

If Ferguson, who had fought cleaner than most, was hated to such an extreme, we can readily imagine how passionately his enemies yearned to kill Tarleton, yet despite always leading from the front and having thousands of bullets directed at him in countless engagements, he was only once lightly wounded. Needless to say the contemporary explanation for this involved intense speculation about a pact with the devil, but a more mundane reason may be that he kept moving when under fire and that the long hunting rifle, although far more accurate than the musket, was still not a precision weapon. Even the legendary Timothy Murphy took three shots at about 200 yards to hit the immobile Simon Fraser at Bemis Heights. Only an infinitesimal number of bullets ever found a human target, and the standard rifles versus bayonets explanation for King's Mountain is part of a very odd American tendency to attribute military success to technology, rather than to the spirit of the men involved. This is not the place to pursue that intriguing theme, and it is mentioned only to explain why the battle was more significant than mere numbers would indicate – in a toe-to-toe contest between equal forces the Americans had been overwhelmingly victorious, largely offsetting the moral effect of Camden.

In recognition of this and alarmed by reports that Ferguson had been overwhelmed by as many as 3000 men, Cornwallis retreated seventy miles from Charlotte to Winsboro, abandoning an outpost where he was closely beset by an aggressive enemy for a Loyalist stronghold where the sick might recover during the winter. A glance back at MAP 20 (p. 156) will show how the tempo of war slowed, with only three major operations mounted against the partisans, the first being the one we have already seen, involving the meeting between Wemyss and Sumter. The second gave Marion the nickname by which he is remembered and featured Tarleton, now recovered from his illness. Cornwallis sent the British Legion to hunt down Marion, who was at this time more troublesome to him than all the other partisan leaders put together. Tarleton employed considerable cunning as well as his trademark speed, but Marion proved faster and was kept well informed by the inhabitants of the marshy area between the Santee and the Pee Dee. They paid the price in ruined livelihoods in a campaign of punitive arson, cut short when Tarleton received an urgent summons to return from Cornwallis. 'Come my boys!' he said. 'Let us go back, and we will find the Gamecock. But as for this damned old fox, the devil himself could not catch him'.

The reason for Tarleton's recall was that the setback at Fishdam Ford had not slowed Sumter down and Cornwallis now trusted nobody else to deal with him. Tarleton did catch up with Sumter again, but it was not to be another Fishing Creek. Cornwallis had given him a battalion of the 71st and the men of the 63rd previously commanded by Wemyss, which together with the 190 dragoons and mounted infantry he brought back from the fruitless pursuit of Marion gave him about 540 men against upwards of 1000 men now riding with Sumter. Informed Tarleton was coming after him, Sumter consulted his colonels and they agreed to take up a defensive position at Blackstock's Farm, twenty miles north of Ninety-Six, and wait for Tarleton to dash himself against it. This he duly did on 20 November, leaving the Highlanders and guns behind to attack only with his cavalry and 80 men of the 63rd. They were shot to pieces, losing 92 killed and 76 wounded out of 270 engaged. Among the mortally wounded was Lieutenant John Money, loved like a son by Cornwallis, whom Tarleton dismounted to lift onto his own horse while under fire from more than a hundred riflemen. We can gauge the distance by the fact that Sumter, who rode forward at this time, was hit in the chest and nearly killed by six shotgun pellets, a load only fired from muskets at very short range, from the volley fired by the 63rd to cover the rescue of their commanding officer.

Twelve days later Nathanael Greene arrived to take over the 2000-man army Horatio Gates had not only managed to reassemble at

Hillsboro, but with commendable enterprise had marched forward to occupy Charlotte after Cornwallis abandoned it. More exculpatory piffle has been written about Greene than any other general in this war. He was absent from his command when disaster struck at Brooklyn Heights, he did not remain with his men when Fort Washington came under attack, he was competent under Washington's eye at Trenton and the Brandywine but mishandled independent command at Germantown. Most notably, he was the deeply corrupt quartermaster-general of the Continental Army between 1778 and 1780, the period of its greatest privation. In the South he lost every battle he fought despite invariably enjoying significant numerical advantage and subordinates who included some of the most talented American cavalry and guerrilla commanders of the war.

To the argument that he was faced with a British officer corps raised from birth to the task, one has only to contrast Greene with the semiliterate Daniel Morgan, who was summoned out of retirement after Camden. Without disrespect to the talents of the partisan leaders, the only senior Continental officers whose presence on the formal battlefield was inspirational were Arnold, Morgan and Wayne. We have seen how this power was earned, the casuistry of labelling the Loyalists 'British' and, crucial to the whole Foundation Myth, the sleight of hand employed to explain away the disparity between British and American officer casualties by reference to marksmanship. If the Loyalists could be turned into line regiments as good as any from the British Isles during the course of this long war, it should not have been beyond the capabilities of the Continental Army to do the same.

Morgan was of the same stamp as New Hampshire's Stark, but with the professional misfortune of being a Virginian in an army where advancement for men of that state was blocked by gentry overpromoted early in the war. It was a perversion of democracy to allot field command in a life and death struggle according to a strict proportionality among the states, but the blame also lies with Washington. Morgan was promoted and given field command quickly enough when it became apparent the situation in the South called for talent. This was to be displayed when Greene divided the army shortly after he assumed command, normally a recipe for disaster in the presence of an aggressive enemy. It was also incoherent in terms of the strategy he already had in mind, and was eventually to pursue. Greene had ordered all the relevant river crossings surveyed in preparation for a retreat across North Carolina, to draw Cornwallis after him as Schuyler had done to Burgoyne, gaining strength and numbers as he fell back on his depots in Virginia, while his opponent would be correspondingly weakened by partisan raids against his lengthening line of communications.

Greene's explanation for sending Morgan west with a 'Flying Army' of light infantry and cavalry while he took the rest to Cheraw (where he detached Harry Lee with a legion of 280 horse and foot to join Marion on the lower Pee Dee) was that this presented Cornwallis with the choice of marching either against one or the other, leaving himself vulnerable to the rear in either case. Perhaps, but by advancing to Charlotte Gates had forced Cornwallis to keep his own army concentrated, to the great benefit of the South Carolina partisans, and Greene's move sacrificed that advantage. In the first of several indications that he was more concerned with asserting Continental authority than he was in bringing the campaign to a speedy conclusion, before leaving Charlotte he wrote a letter to Sumter that can only be read as a studied insult. 'You may strike a hundred strokes and reap little benefit from them unless you have a good army to take advantage of your success', he wrote airily to the man who had fought on alone after the miserable showing of that 'good' army in the first half of 1780. He continued (my emphasis):

> The enemy will never relinquish their plan, *nor the people be firm in our favour* until they behold a better barrier in the field than a volunteer Militia who are one day out and the next at home . . . Plunder and depredation prevail so in every quarter I am not a little apprehensive all this country will be laid waste. Most people appear to be in pursuit of private gain or personal glory. *I persuade myself that though you may set a just value upon reputation your soul is filled with a more noble ambition.*

Alas nobody recorded the reaction of a man who had sacrificed every possession and almost his life, not to mention his soul, at being thus patronized by a Yankee who had been filling his family's pockets at the army's expense for the preceding two years. Sumter chose to

eat his revenge cold. When Greene returned in April 1781 he found
Marion and Pickens willing to work with him, but the senior officer
in the army of South Carolina waged his own war of independence
and left Greene to demonstrate how good his army was at Hobkirk's
Hill, Ninety-Six and Eutaw Springs. The canonical accounts blame
Sumter's 'bristling' pride for this, but the fault can more justly be
attributed to the man who rubbed his fur the wrong way.

10

CAROLINAS' ENDGAME

WITH THE EXCEPTION of Campbell's Virginia frontiersmen the Over Mountain Men took no further part in the war save to defend their settlements against the Indian raids Cornwallis now authorized Brown and his collaborators to coordinate. That he did not do so sooner to prevent the mobilization against Ferguson is not the least of the question marks around his generalship. It was doubly too late because the Creek and the most combative Cherokee warriors, who had formed their own society at Chicamauga, were fully engaged in support of the losing struggle to hold West Florida against Bernardo de Gálvez, the aggressive young Spanish governor of Louisiana, who captured Manchac, Baton Rouge and Natchez soon after Spain declared war in 1779, and Mobile on 14 March 1780 (see MAP 1). Pensacola and the Bahamas fell in 1781, but by then Cornwallis had undone the whole British position in the South. The troops committed to the Caribbean/Gulf of Mexico theatre were mainly Americans recruited from Continentals captured at New York, Philadelphia, Charleston and Camden. Men who had thought to escape death on prison hulks found it far from home in barracks located in the least healthy land available on the islands, or on futile missions around the Gulf coast.

The deep background to the operational decisions taken by Cornwallis in 1781 was that if Greene refused to attack him, attrition by disease and at the hands of the partisans alone might oblige him to withdraw to the coastal enclaves and abandon the interior of South Carolina. There was evidently no glory to be won by continuing to

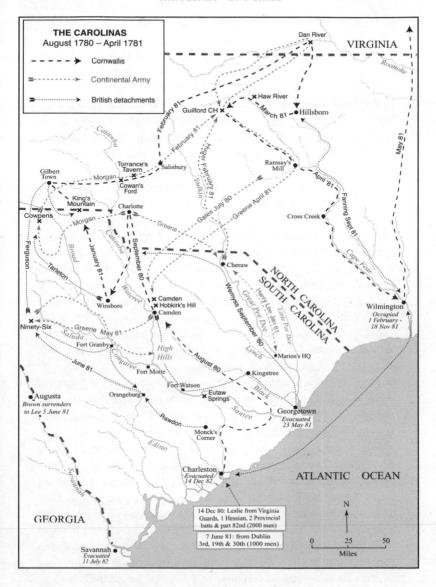

THE CAROLINAS
August 1780 – April 1781

- - - → Cornwallis
- - - → Continental Army
- - - → British detachments

VIRGINIA

Dan River
Roanoke

Haw River
March 81
Hillsboro
Guilford CH
Catawba
February 81
February 81
Torrance's
Tavern
Salisbury
Ramsay's
Mill
Higher February 81
Yadkin
April 81
Gilbert
Town
Morgan
Cowan's
Ford
King's
Mountain
Charlotte
Ferguson
Cowpens
Morgan
Greene
Gates July 80
Greene April 81
Cross Creek
May 81
Fanning Sept 81
Cape Fear
Tarleton
January 81
Broad
Catawba
Wateree
September 80
Cheraw
NORTH CAROLINA
SOUTH CAROLINA
Wilmington
Occupied
1 February –
18 Nov 81
Ninety-Six
Greene May 81
Winsboro
Camden
Hobkirk's Hill
Camden
Wemyss September 80
Harry Lee Jan 81
Little Pee Dee
Great Pee Dee
Saluda
Fort Granby
High
Hills
Congaree
Fort Motte
August 80
Lynch
Marion's HQ
Kingstree
June 81
Fort Watson
Black
Augusta
Brown surrenders
to Lee 5 June 81
Orangeburg
Eutaw
Springs
Santee
Rawdon
Georgetown
Evacuated
23 May 81
Monck's
Corner
Edisto
Charleston
Evacuated
14 Dec 82
ATLANTIC OCEAN

Savannah
Evacuated
11 July 82

GEORGIA

Savannah

14 Dec 80: Leslie from Virginia
Guards, 1 Hessian, 2 Provincial
batts & part 82nd (2000 men)

7 June 81: from Dublin
3rd, 19th & 30th (1000 men)

N

0   25   50
Miles

MAP 25

wage an irregular war, and military honour could not be reconciled with the methods involved. Discipline was crumbling as men previously severely punished for it were encouraged to loot and burn, leaving women and children homeless at the mercy of marauding gangs of outlaws. Freed slaves repaid their white owners' indifference to their own humanity less than they might have, and far less than white fears projected onto them, but they added a further element of potentially career-ending scandal to the situation. The opportunity offered by Greene's division of his army was too good to miss, and Cornwallis moved swiftly against Morgan without waiting for 2000 reinforcements under Major-General Alexander Leslie, who had arrived in Charleston from Virginia in mid December. These included a 700-man brigade of Guards, a battalion of 450 Hessians and six companies of the 82nd, whose comrades had rendered such sterling service at Penobscot. Before they arrived, Cornwallis marched from Winsboro towards King's Mountain, midway between the two halves of the enemy army, and sent Tarleton to drive Morgan towards him.

Tarleton's force was built around a core of 250 British Legion infantry and the same number of dragoons, plus 60 troopers of the 17th Light Dragoons and about 50 North Carolina Loyalist scouts. With them went 180 line infantry of the 7th and 263 of the 1/71st, with a further 69 Highlanders in a light infantry battalion completed by about 40 men each from the 16th and the remains of the Prince of Wales Loyalists. Morgan had about 1600 men, the infantry core provided by two brigades of about 300 each, one of Virginians containing a high percentage of Continentals who had re-enlisted as Militia or state troops, and another of Maryland-Virginia-Delaware Continental light infantry commanded by Lieutenant-Colonel John Howard, a wealthy Maryland landowner and the outstanding American infantry commander of the war. William Washington commanded 82 Continental dragoons, plus 45 mounted volunteers given sabres just before the battle. The largest single contingent of Militia was brought in by the McDowells, but the great majority were small parties of men who had made their own way from across the South Carolina and Georgia back country in response to an appeal by Andrew Pickens, whom Morgan appointed to command them all.

After one of his trademark overnight marches Tarleton caught up

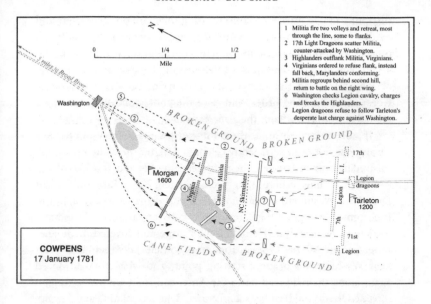

N

| 0 | 1/4 | 1/2 |

Mile

1 Militia fire two volleys and retreat, most
   through the line, some to flanks.
2 17th Light Dragoons scatter Militia,
   counter-attacked by Washington.
3 Highlanders outflank Militia, Virginians.
4 Virginians ordered to refuse flank, instead
   fall back, Marylanders conforming.
5 Militia regroups behind second hill,
   return to battle on the right wing.
6 Washington checks Legion cavalry, charges
   and breaks the Highlanders.
7 Legion dragoons refuse to follow Tarleton's
   desperate last charge against Washington.

3 miles to Broad River

Washington

BROKEN GROUND   BROKEN GROUND

Morgan
1600

Virginia

Carolina Militia

NC Skirmishers

17th

L. I.

Legion
dragoons

Legion

Tarleton
1200

7th

71st

Legion

CANE FIELDS   BROKEN GROUND

BROKEN GROUND

COWPENS
17 January 1781

MAP 26

with Morgan at the Cowpens, that place of fateful reunion for the
men who destroyed Ferguson's command, and launched an immediate
dawn attack. The battle that followed has an exceptionally diligent
chronicler in Lawrence Babits, whose book is a model for the genre.
MAP 26 oversimplifies the reality he explores in much greater detail,
as all static presentations of highly fluid events must, but identifies
the main phases. Tarleton was to find he was faced not with an opponent forced into battle against his will, but with one who had chosen his
ground and his tactics carefully. Morgan deployed a line of skirmishers
across a chokepoint formed by areas of ground impassable to cavalry,
behind them the bulk of the Militia with one wing advanced, under
orders to fire two aimed rounds each and then retreat through and
around the line infantry formed up 150 yards behind them.

During the night before the battle Morgan went to all the Militia
campfires and repeated the same message – he did not want them to
cross bayonets with the British regulars, which both he and his listeners
knew could only have one outcome. Their task was to erode redcoat

discipline in two ways – by concentrating their fire on the officers and by drawing them into a premature charge. As to the first, ten British officers were killed and twenty-nine wounded in the whole battle, and all precedent argues that most of these would have fallen in the melee at the end. As to the second, the British infantry approached the Continentals in good order, and once the chokepoint was passed the 71st advanced to outflank the American line.

If not entirely unsung, the contribution made by Washington's cavalry has not been sufficiently celebrated. After the Militia fell back, misunderstood orders led them to regroup beyond the left of the Continental line, where they were scattered by Tarleton's Light Dragoons. Washington counterattacked and drove off the 17th, not in itself remarkable given a greater than two-to-one numerical superiority. What followed was. He halted the charge and covered the further retreat of the Militia. Morgan rode back to help rally them at a point near Washington's original starting point, and when they advanced again along the road leading to the American right wing Washington screened them, and beat back a fifty-man detachment of Legion cavalry that might otherwise have scattered them again. To round off a good day's work he then charged the 71st in the flank and in the last stages of the battle crossed sabres with a British officer whom legend, alas unsupported by contemporary evidence, would have it was Tarleton himself.

Morgan admitted the *coup de grâce* came as a result of an accident, but he had earned his luck. Howard ordered the outer Virginian companies to refuse the flank threatened by the 71st, to swing back like a door to form an obtuse V with the rest, who were supposed to remain in place. Instead the whole brigade fell back, and Howard ordered the light infantry to conform, creating the impression of a general retreat. This induced the British infantry to break ranks and pursue, leading to a demoralizing dislocation of expectations when the Americans turned, unleashed a crashing volley and followed it up with a bayonet charge. In an instant three regiments that moments before had been advancing in total certainty of victory became a disorganized mass of exhausted, frightened men intent on surrender. The Highlanders stood a while longer, coolly refusing their left in the face of Washington's charge, but were compelled to surrender when enveloped by Pickens' men. Behind the crumbling centre the contagion of panic reached beyond bullets to unman the men who had performed prodigies of valour and endurance for Tarleton in the past. In his own words:

> In the last stage of the defeat [I] made another struggle to bring [my] cavalry to the charge. The weight of such an attack might yet retrieve the day, the enemy being much broken by their late rapid advance; but all attempts to restore order, recollection, or courage, proved fruitless. Above two hundred dragoons forsook their leader and left the field of battle.

Fourteen Legion officers and forty men, mainly from the 17th, followed him into the heart of the melee, but they were too few, too late. In the early stages of the rout Washington got ahead of his men and three British officers turned back to engage him, breaking his sabre, pistolling his horse and checking the pursuit. As the survivors of Tarleton's charge rode past their baggage train they added a number of casualties to the final toll by hacking down their own scouts, who were in the process of looting it. British losses were 210 killed and 710 captured, of whom 179 were wounded. Morgan reported 12 killed and 60 wounded among the two line brigades, and an undifferentiated 80 casualties among the Militia, an honourably large proportion of them officers. The two 'grasshoppers' (3-pounders mounted on legs instead of wheels) lost by Tarleton had been captured with Burgoyne at Saratoga and retaken at Camden. The British were to retake them again at Guilford Courthouse two months later, before losing them for good at Yorktown. It would be nice to know if they were preserved somewhere.

Tarleton rejoined Cornwallis with a little more than 300 men, very few of them Highlanders although theirs were the only regimental colours salvaged. They never forgave him, and his memoirs were immediately refuted by Roderick Mackenzie of the 71st, who had served under him at Blackstock's and Cowpens. 'I leave to Lieutenant Colonel Tarleton', he sneered, 'all the satisfaction which he can enjoy, from relating that he led a number of brave men to destruction, and then used every effort in his power to damn their fame with posterity'. His memoirs aside, Tarleton made no egregious errors apart from the decision to keep back four-fifths of the Legion dragoons as a tactical reserve. He simply ran into a better combination of soldiers and officers than any previous experience in America could have prepared him for. We have already discussed the contribution made by Washington's cavalry, but no less outstanding was the manner in which Pickens and the other Militia commanders returned their men to battle after they had suffered the shattering experience of being ridden down, rarely possible even with regular troops. Howard's alertness and tight control of the line turned a potentially disastrous misunderstanding into the decisive manoeuvre of the day, but the firm basis for all they did was Morgan's keen eye for terrain, ability to make every man under his command understand what was required of him, and intelligent antici-pation of what his opponent would do. He was to take sick leave again just over three weeks later, when once more under Greene's direct command, and was to find it impossible to join La Fayette in Virginia, in both cases overcome by a crippling sciatica that did not trouble him in the slightest when he was everywhere he needed to be at Cowpens, nor when there was the prospect of fighting Tarleton again outside Petersburg, nor indeed during the rest of his very active life.

As soon as Leslie's reinforcements and Tarleton's remnant joined him, Cornwallis erupted in pursuit of Morgan's army and the 800 prisoners he was shepherding to the north as fast as he could drive them. At Cheraw, Greene recalled Harry Lee and ordered Huger to lead the army to Salisbury, while he himself rode with only a personal escort to join the now unarguably Flying Army at the Catawba, to direct it towards the same rendezvous. Morgan was reluctant to march across open country with Cornwallis hot on his heels, and would have preferred to seek the safety of the Blue Ridge Mountains. He did not share Greene's belief that the army would gather strength as it retreated, and he was proved right. The North Carolina Militia did not turn out in the numbers Greene hoped for, and both wings of the army lost a substantial number of Virginia Militia upon the expir-ation of their term of enlistment at the end of January. When we consider Cornwallis twice lost a day's march by directing his army in the wrong direction against the advice of local Loyalists and still came close to trapping the American rearguard on several occasions, it is difficult to see why Greene's strategy has been so celebrated.

In fairness Greene's plans nearly came unstuck because his opponent now did something nobody could have predicted. On 28 January Cornwallis converted the whole army into light infantry by the drastic expedient of burning the baggage train – even the rum! This was unheard of in a century when officers and men alike regarded their creature comforts as sacrosanct, and only a general secure in the knowledge his men adored him would have dared to do it. Its practical effect was somewhat diminished by retaining some wagons and the artillery, but it was good psychology to let the soldiers see their officers' luxuries go up in smoke. The do or die spirit of the moment was captured by the exhilarated hyperbole of Brigadier-General Charles O'Hara, commander of the Guards, in a letter to his patron the Duke of Grafton:

> In this situation, without baggage, necessaries, or provisions of any sort for officer or soldier, in the most barren inhospitable unhealthy part of North America, opposed to the most savage, inveterate perfidious cruel enemy, with zeal and with bayonets only, it was resolved to follow Greene's army to the end of the world.

Three days later this spirit was put to the test at Cowan's Ford on the Catawba, where Generals Cornwallis, Leslie and O'Hara all rode their horses into the storm-swollen river, under heavy fire from several hundred riflemen under the command of William Davidson, the senior active Militia officer in North Carolina. The horses of all three generals were shot, and both Leslie and O'Hara tumbled downstream until rescued by human chains formed by their men, but the crossing was made and Davidson was killed – by a shot fired from the other bank of the river, some 200 yards away. Tarleton caught up with the retreating Militia at Torrance's Tavern and taunted his dragoons to 'Remember Cowpens'. Foes with rain-dampened weapons were more to their taste and they rode the unfortunate men down. How many were killed is as usual a matter of dispute, but the effect is not. The British Army marched from the Catawba to the Yadkin, through Cleveland's stamping ground and avowedly the most hostile part of North Carolina, without suffering a single loss to partisan harassment.

The sacrifice made by Davidson and his men to cover the retreat of the Continentals casts a cold light on Greene's incessant denigration of the Militia. Upon finding that weapons stored in Salisbury were in poor condition he wrote contemptuously 'these are the happy effects of defending the country with Militia from which the good Lord deliver us!'. But what were he and his Continentals doing that was so felicitous? South Carolina had been abandoned, a British Army committed to living off the land was cutting a swathe through the heart of Rebel North Carolina, and the two parts of Greene's own army had failed to rendezvous at Salisbury and were now marching by separate routes to Guilford, less than fifty miles from the capital at Hillsboro. It was not only British generals who refused to adjust their aspirations to the resources available. The following was written by Cornwallis, but could as easily have been from the pen of Greene:

> Our experience has shown us that their numbers are not so great as had been represented and that their friendship was only passive; for we have received little assistance from them since our arrival in the province, not above two hundred have been prevailed upon to follow us . . .

Both men shaded the truth. Neither of them had the time or the inclination to incorporate any significant number of untrained volunteers into their armies, and what they were looking for was supplies and information from people to whom they could not even offer the prospect of protection. Cornwallis had already made plain his distaste for the forces assembled by officers like Ferguson and Brown, and his march across North Carolina with the British elements of his army, leaving the Loyalists behind to continue the struggle against the partisans, confirmed it. His false marches were a product of the same contempt for the locals, and this in turn lead to failure at the Dan where the American light troops, under the command of Otho Williams since Morgan's retirement, got across only hours before O'Hara's Guards arrived. Cornwallis also lacked adequate information because he did not use Tarleton's troopers to screen his advance, the most basic light cavalry function. Since the Legion dragoons had shown at Cowpens that they could not be trusted to cover a retreat, Cornwallis must have been keeping them in reserve to complete the destruction of the enemy army after a climactic battle, as they had after Camden.

With Washington shepherding the Cowpens prisoners deep into Virginia, Harry Lee had the task of screening for Williams and the light infantry. Lee's memoirs are too melodramatic for modern tastes, but there is no better account of the cliff-hanging events at the Dan on 14–15 February, when he had the grace to admit a momentary lapse in vigilance that would have had drastic consequences if his pursuers had been cavalry instead of the Guards. As it was, faced with yet another river crossing and beyond it the manpower and resources of Virginia, Cornwallis fell back on Hillsboro, followed at a discreet distance by Lee's Legion. Only now did Cornwallis issue the usual proclamation, and a party of about 300 Loyalists under Dr John Pyle responded. They had the misfortune to encounter a green-coated Legion at Haw's River and to assume it was Tarleton's, in which belief they were encouraged by Harry Lee until his men were fully in among them, when at a signal they rode into the unsuspecting men and killed a third of them on the spot. More were murdered after the prisoners were handed over to the local Militia. Even more disastrously, on 4 March another party of Loyalists was set upon by Tarleton as it approached the British camp, after which the rest stayed home. Most were not really 'Loyalists' at all, but men disgusted by the arbitrariness and corruption they had endured since 1775. The competition is fierce, but the revolutionaries in North Carolina seem to have been the most despised of all the groups that seized power in 1775.

Events now moved towards the battle Cornwallis had marched 200 miles to fight, and which was supposed to crown Greene's strategy with another Bemis Heights. Neither commander achieved his purpose. Greene was later to warn La Fayette that Cornwallis was a 'Hannibal', which must have made the great Carthaginian turn in his grave. Believing himself outnumbered even more than was actually the case, the Cornwallis solution to Greene's three-layered defence was a brutally unsubtle frontal assault, which succeeded at Phyrric cost only because of the outstanding quality of the human material he hurled through dense woods, uphill, at Guilford Courthouse. On 15 March 1781 the redcoats displayed a heroism and dogged determination equalled but never surpassed on any other of the countless far-flung battlefields where so many of them lie buried and forgotten (see MAP 27).

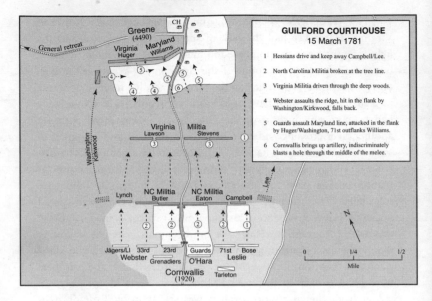

GUILFORD COURTHOUSE
15 March 1781

1 Hessians drive and keep away Campbell/Lee.

2 North Carolina Militia broken at the tree line.

3 Virginia Militia driven through the deep woods.

4 Webster assaults the ridge, hit in the flank by
   Washington/Kirkwood, falls back.

5 Guards assault Maryland line, attacked in the flank
   by Huger/Washington, 71st outflanks Williams.

6 Cornwallis brings up artillery, indiscriminately
   blasts a hole through the middle of the melee.

MAP 27

Greene sought to adapt the scheme Morgan had employed, although the terrain he chose consisted of two clearings separated and surrounded by dense woods, which meant the three parts of his army fought out of sight of each other. Greene either failed to appreciate the compressed spring effect Morgan had devised, or else he overloaded his first line to prove a point. On 11 March about 2000 North Carolina Militia joined Greene under John Butler and Thomas Eaton. Many of these men had served as the Praetorian Guard of the Caswell regime, efficient at keeping the civilian population down but unproven in battle. Caswell's successor Thomas Burke had refused all assistance during the retreat, and the belated arrival of these well fed and superbly equipped men may have caused the iron to enter Greene's soul. He put them in the front line overlooking a wide clearing around several cultivated fields. On either flank he stationed Virginia riflemen, about 200 each under the command of William Campbell of King's Mountain fame and Charles Lynch of the eponymous Law. Flanking Lynch was Washington with 86 Continental dragoons and about 110 Delaware light infantry under Robert Kirkwood, probably the best infantry in the Continental Army under one of its most experienced regimental commanders. Lee's Legion of 82 infantry and 75 dragoons formed outside Campbell. Morgan had used terrain to ensure the Militia fell back as he wished, Greene tried to use men instead.

The second line, about 350 yards behind the first and in the deep woods, was formed by two Virginia Militia brigades of about 600 men each under Robert Lawson and Edward Stevens. Stevens, whom last we saw swept away by his men at the Camden panic, was determined to prevent a repetition and stationed picked marksmen behind the line with orders to shoot anyone who ran. Finally Greene placed his regulars – 800 Virginians under Huger and 720 Marylanders under Williams – at the top of a ridge overlooking the second area of culti-vated fields, and sent two of his four 6-pounders to support the first line, retaining the other two and the grasshoppers captured at Cowpens on the ridge. The front line alone outnumbered the entire British force by more than 800 men and, possibly in conscious imitation of Hannibal's masterpiece at Cannae, Greene had flanked his least valued troops with some of his best. Alas poor Greene, although the scheme was technically sound he lacked the spark – call it charisma or just luck – which sets the great commanders apart from the also-rans.

Every historian of this battle quotes Sergeant Lamb's eloquent description of the heart-stopping moment when the 23rd approached the North Carolina line and so shall I, for there is no better evocation of the moral demands of combat in the black powder era:

> . . . when we arrived within forty yards of the enemy's line, it was perceived that their whole force had their arms presented, and resting on a rail fence, the common partitions in America. They were taking aim with the nicest precision. At this awful period a general pause took place; both parties surveyed each other with the most anxious suspense. Nothing speaks <u>the General</u> more than seizing on decisive moments: Colonel Webster rode forward in front of the 23rd regiment, and said, with more than his usual commanding voice, '<u>Come on, my brave Fuziliers</u>'. This operated like an inspiring voice, they rushed forward amidst the enemy's fire; dreadful was the havoc on both sides.

Such was the impetuosity of the advance that not only were the North Carolinians driven back in disorder, but the 321-man Hessian Bose regiment managed to come between them and the flank guard formed by Campbell and Lee, who were thereafter kept out of the battle, while on the left a mere 164 Jägers and light infantry refused the flank against Kirkwood, Lynch and Washington. The 33rd, 23rd and 2/71st went into battle respectively 334, 238 and 244 strong, the Guards in two battalions of about 200 each. Most graphic reconstructions of the battle follow Lee in putting one battalion of the Guards on the far right of the British line, and despite his obvious interest in showing himself facing overwhelming odds there is other contemporary evidence to support it. However, I believe it improbable Cornwallis would have left O'Hara, a close friend and the brigadier-general of the Guards, in command of only one battalion and the map (p. 210) assumes the two Guards battalions were kept together to break through whatever lay beyond the trees.

The fight in the woods against the Virginians was protracted, and although Stevens fell with a shattered femur he had the satisfaction of seeing his men give a good account of themselves. Emerging from the woods, first Webster and then O'Hara paused to regroup their men before charging up the hill at the Continentals. Leslie's regiments had diverged and the 71st had become more dispersed than the others, with the result that the British made three uncoordinated attacks, with Webster thrown back before O'Hara could advance, and the Highlanders marching to outflank the American line too late to prevent a concentration of fire on the Guards. Few present would have disagreed with Tarleton's judgement that it was 'one of the most hazardous, as well as severe battles that occurred during the war . . . a defeat of the British would have been attended with the total destruction of Earl Cornwallis's infantry, whilst a victory at this juncture could produce no very decisive consequences against the Americans'. In defence of Cornwallis the battle permitted him to retreat unharassed from an extremely exposed situation, and made Greene's subsequent operations more tentative than they might otherwise have been. That Cornwallis should not have put his army in such a position is unarguable, but by mid March 1781 he really had no choice.

Every unit on the field, American and British alike, recoiled at one time or another, but to claim a moral victory for an army that lost its guns and retreated before one less than half its size, and which reported more than 1000 men missing in addition to 79 dead and 184 wounded, is to put a novel interpretation on the concept. The British had only 26 missing, but 150 were mortally wounded including the gallant Webster, with a further 360 less seriously wounded including O'Hara, whose artilleryman son was killed, and Tarleton who had two fingers shot from his right hand when riding down Campbell's riflemen after they were abandoned by Lee. Night and torrential rain fell before supplies or medical staff could reach the field, and Lamb remembered the exhausted survivors, without shelter or food, unable to sleep because:

> The cries of the wounded, and dying who remained on the field of action during the night, exceeded all description. Such a complicated scene of horror and distress, it is hoped, for the sake of humanity, rarely occurs, even in a military life.

Both commanders-in-chief repeatedly rode into situations where they could have been killed or captured, but without doubting Greene's courage any more than his theoretical skill, he lacked the killer instinct possessed by Cornwallis in such abundance. At the end, if Greene had thrown in Huger's previously uncommitted 4th Virginia instead of using it to cover the retreat the battle almost certainly would have gone the other way. The consensus among his opponents of all ranks was that after reaching so deeply into their reserves of stamina and courage they had no more to give. Likewise during the subsequent British withdrawal to the Cape Fear River it should have been possible for an army that still greatly outnumbered them to do more than simply follow at a prudent distance. The error of believing the Militia would turn out to harass the enemy as they had in the North was now revealed. Greene found North Carolina no more welcoming in 1781 than Kalb and Gates had in 1780, and both armies were happy to leave it.

Greene now turned south leaving the back door to Virginia unguarded. It is a profound mystery how this can ever have been portrayed as the culmination of his plan, which had been to defeat Cornwallis so far from his South Carolina bases that he could not recover. Nor, in strictly military terms, did it make any strategic sense whatever to give Cornwallis unimpeded access to the heart of the richest and most populous of the United States. It is best seen as part of the political agenda Greene followed from the first, with the strong presumption that he was acting on oral instructions from George Washington. North Carolina clearly would go with whichever side won the war but South Carolina and Georgia, with their powerful indigenous resistance movements, were another matter. After the arrogant behaviour of the slavocrats in 1775–79 and their abject showing thereafter, the most likely result of leaving the far South to its own devices was not the restoration of British authority but the more socially dangerous emergence of a populist if not also an actively separatist regime, which at the very least would greatly complicate a general settlement between the United States and Britain.

Before following Greene south let us consider the effect on Cornwallis of unexpectedly finding himself with an alternative to returning south by sea with his tail between his legs. We shall discuss the merits of shifting the principal theatre of war to Virginia in the next chapter, but Cornwallis was as much driven north by reluctance to resume the war of attrition in South Carolina as he was drawn by the prospect of easier pickings around the Chesapeake. He had made a serious operational error by assuming he would be able to sustain the army in the strongly Loyalist area between Ramsay's Mill and Cross Creek, if necessary supplemented with supplies shipped up the Cape Fear River from Wilmington, which he had ordered seized before embarking on his charge into North Carolina. Upon finding the downtrodden Highlanders of the Cross Creek area without the means or the disposition to offer him significant support, he also belatedly discovered the Cape Fear was not the easily navigable artery he had believed. During the march to Wilmington he had plenty of time to appreciate the likely effect on his career of returning to Charleston, and to conclude this was the result not of his own errors but of Clinton's wish to discredit him. Thence to disobeying the orders of his hierarchical superior was but a step, prefigured in the letter he wrote to Clinton from Wilmington on 10 April:

I cannot help expressing that the Chesapeake may become the seat of war, even (if necessary) at the expense of abandoning New

Light Cavalry Apollo – Banastre Tarleton

ABOVE 'Baron' Friederich von Steuben drilling troops at Valley Forge

Killer Instinct – Charles, Marquess
Cornwallis

He had a cunning plan –
Nathanael Greene

He had a better one – Daniel Morgan

Victor at Yorktown – François-
Joseph, Comte de Grasse

Balance Redressed – the Battle of the Saintes

'Oh God! It's all over!' – the surrender at Yorktown

Out of Pawn – George, Baron Rodney post-war

York. Until Virginia is in a manner subdued, our hold of the Carolinas must be difficult, if not precarious. The rivers in Virginia are advantageous to an invading army; but North Carolina is of all the provinces in America the most difficult to attack (unless material assistance could be got from the inhabitants, the contrary of which I have sufficiently experienced), on account of its great extent, of the numberless rivers and creeks, and the total want of interior navigation.

Both Cornwallis and Greene failed to achieve their primary objective, which was the destruction of the other's army. What they did and more so what they wrote thereafter was conditioned by a desire to conceal this fact. Of the two Cornwallis was the more evidently motivated by considerations of a personal nature, while his disloyalty to Clinton was condoned to the point of encouragement by Germain. Washington's overt respect for civilian supremacy and the will of Congress aside, the war at last settled into a pattern where on the American side there was a single guiding intelligence – his own – while the British fell victim to command chaos. The blame for this was widespread and how one apportions it is a function of personal prejudice. I believe mine has been apparent throughout – it was a systemic failure, the product of a long tradition of muddling through to avoid the political consequences of efficiency.

Having devised a plausible explanation for refusing to obey orders while avoiding the humiliation of returning to Charleston, Cornwallis marched north into our next chapter, leaving South Carolina and Georgia in the hands of Colonel Nisbet Balfour, previously the commander at Ninety-Six, whom Cornwallis ordered to take over in Charleston before he marched into North Carolina. Just as he had played little active part in the operations conducted from Ninety-Six by the New Yorkers under Cruger, so now Balfour conformed to the wishes of his nominal subordinate Lord Rawdon, who was with a predominantly Loyalist field army at Camden. Greene marched directly towards the outpost, detaching Lee once more to operate with Marion against the British line of communications, which they did spectacularly on 23 April 1781 when they took Fort Watson (see MAP p. 201) without artillery by building a tower from which riflemen brought the interior of the work under fire. They also prevented 600 men, detached under Guards Lieutenant-Colonel John Watson for operations against Marion, from rejoining Rawdon at Camden before Greene arrived with 1550 men, all Continentals with the exception of 250 North Carolina Militia. Finding Camden too hard a nut, he withdrew a mile and a quarter to Hobkirk's Hill to await the reinforcements he expected from Pickens, and hoped in vain to receive from Sumter. In the evening of 24 April Greene was rejoined by his artillery, three 6-pounders earlier sent back twenty miles for safe-keeping while he marched to the east of Camden in response to a false report that Watson was approaching from that direction.

The fickle finger of fate at Hobkirk's Hill was condensed in the figure of a young deserter from the Maryland line, captured in British uniform at Fort Watson, who persuaded Lee he was a prisoner who had donned the red coat only to facilitate an eventual escape. He returned just long enough to make a note of Greene's numbers before deserting again – prior to the arrival of the guns. Armed with otherwise accurate information Rawdon assembled 800 men, including 150 walking sick and wounded, and marched out to do battle in the early morning of 25 April. The only non-American unit in his army was a part-battalion of the 63rd, the rest being his own 2nd American (Volunteers of Ireland), the 3rd American (New York Volunteers) and 4th American (King's Americans), plus sixty New York and South Carolina dragoons led by a Massachusetts Loyalist with the distinguished but ominous name of John Coffin. Rawdon's advance was unexpected, but Greene had covered the approaches from Camden with Kirkwood's Delaware Regiment in two redoubts, and had time for the unhurried deployment of two battalions of the Virginia Line under Huger on the right and two of the Maryland Line under Williams on the left, masking his guns at the centre, with the North Carolina Militia and William Washington's eighty Continental dragoons in reserve (see MAP 28).

Once again Greene fell into the trap of overelaboration. The first stage, involving an oblique march by the inner battalions to unmask the guns, was smartly done and came as a nasty surprise to Rawdon, more so to the men of 3rd and 4th American who received several salvoes of grapeshot and fell back. Encouraged by this Greene gave orders for a general attack, with the outer battalions extending to

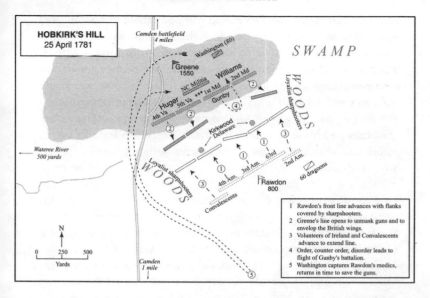

MAP 28

envelop Rawdon's flanks. Precisely what happened next is unclear, save that Rawdon had posted riflemen in the woods on either flank with orders to snipe the enemy officers, which it seems they did with some success once the range shortened. 2nd Maryland and 4th Virginia were then outflanked in turn and halted when Rawdon sent the Convalescents and 2nd American to extend his line. At the left centre 1st Maryland was advancing with confidence to attack with the bayonet until Colonel John Gunby ordered it to halt, either to correct alignment or because it had got ahead of its sister battalion. Something snapped and Gunby's men fled, precipitating a general panic that only a stubborn stand by 5th Virginia saved from becoming a complete rout.

Meanwhile, as austerely noted by Fortescue, Washington 'had been busy with the task (rather strange in a leader of cavalry) of capturing the British medical staff'. He rode back in time to save the guns, paroling the medical officers but somehow shepherding 50 prisoners with him. Greene's guns were responsible for the great majority of Rawdon's 38 killed and 170 wounded, 26 per cent of all the men engaged. The North Carolina Militia had not paused to find out why their Continental colleagues were in flight, so all of Greene's 18 killed, 108 wounded and 138 captured, 22 per cent of the line, were irreplaceable veteran infantry. These are unusually high proportions, testimony to the extremely close range at which much of this battle was fought – for example, 1st Maryland was only yards away from the 63rd when the fateful order was given. Greene made Gunby the scapegoat, but the blame was his for expecting officers and men, while under fire, to switch at a moment's notice from a previously discussed defensive scheme to an ambitious attack for which they had received no preparation.

Following Cornwallis's decision not to return to South Carolina there was no question of attempting to hold the hinterland with half the force that had previously proved inadequate for the task, and if Germain in London entertained the fantasy – nurtured by Cornwallis – that the Carolinas were pacified, nobody in America shared it. The Carolina Loyalists, repeatedly encouraged to rally round the flag with assurances that His Majesty's forces had returned to stay, were cold-bloodedly sacrificed on the altar of one man's impatience with a situation that offered him no prospects for glory and advancement. It was a disgraceful deed done for the meanest of reasons, leaving Rawdon to salvage what he could with barely a week's warning that Greene was marching south. Hobkirk's Hill bought time to retreat from an untenable position, which Rawdon began on 10 May and completed two weeks later when he reached Monck's Corner without losing a wagon or a man. The retreat was supposed to be part of a coordinated withdrawal from all outposts to concentrate forces at Savannah and Charleston, but the couriers to Augusta, Ninety-Six and the forts along the Congaree were intercepted by the partisans, and all were besieged before the garrisons could escape. The only secure communications were now by sea, which enabled the orderly evacuation of Georgetown on 23 May, recognition that Marion had won and the British lost all hope of controlling the Pee Dee.

The principal obstacle to a clean sweep of the hinterland was Greene's continuing effort to force the partisan leaders to recognize him as commander-in-chief. Sumter never did, and opened his own campaign by taking a swipe at Fort Granby before riding to the British outpost at Orangeburg on the upper Edisto on 11 May. The small Loyalist garrison surrendered upon being summoned and was therefore spared. Fort Motte, held by 150 regulars, fell to Marion and Lee the following day after a four day siege. After the surrender Marion came upon some of his men about to hang Levi Smith, a Loyalist magistrate, who reported an incident that nicely identifies the practical reasoning underlying the laws of war:

> I had nearly taken farewell of this world, when I perceived General Marion on horseback with his sword drawn. He asked in a passion . . . who ordered them to hang any person. They replied, 'Colonel Lee'. 'I will let you know, damn you, that I command here and not Colonel Lee. Do you know if you hang this man Lord Rawdon will hang a good man in his place, that he will hang Sam Cooper who is to be exchanged for him?

Only British possession of hostages and a new willingness to execute them if one of their own were killed after surrender forced the partisan leaders to impose some restraint on their followers, After Loyalist Colonel James Grierson was murdered while in Continental custody Greene denounced the act as 'an insult to the arms of the United States and an outrage upon the rights of humanity'. Indeed it was, and the British hanged Militia Colonel Isaac Hayne for it, and also for trying to kidnap Militia Brigadier-General Andrew Williamson, whose offence was to have honoured his parole. The American war witnessed the birth of the now well-established tradition of British politicians giving comfort to the enemy by moral posturing at the expense of their own compatriots, and on this occasion the Duke of Richmond falsely claimed that the local Loyalists condemned the Hayne hanging. This drew an address to the king from leading South Carolina Loyalists, which listed more than 300 of their comrades killed after surrender and stated that a policy of strict retaliation should have been implemented years earlier.

The tensions between Continental and Partisan officers evident in Marion's intervention to spare the life of Levi Smith now boiled over. When Lee took Fort Granby on 15 May, Sumter wrote a protest to Greene, saying it would have been 'for the good of the public to do it without regulars'. Upon receiving a reply asserting Greene's right to direct operations Sumter resigned his Continental Army commission. This was followed by an altercation over horses between Greene and Marion, which ended when Marion threatened to resign and take his case to Congress. Greene backed down in both cases and desisted from the folly of trying to give orders to men whose personalities were defined by their independence of spirit. There was to be no 'Continental' solution imposed on South Carolina, which would lead the way out of the Union in 1861 by firing on a Federal fort in the Charleston estuary named for . . . Thomas Sumter.

Greene detached Lee to operate with Pickens against Brown in Augusta while he himself marched against Cruger at Ninety-Six. Both sieges began on 22 May, and on 5 June after heroic resistance Lee granted Brown's request for the honours of war in 'sympathy for the unfortunate and gallant of our profession'. The partisans swore to assassinate Brown anyway, but Lee ordered Pickens to send him under guard to Charleston so that 'the laurels acquired by the arms of America [should not be] stained by the murder of a gallant soldier who had committed himself to his enemy on their plighted faith'. In Lee's code Levi Smith could be hanged because the garrison at Fort Motte had refused a summons to surrender and caused him unnecessary casualties. Brown, who had bowed in time to the inevitable, was sacrosanct, as was the life of one of Brown's men who revealed, after the surrender, that he had entered Lee's camp pretending to be a deserter in order to give him misleading information.

Things did not go so well for Greene at Ninety-Six, where he followed the advice of the engineer Tadeusz Kosciuszko. It is probably as well the fortifications designed by Kosciuszko at Bemis Heights and West Point were never put to the test, for he proved at Ninety-Six to be ignorant of the most basic principles of siege warfare. Cruger's garrison held out until 19 June, when Greene lifted the siege on learning that Rawdon, with reinforcements recently arrived from Ireland, was marching to the relief of the place. After doing so Rawdon shadowed Greene's movements along the Congaree until the two armies took a break from the blasting summer heat respectively at Orangeburg and the High Hills of the Santee. Rawdon became seriously ill and handed over command of the field army to Lieutenant-Colonel Alexander Stewart of the 3rd, one of the newly arrived regiments.

Another was the 19th, which included the nineteen year-old Lieutenant Edward, Lord Fitzgerald, son of Ireland's grandest grandee, the Earl of Kildare and Duke of Leinster. As 'Citizen Lord' Fitzgerald and leader of a group of would-be revolutionaries inspired by the French Revolution, he was to die of septicaemia from wounds received while stabbing to death the officer who came to arrest him in 1798. It would be tidy to claim his democratic sensibilities were first awakened by his experiences in America, but he saw only the struggle in the South and was not impressed by what he saw of American democracy at work. Fitzgerald's regiment was a protagonist at Quinby Bridge on 17 July, the first and last occasion where Sumter had the opportunity to show what he could do in formal battle. With Marion and Lee under his command he mounted an all-out assault, without waiting for his own artillery piece to come up, on an infantry square with its flanks covered by buildings and its front by a howitzer. Although Lee had earlier disobeyed orders and permitted the enemy to escape across the bridge, the bloody failure of the final assault caused even one of Sumter's longest-serving lieutenants to swear never to serve under him again. It was the end of Sumter's military career but the legal repercussions continued for years, until finally both Carolinas passed a law holding him harmless for the pillaging and slave-stealing that had for so long underwritten resistance in the South.

Fitzgerald's introduction to combat came when serving with the light infantry at Eutaw Springs, the last of the major engagements fought in South Carolina, where he was severely wounded. A runaway slave called Tony Small found him and nursed him back to health, to remain his lifelong companion. Although the one in which Greene enjoyed the smallest numerical superiority, this was the nearest he came to a victory in the field,. Having tried the defensive at Guilford and the defensive-offensive at Hobkirk's Hill, he now abandoned cunning plans and put his faith in the shock of an outright attack. He even achieved surprise by a deft march north from the High Hills to cross the Watcree at Camden before turning south to cross at the Congaree fork. The manoeuvre caused Stewart, who had been covering Greene from the other side of the Santee, to lose touch and fall back along his line of communications to Eutaw Springs, a few miles from the ruins of Marion's and Sumter's plantations as such and an almost incredibly appropriate place to fight the last major battle for South Carolina.

Stewart was not an opponent of the calibre to which Greene had become painfully accustomed and would have suffered tactical as well as operational surprise were it not for a fortuitous encounter between the vanguard of the Continental Army and a troop of Coffin's dragoons guarding a party of foragers. Greene advanced in two strong lines with two 6-pounders at the centre manhandled forward ahead of the North Carolina Militia, led by the volunteer François, Marquis de Malmédy, whose previous battle honour had been the command of what Cornwallis called a 'gang of plunderers'. On Malmédy's left were Pickens' Militia, and on their left some of Sumter's men, the cavalry under the command of the very wealthy Wade Hampton, who had signed an oath of allegiance to the king in 1780 and was now anxious to save his lands by proving his commitment to the revolutionary cause. On Malmédy's right were Marion's Militia, and outside them Harry Lee's Legion. The second line was formed by the Maryland Continentals under Williams on the left, at the centre the Virginians under Richard Campbell, yet another member of the clan that contributed so many to both sides of our story, and on the right the North Carolina Line recruited and led by the very wealthy Jethro Sumner, whose first battle this was. Kirkwood's Delaware Regiment and William Washington's dragoons formed the reserve (see MAP 29).

Facing them through moderately dense woods Stewart commanded a composite battalion with elements of the 63rd, 64th and the Canadian 84th (Royal Highland Emigrants) at the centre, with two battalions of Loyalists on either side. The larger one on the left was a composite of 1/3rd American (DeLancey's) and Isaac Allen's Provincial New Jersey Volunteers, commanded by the indomitable John Cruger. Cruger's own 2/3rd American was on the right under Major Henry Sheridan, and beyond him at an angle to the line were the flank companies of the British regiments still remaining in the theatre, some 300 men under Major John Marjoribanks. Most unusually he was regarded as the hero of the battle by both sides, but unfortunately a fever killed him forty-five days later. It does great honour to the state of South Carolina that his remains were moved and a memorial placed over

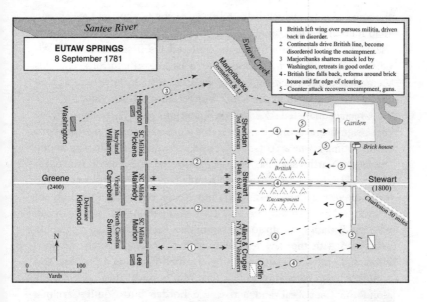

MAP 29

them on the battlefield, now lapped by the waters of Lake Marion, when the dam that created the lake was topped out.

The battle went as shown in MAP 29, with the American advance overwhelming the British left and centre before succumbing to premature looting in the British encampment. On the right Sheridan and Marjoribanks fell back on a redoubt formed by a brick house and walled garden, from which they led a general counterattack. Although the American retreat was orderly, many men were unable to stand up and others may have died as a result of drinking British government issue rum without diluting it first. Barring those involving Indians it was the most ferocious battle of the war. Stewart lost 85 killed, 351 wounded and 430 captured (including the foragers surprised by Lee) – half his army. Greene lost his guns, 139 killed and 375 wounded, of whom 17 and 43 respectively were officers, and perhaps 200 missing. Of the senior officers Campbell was killed and Washington wounded and captured. The blood-price of epaulets was magnified because the loss of charismatic officers often led to the subsequent dissolution of the units they led, which helps to explain why Greene had fewer than 1000 men under his command ten days later when the army regained the High Hills. A month later he suffered his first mutiny and was compelled to have a man shot inside a hollow square formed by his comrades, but by then the events we shall turn to next had decided the issue not merely in the South but for all of North America.

Greene conducted other minor operations after Eutaw Springs, the most significant being to counter the depredations of two die-hard British officers, one a Scots regular and the other a Loyalist, operating mainly in North Carolina. The occupation of Wilmington was never intended to do more than create a supply base to support Cornwallis's army along the Cape Fear River, but it was entrusted to Penobscot veteran Major James Craig and four companies of his own 82nd, who more than lived up to the reputation for operational originality associated with the new regiments formed in response to this war. He teamed up with David Fanning, a much-persecuted Loyalist, and appointed him colonel of Militia. For nine months they raided freely along the Cape Fear and across the border into South Carolina, encountering widespread support in areas where Cornwallis alleged there was none.

Fanning's most daring achievement came in September 1781 when he led 950 Loyalists on a raid to Hillsboro, where they captured Governor Burke and his entire Council. They then fought their way back to the coast with their captives and a large number of liberated Loyalist and British prisoners. Fanning continued to fight after Wilmington was evacuated in November 1781, and in return for having led thirty-six successful raids in North Carolina and four into South Carolina, the Crown in its munificence allowed him compensation of £60. There is no doubt that with a few more officers like Craig the British Army could have attracted many more like Fanning, but as we have seen the Continental Army was no more welcoming to irregulars unless they accepted a subordination that clipped the wings of their effectiveness. The constant theme of the war in the South was that regular armies, with their bureaucracies and ritualized forms of warfare, felt threatened by irregulars at a far deeper level than the merely tactical.

11

CHECKMATE IN VIRGINIA

IN WORDS THAT WOULD CARRY greater weight had they been
written before 1780, Washington declared 'without a decisive naval
force we can do nothing definitive – and with it everything honourable
and glorious. A constant naval superiority would terminate the war
speedily'. So, of course, would a regular army treated at least as well
as swine, but Washington's early fury at the shameless profiteering
taking place under the guise of patriotism had by now subsided to a
dull resignation. As mutinies wracked the Continental Army and the
python-like coils of the British naval blockade gradually compressed
the economic ribs of his country, Washington was not so much patient
as helpless to influence events once the French had refused to lead an
assault on either Canada or New York. Subsidies aside, the greater
Anglo-French war impinged on the American sideshow directly only
in Virginia, and even there only as the result of a short break in the
constant superiority otherwise maintained by the Royal Navy. The
broader war falls outside our theme and is anyway well covered by
Fortescue and Mackesy, but a brief summary is necessary to put the
Virginia campaign in context.

As far as Vergennes was concerned the main purpose of the war
of revenge was to invade Britain. Only after this proved beyond French
capabilities did an alternative strategy emerge of forcing the Royal
Navy to concentrate in defence of the homeland, leaving the French
free to pick up colonial possessions like so much ripe fruit. That did
not work particularly well either, and when the war ended the French
retained only the island of Tobago and some trading posts in Senegal,

not much to show for five years of worldwide effort. The struggle bankrupted the Bourbon monarchy and finally forced Louis XVI to summon the long-ignored French parliament (Estates General) to ask for money. The British monarchy, of course, had found itself in the same situation 150 years earlier, setting in motion a process during which the already extremely short Charles I was further abbreviated along with his dream of absolutism. Thus also the hapless Louis at the hands of revolutionaries so disgusting they made their American peers seem like the Apostles a fawning posterity was to make of them. There is no ideological or cultural continuity between the two revolutions. The ideas batted about by French thinkers during the eighteenth century were borrowed by some Americans to dress up their grab for money and power, but Anglo-American individualism then as now was anathema to the French.

The Choiseul–Vergennes strategy to humble Britain was the equivalent of a frontal assault on the strongest part of an enemy fortification. British military expenditure was preferentially directed into the navy, proportionally vastly more than France with her long land frontiers could hope to match. French military ideology of the *ancien régime* (usually defined as the period 1661–1789) was also singularly unconducive to the short, sharp war that was all the monarchy could afford. It was devoted to form over, indeed at the expense of, function, and its highest expression was the siege. There is a lively debate within the military history community whether the strict geometric shapes of the bastioned fortifications with which Sébastien le Prestre de Vauban expensively adorned the eastern French frontier were dictated by the demands and limitations of contemporary artillery or were built because they looked so pleasing, and to reduce attack and defence to elegant mathematical equations. The French ideal was to make war according to a set of rules with a predictable outcome, and a commander's skill measured by how well he manoeuvred to avoid being forced to engage in uncertain battle. When this mentality was exposed to wind, wave and tide as well as a more experienced if not generally more skilful opponent the outcome was indeed predictable, although not to the benefit of French arms.

Despite enormous expenditure since the War for Empire the French Navy could not, by itself, win the control of the English Channel necessary to land *and maintain* an invasion force. This required the collaboration of the Spanish Navy and this was the undoing of the 1779 invasion plan, potentially the most serious threat to British independence since the Spanish Armada of 1588. An inconclusive clash off Ushant with the British fleet under Vice Admiral Augustus Keppel in July 1778 improved French prospects by creating a bitter division within the Royal Navy between the Sandwich faction ('Montagus') and the Keppelites ('Capulets'), with the result that the only senior admiral who would accept command of the Home Fleet in 1779 was the antique Sir Charles Hardy, previously governor of Greenwich Hospital. He was, however, a spring chicken next to the Spanish Admiral Don Luis de Córdoba, and by the time French Admiral Louis Guillouet, Comte d'Orvilliers, had waited for him and devised a system to operate together with the thirty-four Spanish ships of the line and with due regard for Córdoba's pride, his own fleet of thirty was undone by epidemics. The grand enterprise collapsed after some futile manoeuvring in which the usual roles were reversed, with Hardy holding back his thirty-four ships of the line and Orvilliers unable to force a decision.

In September the Scots slaver and pirate John Paul alias Jones, flying the stars and stripes on a mainly French-manned converted East Indiaman renamed *Bonhomme Richard* in honour of Benjamin Franklin, author of *Poor Richards Almanack*, defeated the frigate HMS *Serapis* in a savage battle off the coast of Yorkshire at Flamborough Head. It was the sole significant victory won by the Continental Navy during the entire war and thus an iconic event of some importance. His later career included service in the navy of the freedom-loving Catherine the Great of Russia, finally fleeing St Petersburg to evade an allegedly fabricated accusation of rape. What may have been his remains were exhumed from a built-over Paris cemetery in 1905 and escorted across the Atlantic by the US fleet for deposit in a magnificent crypt at the Annapolis Naval Academy. Not many other career criminals have been similarly honoured.

As far as the American war was concerned the French wished not only to draw substantial British naval assets away from Europe but also to keep them further divided between the defence of the West Indies and the North American mainland. Operations were conditioned by horrendous winter weather in the North and the summer hurricane season in the South. We have seen that things did not go well for the fleet dispatched under Estaing to keep the British busy in America while the grand plan was put in motion. After a slow passage from Boston Estaing arrived a day too late to prevent the loss of St Lucia to the expedition sent from New York under Grant, but in combination with François, Marquis de Bouillé, the aggressive governor general of the French Antilles who had already captured Dominica, he took Grenada and St Vincent in June 1779. At Grenada he was attacked by Rear Admiral John 'Foul Weather Jack' Byron, who had been prevented by one of the violent storms that dogged his career from intercepting Estaing on his way to New York in 1778. Estaing had much the better of the engagement but failed to deliver the killing blow, saving his fleet for disease, defeat and humiliation at Savannah and Charleston. The three islands were a negligible gain when set against the result of sinning against the principle of concentration. It was a serious strategic error to send Estaing and subsequent reinforcements to the West Indies at a time when French naval forces should have been fully committed to gaining control of the English Channel. By doing so, operations in the Channel became hostage to the late entry of Spain into the war and the even later response of the Spanish fleet.

The enterprise of England abandoned, French naval operations in 1780–81 were more tightly focused. Joint operations with the Spanish against British bases in Minorca and Gibraltar were a price that had to be paid for the alliance, and drew a powerful fleet under Vice Admiral George Rodney in January 1780. On the way Rodney captured a large Spanish convoy off Cape Finisterre and roundly defeated a Spanish squadron off Cape St Vincent, but after the relief of Gibraltar most of the fleet sailed home, leaving Rodney to sail on with only four ships of the line to join Hyde Parker's seventeen in the West Indies. Unknown to Rodney he was five days behind a massive fleet of twenty-three under Vice Admiral Luc-Urbain, Comte de Guichen, which arrived off Martinique on 22 March. This massive dispersal of effort achieved even less for the French than Estaing had managed. Guichen was tied by instructions ordering him to risk nothing, so after successfully evading two attempts by Rodney to bring him to battle off Martinique he sailed home in August leaving ten of the line at Haiti for convoy duties.

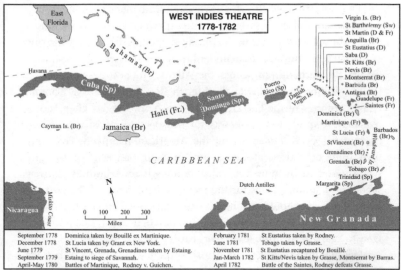

WEST INDIES THEATRE 1778-1782

East Florida

Bahamas (Br)

Havana

Cuba (Sp)

Cayman Is. (Br)

Haiti (Fr.)

Jamaica (Br)

Santo Domingo (Sp)

Puerto Rico (Sp)

Danish Virgin Is.

Virgin Is. (Br)
St Barthelemy (Sw)
St Martin (D & Fr)
Anguilla (Br)
St Eustatius (D)
Saba (D)
St Kitts (Br)
Nevis (Br)
Montserrat (Br)
Barbuda (Br)
Antigua (Br)
Guadelupe (Fr)
Saintes (Fr)

Leeward Islands

Dominica (Br)
Martinique (Fr)
St Lucia (Fr)
StVincent (Br)
Grenadines (Br)
Grenada (Br)
Tobago (Br)

Barbados (Br)

Windward Is.

Trinidad (Sp)
Margarita (Sp)

CARIBBEAN SEA

Dutch Antilles

Nicaragua

Miskito Coast

N

0   100   200   300
Miles

New Granada

September 1778	Dominica taken by Bouillé ex Martinique.	February 1781	St Eustatius taken by Rodney.
December 1778	St Lucia taken by Grant ex New York.	June 1781	Tobago taken by Grasse.
June 1779	St Vincent, Grenada, Grenadines taken by Estaing.	November 1781	St Eustatius recaptured by Bouillé.
September 1779	Estaing to siege of Savannah.	Jan-March 1782	St Kitts/Nevis taken by Grasse, Montserrat by Barras.
April-May 1780	Battles of Martinique, Rodney v. Guichen.	April 1782	Battle of the Saintes, Rodney defeats Grasse.

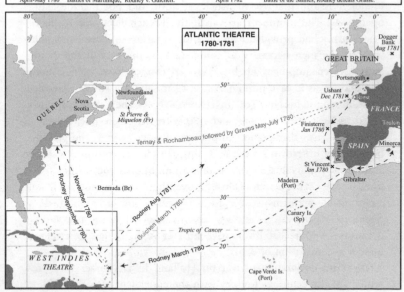

ATLANTIC THEATRE 1780-1781

80°   60°   50°   40°   30°   20°   10°   0°

Dogger Bank *Aug 1781* ×

GREAT BRITAIN

Portsmouth •

50°

QUEBEC

Nova Scotia

Newfoundland

St Pierre & Miquelon (Fr)

Ushant *Dec 1781* × Brest

FRANCE

Toulon

Finisterre *Jan 1780* ×

SPAIN

Minorca

Portugal

Ternay & Rochambeau followed by Graves May-July 1780

40°

Bermuda (Br)

Rodney Aug 1781

Rodney November 1780

Rodney September 1780

Guichen March 1780

St Vincent *Jan 1780* ×

Madeira (Port)

Gibraltar

30°

Tropic of Cancer

Canary Is. (Sp)

WEST INDIES THEATRE

Rodney March 1780   20°

×

Cape Verde Is. (Port)

MAP 30

The distraction of British attention had a beneficial result further north, where a fleet of seven of the line under the hereditary knight Rear Admiral Charles-Henri de Ternay shepherded a convoy carrying 5500 men and a full siege train under Lieutenant-General Jean-Baptiste, Comte de Rochambeau, across the Atlantic to occupy Newport on 10 July. Sailing in parallel to the French fleet Rear Admiral Thomas Graves with six of the line arrived in New York the day after Ternay reached Newport, but there was no prospect of decisive action to prevent a French lodgement on the American mainland. Following their joint operations at Charleston, rancour between Clinton and Arbuthnot had by now reached a point where Arbuthnot actively sabotaged Clinton's plans for the recovery or defence of the port the admiral judged should not have been abandoned in the first place. There are other strong claimants, but the cognoscenti consider mid 1780 to mark an historic low in British interservice cooperation.

Happily for the immediate British situation in North America the French mission, that sacred article of faith, did not include active operations. The imminent arrival of the French fleet and Rochambeau's army had provided Clinton with a reason to leave Cornwallis without the men necessary to complete the conquest of the South, and their encampment on his doorstep cannot have been entirely unwelcome, as it gave him an excuse to maintain a strong defensive position around his New York investments. Not to be outdone, Rodney sailed to New York in September 1780 with ten of the line, reversing the usual seasonal migration in pursuit of prize money, the pickings being better off North America. Having plundered Arbuthnot's stores and taken two invaluable frigates plus an additional 400 seamen from him, Rodney sailed south again in November. One cannot say it was a remarkable performance, for it was typical of an officer who fled his creditors to Paris in 1775 and was able to flee back again in 1778 only because old Maréchal Biron gave him enough money to escape a further accumulation of debts.

Britain's declaration of war on Holland in December 1780 presented the impecunious Rodney with the equivalent of roast suckling pig to the starving in the form of the Dutch island of St Eustatius, the bulging heart of contraband trade with America. The declaration was rushed to pick off the Dutch before they could ratify membership of the Russia-led League of Armed Neutrality, but the timing was also influenced by knowledge of a fat convoy due to depart St Eustatius in January. Rodney and land forces commander Major-General John Vaughn moved with uncommon speed to capture both island and convoy in the first week of February 1781. To nobody's surprise the greater part of the spoils belonged to British merchants, who were further aggrieved when the convoy bearing it back to Britain was intercepted by the French. They persecuted Rodney and Vaughn in the law courts for years, citing principles similar to the language of natural rights employed by the Americans and by the League of Armed Neutrality. The Law Lords finally decided that supplying the enemies of the nation was not, on balance, something to be encouraged, but the prolonged proceedings are a reminder that Common Law, once upon a time, protected citizens from the agents of the state.

While Rodney was overseeing preparations for shipping home what he fondly believed would be his nest egg he delegated his official duties to Rear Admiral Samuel Hood. Not content with that dereliction, he also ordered Hood to abandon the windward station off Martinique to ensure the small French squadron anchored there should not interfere with the departure of his loot. As a result Hood was unable to intercept a giant convoy from France escorted by twenty of the line under the command of Vice Admiral François-Joseph, Comte de Grasse. This was Vergennes's last throw in the Americas. It had dawned on him that the British tax and credit structure was not going to collapse and in some desperation he wrote to warn the Spanish there might not be a *mañana*: 'The war has gone too slowly; it is a war of hard cash and if we drag it out the last coin may not be ours'. Some of the last coins were sent to Rochambeau to enable Washington to keep 15,000 men under arms, much of the rest invested in the Grasse expedition. The cost of Rodney's obsession was Grasse's capture of Tobago in June, leaving the British in possession only of Barbados and St Lucia among the string of strategically vital islands to windward of the whole Caribbean basin.

Thus the oceanic background to the climax of the land war in North America. In February 1781 Germain was at last able to obtain the signature of king and cabinet to an order categorically directing

Clinton to implement the Southern strategy, although it will be noted they were careful not to order him to abandon New York (my emphasis):

> The recovery of the southern provinces, and the prosecution of the war by pushing our conquests from south to north is to be considered the chief and principal object for the employment of *all the forces under your command.*

Although Germain was right to observe 'that the American levies in the King's service are more in number than the whole of the enlisted troops in the service of the Congress', as we have seen the realities on the ground were not as Cornwallis had led him to believe, and the imbalance of enlisted Americans was soon corrected by the French subvention. The Southern strategy might have worked if whole-heartedly adopted a year earlier, but following the fall of Charleston Clinton left Cornwallis with only 30 per cent of all the forces in the colonies. In December 1780 he sent 1900 to the Chesapeake, 2400 in March and 1900 in May 1781, but even in the face of unequivocal orders to do so from the highest authority he adamantly refused to make it the main seat of war. The returns he concocted in mid 1780 tell a sad story: 7207 of the 10,204 effectives in primitive, deeply unhealthy South Carolina, Georgia and Florida were judged fit for duty, against only 14,285 of 20,048 around New York. If true these figures denounce Clinton's administrative incompetence, if not his moral cowardice.

This said the strategy of an advance from the South was always inferior, in strictly military terms, to a direct strike against Virginia, Maryland and Delaware, the glue holding the thirteen colonies together. All sat uneasily atop large slave populations and all were equally vulnerable to amphibious operations in the Chesapeake Bay and along the great rivers draining into it. The destruction of about forty plantations in Virginia and about half that number in the other two states would have erased the economic base of the American upper class – and there was the rub. All wars end, and Lord North was alert to the need for an exit strategy. To destroy the power base of the emerging American aristocracy was not only socially distasteful but would create a political hydra with which it might be impossible to negotiate at all. Whatever Germain might think and hope, North regarded the formal cession of sovereignty over the colonies to a class with values similar to his own as infinitely preferable to the total collapse of civil order that must follow the social decapitation of the rebellion.

As though to underline how viciously illiberal the American populists and their British supporters were outside a narrow concern for the rights and privileges of Protestant Englishmen, in mid 1780 the North administration weathered an episode of mob violence ideologically comparable to the revolt of Massachusetts and with more than a passing resemblance to the Paris riots nine years later that ushered in the French Revolution. In 1778 the government passed the Catholic Relief Act, which absolved Roman Catholics from taking the religious oath on joining the army, a matter of no small importance when the army needed to recruit as many French Canadians, Irishmen and Highlanders as possible on both sides of the Atlantic. In 1780 Lord George Gordon, like his descendant Lord Byron mad, bad and dangerous to know, organized the Protestant Association around popular fears that the Catholics in the army constituted a papal fifth column, and invoked the Glorious Revolution by tying this to fears of royal absolutism. In June he led a crowd of about 60,000 to the House of Commons to present a petition for the repeal of the Act, which rapidly degenerated into the largest riot the metropolis ever experienced.

Catholic chapels and the homes of leading Catholics, along with those of Lords Savile and Mansfield, advocates of the Act, were burned, while those of Lords Rockingham and Devonshire were kept from the torch only by armed force. The watch houses and tollgates of what passed for civilian police were destroyed, the prisons burst open and their denizens joined assaults on the Bank of England and the Navy Pay Office. London was at the mercy of the mob for a week until the king, commenting that there was at least one magistrate in Britain prepared to do his duty, authorized the use of armed force. The 5th and 11th Dragoons, a battalion of Guards, the 18th and 52nd of Foot and Militia from as far away as Yorkshire marched into London and killed between 300 and 700 people. Twenty-five others were hanged. John Wilkes was in command of the Militia outside the Bank of England and marked the end of a long career as the darling of the mob by ordering them to fire into the crowd. However not all the opposition leaders would admit to the dangers of the fire they had been playing with for so long. Once the danger was past Lords Shelburne, Richmond and Grafton denounced the use of soldiers to suppress the riot as an infringement of the Bill of Rights.

Even if only subconsciously, consideration of the overriding need to maintain order meant that the last British military effort in America was as compromised as all the rest by nuances a later age may have difficulty in fully appreciating. It was among the last of the limited wars, which never approached the uncompromising barbarity of those waged in the name of religion or secular ideology. An indication of how far it was from total war came in April 1781 when the manager of George Washington's estate at Mount Vernon went aboard a British warship on the Potomac to negotiate payment for some runaway slaves and to spare the plantation dwellings from the torch. Washington rebuked the man for setting a bad example, but the point is surely that although it could have been done at any time, it did not occur to the British high command to order the destruction of the enemy commander-in-chief's property, and that a junior ship's captain did not think doing so would lead to advancement.

Another dimension to the final operations of the war comes from the weight of history. The grey, italicized places in MAP 31 are just a few locations redolent of destiny: Jamestown, the first permanent English settlement in North America; Malvern Hill, Fredericksburg, Chancellorsville, The Wilderness and Spotsylvania, places where Robert E. Lee savaged successive Union commanders in the next civil war; Guinea where the great Stonewall Jackson crossed over the river to rest in the shade of the trees. Places fought over in both wars include Richmond, Petersburg, Hanover, Williamsburg, Yorktown and the mouth of the James River, where the CSS *Virginia* and the USS *Monitor* fought the first battle between ironclads. Although such places are common in Europe, the peninsula between the Potomac and the James Rivers is the only one in the New World where the bones of soldiers lie in multigenerational layers, emphasizing the centrality of Virginia to the first 250 years of American history.

As a man clinging to a post for which he was unfitted Clinton possibly merited the contempt in which he was held by Germain, his

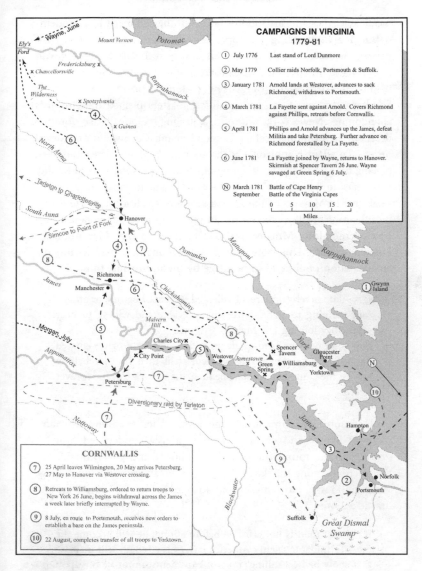

CAMPAIGNS IN VIRGINIA
1779-81

① July 1776   Last stand of Lord Dunmore

② May 1779   Collier raids Norfolk, Portsmouth & Suffolk.

③ January 1781   Arnold lands at Westover, advances to sack Richmond, withdraws to Portsmouth.

④ March 1781   La Fayette sent against Arnold. Covers Richmond against Phillips, retreats before Cornwallis.

⑤ April 1781   Phillips and Arnold advances up the James, defeat Militia and take Petersburg. Further advance on Richmond forestalled by La Fayette.

⑥ June 1781   La Fayette joined by Wayne, returns to Hanover. Skirmish at Spencer Tavern 26 June. Wayne savaged at Green Spring 6 July.

Ⓝ March 1781   Battle of Cape Henry
September   Battle of the Virginia Capes

0   5   10   15   20
Miles

CORNWALLIS

⑦ 25 April leaves Wilmington, 20 May arrives Petersburg. 27 May to Hanover via Westover crossing.

⑧ Retreats to Williamsburg, ordered to return troops to New York 26 June, begins withdrawal across the James a week later briefly interrupted by Wayne.

⑨ 8 July, en route to Portsmouth, receives new orders to establish a base on the James peninsula.

⑩ 22 August, completes transfer of all troops to Yorktown.

MAP 31

naval colleagues and his subordinates, but they all merit like condemnation for withholding the formal loyalty due his rank, if not his person. As such men do, he did his best to reconcile his orders with a paralyzing fear of failure, but there would never be enough troops to hold the perimeter around New York and also to implement the Southern strategy. Just as his political masters pushed him towards abandoning New York without assuming responsibility for the decision, so Clinton carefully avoided giving Cornwallis categorical orders. To adapt Napoleon's adage about victory and defeat, all were playing the familiar political game of avoiding personal accountability while positioning themselves to take the credit for any success there might be. In May 1779 Clinton had sent an expedition to seize Portsmouth and Norfolk at the mouth of the James River, an area last held by Governor John Murray, Earl of Dunmore, in 1775. Like Abraham Lincoln in 1863 Dunmore issued a proclamation announcing the emancipation of all held in bondage by the insurgents, thus:

> 1775 – I do hereby declare all indented servants, negroes, or others, (appertaining to Rebels) free that are able and willing to bear arms, they joining His Majesty's troops.
> 1863 – all persons held as slaves within any State or designated part of a State the people whereof shall then be in rebellion against the United States shall be then, thenceforward, and forever free.

Dunmore's proclamation hit the rawest of nerves among the champions of liberty and virtue. Congress piously condemned him for 'tearing up the foundations of civil authority and government', but the reaction among the slavocrats was hysterical. From Boston, George Washington wrote to Congressman Richard Lee urging immediate and drastic action:

> If . . . that man is not crushed before Spring, he will become the most formidable enemy America has – his strength will increase as a snow ball by rolling, if some expedient cannot be hit upon to convince the slaves and servants of the impotency of his designs . . . nothing less than depriving him of life or liberty will secure peace in Virginia.

Dunmore was duly driven from Norfolk in December and spitefully ordered the firing of the town on New Year's Day, 1776. He then withdrew his 500 Loyalist troops, including an 'Ethiopian Legion' of freed slaves, to Gwynn Island where an outbreak of smallpox reduced the force still further, and from which it was driven in July. During the years that followed Virginia lapsed into an unconscionable complacency under the governorship of Thomas Jefferson, with the result that in May 1779 a raid under the outstanding Commodore George Collier captured Hampton, Norfolk, Portsmouth and Suffolk against negligible opposition. About 150 privateers and merchant ships were captured or burned, a Continental Navy frigate destroyed on the stocks and tobacco, artillery and general supplies worth in the region of £2,000,000 carried off. There followed another lull of eighteen months during which the attention of the Virginia authorities became increasingly distracted by the war in the South, setting the stage for the return of Brigadier-General Benedict Arnold to active operations wearing his new coat.

Clinton dispatched Arnold with an all-Loyalist force of 1600 men including Arnold's own American Legion and the 1st American (ex-Queen's American Rangers) still led by the durable Colonel John Simcoe. Pausing to seize and garrison the ports at the mouth of the James, Arnold embarked his men on captured boats and sailed up the river to Westover, thence overland to Richmond, which he occupied on 7 January 1781. The next day Simcoe surprised and routed Virginia Militia seeking to cut off Arnold's retreat at Charles City, and after plundering the surrounding countryside the raiders withdrew to Norfolk with goods later valued by a prize court in excess of £1,000,000. News that Arnold was ravaging his own state roused Washington to a rare passion and he dispatched some 1200 New England and New Jersey Continental light infantry under La Fayette to provide stiffening for the Virginia Militia. At the same time he prevailed on Commodore Charles-René Destouches, commander of the French fleet at Newport after the death of Ternay from typhoid, to cooperate in a joint operation to trap Arnold.

Destouches sailed on 8 March with eight of the line followed thirty-six hours later by Arbuthnot with the same number from his base at Gardiner's Point on Long Island. Arbuthnot got to the

Chesapeake first thanks to the antifouling copper sheathing with which the Royal Navy was in the process of equipping its ships. The battle fought off Cape Henry on 16 March did not lead to the capture of enemy ships, the measure by which the British measured success, but from the French point of view Arbuthnot accomplished his mission by preventing Destouches from entering the bay. Clinton, by now in receipt of the order from king and cabinet to make the South 'the chief and principal object' of operations, dispatched a further 2000 men under Major-General William Phillips, whom last we saw in charge of Burgoyne's artillery and who had been exchanged along with Riedesel for Benjamin Lincoln the preceding October. Clinton's hope was that a major threat to Virginia would draw Nathanael Greene north. Instead, as we have seen, it drew Cornwallis.

Phillips sailed up the James to City Point, where his vanguard under Arnold defeated the last substantial body of Virginia Militia retained for the defence of the state, and took Petersburg on 25 April. A further advance towards Richmond was halted at Manchester when La Fayette unexpectedly put in an appearance on the other side of the James. Phillips fell back on Petersburg where he died of typhoid on 13 May, leaving Arnold to complete what one authority considers the most comprehensive looting and destruction of the entire war before he was recalled to New York. Before he died Phillips received a letter from Cornwallis written the same day he avoided informing Clinton of his intention to march north, in which he showed his hand:

> Now, my dear friend, what is our plan? Without one we cannot succeed, and I assure you that I am quite tired of marching about the country in quest for adventures. If we mean an offensive war in America, we must abandon New York and bring our whole force into Virginia; we then have a stake to fight for and a successful battle may give us America. If our plan is defensive, mixed with desultory expeditions, let us quit the Carolinas (which cannot be held defensively while Virginia can be easily armed against us) and stick to our salt pork at New York, sending now and then a detachment to steal tobacco, etc.

Once the march began the noble earl's disdain for theft evaporated and Tarleton's dragoons fanned out to loot all the tobacco stocks between the Dan and James Rivers. The etceteras included enough horses to mount the whole army and thousands of slaves who escaped to join the column, explaining both the speed and the lack of stragglers during the march. Ewald later described how the army, by then including the Phillips corps, appeared to him:

> The army appeared similar to a wandering Arabian or Tatar horde . . . Every officer had four to six horses and three or four Negroes, as well as one or two Negresses for cook and maid. Every soldier's woman was mounted and also had a Negro and a negress on horseback for her service . . . every soldier had his Negro, who carried his provisions and bundles. This multitude always hunted at the gallop, and behind the baggage followed over four thousand Negroes of both sexes and all ages. Any place this horde approached was eaten clean, like an acre invaded by a swarm of locusts.

He might more accurately have compared it to a medieval *chevauchée*, the sort of punitive raid deep into enemy territory associated with the Crécy and Agincourt campaigns of Edward III and Henry V. After the arrival of 1200 reinforcements sent by Clinton before he learned either of Cornwallis's march north or of Phillips' death, there was now an army of about 7500 first-rate troops in Virginia and Cornwallis could go wherever he wanted. For all his bombast he accomplished surprisingly little. After marching around Richmond to Hanover via Westover in the hope of trapping La Fayette, Cornwallis dispatched Simcoe and Tarleton to raid deep into Virginia while the rest of the army marched in a leisurely semicircle back to Richmond. Simcoe's regiment was reinforced by the 2/71st (which had refused to serve under Tarleton) and with 650 men he marched rapidly to Point of Fork, where a major supply depot for Greene's army in the south was guarded by Steuben and 500 Continentals. Steuben withdrew the stores across the James in time, but the supplies were lost when he retreated again after Simcoe tricked him into believing the main army had arrived. Tarleton with 250 mounted men intended to capture Governor Jefferson and the Virginia legislature, which had moved to Charlottesville after abandoning Richmond in April, but they got away with minutes to spare. Again we find the paradox that Tarleton's men did no damage at Jefferson's Monticello mansion apart from helping themselves to his wine cellar. His political career was another matter, and a lesser man might have disappeared from public life after the humiliations of June 1781.

The remainder of the campaign in Virginia has been the subject of such frenzied finger-pointing that it is easy to lose sight of the obvious – from the time Cornwallis set out from South Carolina his actions could only be redeemed by a decisive victory in the field. Failing to achieve this and abetted by Germain, he tried to deal himself a new hand by forcing Clinton to abandon New York. When that failed he was out of options and, like Burgoyne before him, began to look for an 'honourable' way out of the situation he had got himself into. Suddenly obedient to the orders from his commander-in-chief he marched to Williamsburg followed by La Fayette, who had been joined by 1000 Pennsylvanian Continentals under Wayne. With perhaps 2200 Continental and about the same number of Virginia Militia La Fayette was not in a position to do any more. On 26 June he detached a mixed force of infantry and cavalry to attack Simcoe's Rangers at Spencer Tavern, with mixed results, but otherwise this part of the campaign was without serious incident until Cornwallis marched out of Williamsburg to the banks of the James. The reason for the move was an order from Clinton to send troops back to New York, requiring the army to march to Portsmouth for embarkation. Cornwallis encouraged La Fayette to believe he might be able to destroy the British rearguard after the rest of the army had crossed, but once again the decisive battle evaded him and when the trap was sprung at Green Spring on 6 July it only managed to maul Wayne's command, which fought its way out with the loss of 140 men.

During the march to Portsmouth, Cornwallis again detached Tarleton on a long raid beyond Petersburg. This had a magical effect on Daniel Morgan and William Campbell, until then unenthusiastic about responding to La Fayette's appeals for assistance, who gathered their riflemen and marched to Petersburg in the hopes of encountering Bloody Ban. It was not to be, and after a flurry of orders and counterorders from New York Cornwallis settled at Yorktown, posting Tarleton with 1100 men to hold Gloucester Point on the other side of the York River. Clinton's plan was now to establish a permanent base of operations from which, unlike Portsmouth and Norfolk, the whole of Virginia could be raided at will. It was a ridiculous compromise and Cornwallis showed his lack of enthusiasm for it. He made no serious effort to construct earthworks, falsely claiming a lack of entrenching tools, and failed even to harass La Fayette's command at Williamsburg, which he outnumbered by nearly two to one. Everything about his conduct of the last stages of the campaign argues that he was heartily sick of the whole war and was looking for a way out. That came as the result not merely of the cumulative weight of British errors but because Grasse, Rochambeau and Washington achieved a combination of strategic surprise and tactical coordination unprecedented in the age of sail.

The first domino to fall was Grasse's decision to make a brief foray to North America with his whole fleet instead of remaining in the Caribbean to prepare for combined winter operations with Bernardo de Gálvez. On 15 August Rochambeau received a dispatch sent by Grasse from Havana informing him that he would be off the Chesapeake by the end of the month with twenty-four of the line, more than 3000 troops and 1,200,000 livres borrowed from the Spanish – this last a particularly striking example of how the 'everything that can go wrong will' rule was in unusual abeyance for the French at this time. Rochambeau had spent the preceding year struggling to liaise directly with Washington, whom he always treated with the utmost deference, but found it difficult to bypass La Fayette. With the young man away and money in hand to ensure the Continental Army would be able to participate in what would otherwise have been an all-French affair, Rochambeau had little difficulty in persuading Washington to abandon his obsession with an assault on New York. After making a strong feint at Staten Island that convinced Clinton the long-feared assault was at hand, on 19 August 4000 French and 2000 American troops marched south towards Head of Elk, where William Howe had landed his expedition against Philadelphia almost exactly four years earlier. The new commander of the French fleet at Newport, Vice Admiral Jacques-Melchior, Comte de Barras, did not wish to leave his anchorage guarded by the Americans, whom he distrusted totally, but Rochambeau prevailed on him to sail south with eight of the line and the army siege train on the 25th (see MAP 32).

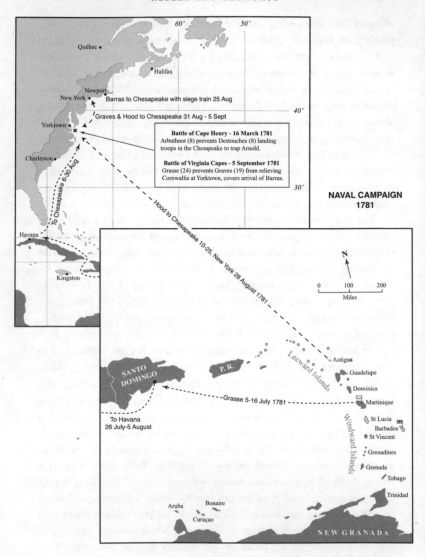

Battle of Cape Henry - 16 March 1781
Arbuthnot (8) prevents Destouches (8) landing troops in the Chesapeake to trap Arnold.

Battle of Virginia Capes - 5 September 1781
Grasse (24) prevents Graves (19) from relieving Cornwallis at Yorktown, covers arrival of Barras.

Barras to Chesapeake with siege train 25 Aug

Graves & Hood to Chesapeake 31 Aug - 5 Sept

To Chesapeake 6-30 Aug

Hood to Chesapeake 10-25, New York 28 August 1781

NAVAL CAMPAIGN 1781

Québec

Halifax

Newport
New York

Yorktown

Charleston

Havana

Kingston

N

0   100   200
Miles

SANTO DOMINGO

P. R.

Leeward Islands

Antigua

Guadelupe

Dominica

Martinique

Grasse 5-16 July 1781

To Havana
26 July-5 August

Windward Islands

St Lucia
Barbados
St Vincent

Grenadines

Grenada

Tobago

Trinidad

Aruba   Bonaire

Curaçao

NEW GRANADA

MAP 32

The next domino fell when Hood sailed from Antigua on 10 August upon learning that Grasse had sailed north from Havana, and his copper-sheathed ships arrived at the Chesapeake on the 25th while Grasse was still labouring along the coast of the Carolinas trailing weeds. Hood, assuming the French admiral must be heading for New York, sailed on. Grasse therefore entered the Chesapeake unopposed on the 30th to disembark his troops, and at last La Fayette was in a position to fight if the hitherto inexplicably passive British chose to make a sally. Instead Cornwallis belatedly set about fortifying York-town, calculating that a show of resistance would suffice until either he was evacuated by the Royal Navy or Clinton finally came south in force. The appearance of the French fleet held out the further possibility that if the worst came he could surrender without undue loss of face amid the civilities of war among gentlemen, in the certain knowledge that Clinton and Graves (who took over when Arbuthnot was recalled in July) would be blamed. Generals, like the senior employees of any other large public or private corporation, are not renowned for the alacrity with which they shoulder responsibility when things go wrong. It is only because they deal in life and death on an exposed stage that we expect better of them.

Graves sailed south with nineteen of the line on 31 August to prevent the junction of the two French fleets. Still unaware that Grasse had done the unthinkable by leaving the West Indies unguarded, when he saw twenty-four of the line emerging from Lynnhaven Bay Graves assumed Barras had beaten him to the Chesapeake. He attacked none-theless, and the battle that followed was the only major French victory at sea since Beachy Head (Bévéziers) in 1690. Measured by its effects Tourville's strategically sterile trouncing of the Anglo-Dutch fleet on the earlier occasion was less significant than Grasse's success in merely warding off Graves, which decided the war in America. Harold Larrabee's study of the battle concludes that Graves was less to blame than he was painted by Hood, but that overall the issue was decided by signalling errors and by the strict standing orders laid down by the Admiralty requiring admirals to bring their entire force to bear parallel with the enemy. As the map above indicates Graves tried manfully to achieve this ideal, an almost impossible feat given the slowness and lack of manoeuvrability of contemporary battleships. Unfortunately

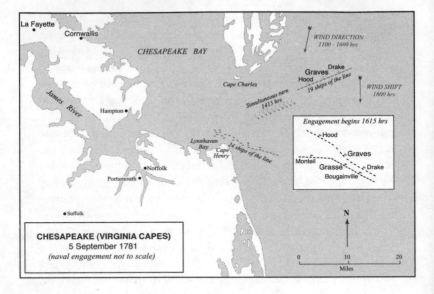

La Fayette
Cornwallis
CHESAPEAKE BAY
WIND DIRECTION
1100 - 1600 hrs
Cape Charles
Drake
Graves
Hood
19 ships of the line
WIND SHIFT
1600 hrs
James River
Hampton
Simultaneous turn
1415 hrs
Engagement begins 1615 hrs
Hood
Lynnhaven
Bay
Cape
Henry
24 ships of the line
Graves
Monteil
Grasse
Drake
Norfolk
Bougainville
Portsmouth
Suffolk
N

CHESAPEAKE (VIRGINIA CAPES)
5 September 1781
(naval engagement not to scale)

0   10   20
Miles

MAP 33

lie signalled contradictory signals both to close with the enemy and
to preserve the line, and the rear seven ships under Hood never got
into gunnery range. Graves' more culpable error came afterwards,
when he lost sight of the need to regain control of the Chesapeake
and pursued the French fleet until on 9 September favourable winds
made it possible for Grasse to break contact and return to the bay.
There he found Barras' fleet, giving him thirty-two of the line to
Graves' nineteen and dooming Cornwallis's command.

The main points of the siege that ensued once Grasse transported
Rochambeau's and Washington's men from Head of Elk to the
Jamestown Peninsula are set out in the map opposite. The three outworks abandoned on 30 September show that Cornwallis knew the
natural defensive line lay along the Yorktown Creek marshes and the
Wormley's Creek ravine, but lacked the men to hold such an extended
perimeter. Instead the ravine provided a ready-made covered way
exploited by Rochambeau's sappers to begin the first parallel less than
a mile from the Yorktown perimeter, rendering the outworks unten-

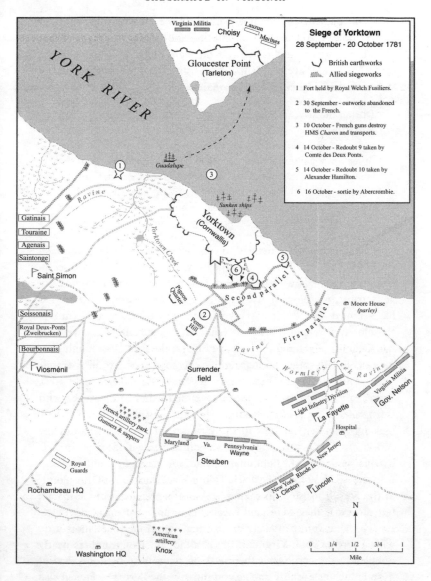

Virginia Militia ⊓ Lauzun
Choisy ⊓⊓ Marines

Gloucester Point
(Tarleton)

Siege of Yorktown
28 September - 20 October 1781

↲ British earthworks
⚓ Allied siegeworks

1 Fort held by Royal Welch Fusiliers.

2 30 September - outworks abandoned
to the French.

3 10 October - French guns destroy
HMS *Charon* and transports.

4 14 October - Redoubt 9 taken by
Comte des Deux Ponts.

5 14 October - Redoubt 10 taken by
Alexander Hamilton.

6 16 October - sortie by Abercrombie.

YORK RIVER

YORK RIVER

Guadalupe

③

Ravine

①

Sunken ships

Yorktown
(Cornwallis)

Gatinais
Touraine
Agenais
Saintonge
⊓ Saint Simon

Yorktown Creek

⑤

⑥ ④

Second parallel

Pigeon
Quarter

First parallel

☐ Moore House
(parley)

Soissonais
Royal Deux-Ponts
(Zweibrucken)
Bourbonnais
⊓ Viosménil

②

Penny
Hill

Ravine

Surrender
field

Wormley's Creek Ravine

Light Infantry Division
⊓ La Fayette

Virginia Militia
⊓ Gov. Nelson

French artillery park
Gunners & sappers

Maryland   Va.   Pennsylvania
Wayne

⊓ Steuben

☐ Hospital

New Jersey

Royal
Guards

New York   Rhode Is.
J. Clinton   ⊓ Lincoln

Rochambeau HQ

N

American artillery
Knox

Washington HQ

0   1/4   1/2   3/4   1
Mile

MAP 34

245

able. One pathetic episode not marked on the map was the expulsion into no-man's land of 'useless mouths', the runaway slaves who had joined the British in their march through Virginia. Joseph Martin, serving with La Fayette's light infantry division, revealingly wrote of this with the usual cognitive dissonance:

> During the siege, we saw in the woods herds of Negroes which lord Cornwallis (after he had inveigled them from their proprietors), in love and pity to them, had turned adrift, with no other recompense for their confidence in his humanity, than the smallpox for their bounty and starvation and death for their wages ... After the siege was ended many of the owners of these deluded creatures came to our camp and engaged some of our men to take them up, generally offering a guinea a head for them.

Even if Cornwallis intended to conduct an active defence, any such plans were rendered moot by smallpox, malaria and camp diseases compounded by lack of fresh food. One of his soldiers lamented 'we get terrible provisions now ... putrid meat and wormy biscuits that have spoiled on the ships. Many of the men have taken sick with ... the bloody flux and diarrhoea. Foul fever is spreading ... we have had little rest night and day'. At the time of the capitulation only 3275 of 4300 British, 2100 German and more than 1000 Loyalists troops were fit for duty. The majority of the men still able to fight were from the previously winnowed-out regiments that had marched with Cornwallis from South Carolina, who may justifiably have felt they had done enough. Thanks to the exquisite tact of Rochambeau the Americans were permitted to play a significant role in the siege, including an assault made by light infantry under Alexander Hamilton alongside one led by Wilhelm Forbach, Count Zweibrucken (or Deux-Ponts, as the French insisted on calling him and his regiment of Germans), but otherwise they were paid spectators at an event managed by the French. The Continental Army contingent numbered at most 3500 with a further 2000 Virginia Militia, although these numbers nearly doubled at the end, when there was no fighting to be done, against 9500 Frenchmen ashore and 25,000 more in the fleet. The French also supplied all the heavy guns and the siege engineers.

The account of the siege written by the Zweibruckener Captain

Ludwig, Baron von Closen, contains the fascinating observation that a quarter of the Continentals were African Americans, and described the all-black 1st Rhode Island Regiment as 'the most neatly dressed, the best under arms, and the most precise in its manoeuvres'. Hamilton evidently agreed, for the light company from this regiment accompanied him in the assault on Redoubt 10. There is food for thought here – Germans fighting for both the French and the British, Irishmen serving in all three armies, almost as many white Americans in the British as there were in a Continental Army in which, of three divisional commanders, one was a French nobleman and another a Prussian mercenary, and which was becoming increasingly dependent on slaves volunteered by their owners to take their place, or by African American paid substitutes. Further proof, if any were needed, how utterly misleading it is to see the events we have been reviewing through the lens of a nationalist consciousness that did not yet exist.

By 10 October, when the French brought the harbour under direct fire and sank HMS *Charon* and several transports, even the prospect of relief from the sea had evaporated. There remained one last, empty act of defiance, a predawn sortie on 16 October by the light infantry under Lieutenant-Colonel Robert Abercrombie which spiked some guns, but bad weather aborted a half-hearted effort during the day to evacuate the men to Gloucester Point, from which another epic cross-country march might have begun. The passionate energy that had carried Cornwallis from South Carolina was gone, and on the morning of the 17th a drummer beat the call for a parley from the parapet of the battered hornwork. The terms of capitulation were generous. The honours of war were denied, as they had been to Lincoln's garrison at Charleston, but Cornwallis was permitted to ship 'such soldiers as he may think proper' to New York. These were supposed to be only the deserters from the Continental Army, an acute embarrassment to Washington, but Cornwallis also shipped out the escaped slaves formally recruited by the British, mainly as Pioneers. The sloop supplied for this evacuation was supposed to carry only 250 men, but more than 600 disembarked in New York. Some of the more demeaning documents in Washington's collected correspondence concern his fruitless subsequent efforts to oblige the British to break their commitment to these men and their families.

On 20 October, four years and three days after the Saratoga capitulation, the British garrison of Yorktown marched out with cased colours while the bandsmen played a popular song, 'The World Turned Upside Down', doubly appropriate because it was first performed on the London stage in one of John Burgoyne's comic operas. When he learned Washington would be taking his surrender Cornwallis developed an indisposition and delegated the duty to O'Hara, who handed his sword to Benjamin Lincoln, delegated by Washington to receive it. Some 850 Royal Navy personnel surrendered directly to Grasse. The mutual respect that followed Saratoga was notably absent at Yorktown, even the common soldiers showing their contempt by smashing their muskets. No sooner were the capitulation proceedings ended than the French officers entertained their British and German peers lavishly and even lent Cornwallis 300,000 livres to pay his troops. Jean-François-Louis, Comte de Clermont-Crevecoeur noted:

> ... when the Americans expressed their displeasure on this subject we replied that good upbringing and courtesy bind men together, and that since we had reason to believe the Americans did not like us, they should not be surprised at our preference.

Hamilton's assault on Redoubt 10 was the last military operation of significance by the Continental Army, although nobody could have imagined it at the time. The British had lost their strategic reserve but still held New York, Wilmington, Charleston and Savannah, none of which could be taken by American arms alone. As though to emphasize that they would offer no further assistance Grasse and Barras sailed for the West Indies, where they were to take three more British islands in the Spring. However the naval pendulum now began to swing inexorably against the French, starting with the defeat of their Dutch allies at the battle of the Dogger Bank on 15 August 1781. This was followed by the capture off Ushant on 2 December of 15 transports from a French convoy escorted by Guichen and intended for operations against Jamaica. The victor was Rear Admiral Richard Kempenfeldt, on board HMS *Victory*, Nelson's flagship at Trafalgar a quarter of a century later. Sadly, this talented officer and 800 of his crew died on 29 August 1782, when with appallingly appropriate symbolism his flagship HMS *Royal George* rolled over and sank in harbour while performing what should have been routine maintenance in port. Finally, in a running fight from 9 to 12 April 1782 Rodney and Hood salvaged the British position in the West Indies by defeating and capturing Grasse at the battle of the Saintes (see MAP p. 229).

Although the improvement in the naval situation conditioned the peace negotiations that followed, when Lord North learned of the capitulation at Yorktown he exclaimed 'Oh God! It is all over!' His political base fell away and finally on 4 March 1782 the House of Commons passed a resolution declaring that all who sought to prosecute the war against the American colonies would be regarded as enemies of their country. The North administration resigned, King George prepared an abdication statement and a new government led by Rockingham took over with real power in the hands of Shelburne, who became Secretary of State for Home, Irish and Colonial Affairs. After Rockingham died four months later the sinuous Shelburne was left to head a government without a parliamentary majority. He was ousted in February 1783 by a Fox-North combination (under the figurehead Duke of Portland), but not before winning a consolation prize or two from the negotiations to end the war his own self-serving Tea Act had precipitated ten years earlier.

CONCLUSION

Although military operations in America virtually ceased after York-town, it was not until February and April 1783 that Parliament and Congress proclaimed an official cease-fire. Within a year the Continental Army was reduced to a rump of 700 men, insurance for nervous politicians but not so for citizens on the frontier. The Indians were not bound by the incomprehensible deals made among white men and more than 1500 settlers were killed between 1783 and 1794, with sizeable Militia forces under the command of Brigadier-General Josiah Harmar and Major-General Arthur St Clair, the latter governor of the North-West Territories, defeated by Miami Chief Little Turtle in 1790 and 1791. The hostiles were finally subdued by a major expedition led by Anthony Wayne, who systematically divided up their territory with stockades until finally crushing them at Fallen Timbers in 1794. By then the British had extracted the maximum benefit from the situation and agreed to give up the forts they had until then illegally maintained to the south of the Great Lakes. This forced the hostiles to sign the Treaty of Greenville of 1795 – with the United States. They had, at least, thwarted the imperial dreams of Virginia and Pennsylvania.

However one calculates who won, there is no disagreement that the Indians were the greatest losers. The Oneida, Mohican and Catawba tribes bought themselves some consideration while the revolutionary generation lived, but by the 1820s all three had been reduced to unsustainably small enclaves on marginal lands surrounded by white immigrants who regarded the original inhabitants of America as intruders. In 1794, the Oneida signed a treaty with the US government giving them protection over their lands in New York and recognition as a sovereign nation, in gratitude for the part they had played in the war of independence. The treaty stipulations were ignored by the state of New York, which imposed dispossessing treaties on them. By 1830 their six million acres were reduced to a paltry thirty-two, and large numbers relocated to Canada and Wisconsin. In 1974 and 1985 the Supreme Court ruled that the New York treaties were illegal and that the Oneida could seek redress through the courts. The Mohicans were harassed and their treaty lands encroached upon until the remnant of the tribe was moved to a mere six square miles of Oneida land in the 1820s, then to Wisconsin where today there is a thriving Munsee-Mohican community. By 1826 the Catawba reservation in South Carolina was down to one square mile, where the descendants of Sumter's scouts lived in abject poverty.

From a precontact population in the millions, by 1900 the Indians were reduced to a culturally destroyed remnant of 250,000. As in Australia and New Zealand, the nineteenth century practice of signing treaties with autochthonous peoples as though with foreign powers has led to some interesting developments of late, but in America their ability to exploit the sensibilities of a more enlightened age is reduced by the effects of history's longest-running social engineering programme, like all its successors designed to reduce people to powerless dependency. When one considers the fate of those who adopted white men's ways, the manner in which the tenuous authority of accommodationist tribal leaders was invariably undermined by Anglo-American bad faith, and that Indian agents were either profiteering scum or missionaries deeply hostile to Indian culture, it is impossible not to sympathise with the warriors who preferred an honourable death in battle. Regardless of its inevitability, the dispossession of the North American Indians makes melancholy reading. The losing wars they fought for their own independence are anecdotes beside the grim truth that when two peoples compete for the same land, the stronger will prevail and the weaker must accept whatever terms it can get.

Among the last acts by the North administration was to put Germain out to pasture as Viscount Sackville. He died eighteen months later, possibly amused to see the men who had hounded him from office remain true to their natures, squabbling and scheming against each other until a new 'king's man' emerged riding a wave of popular disgust. On 31 March 1783 William Pitt, the twenty-four year-old son of the great Chatham, resigned from the Portland administration and declared he was 'unconnected with any party whatever'. Deftly playing their abandoned ideals back upon the one-time firebrands, he introduced a private member's bill proposing the limitation of bribery elections and the disenfranchising of corrupt constituencies, including his own at no longer populated Old Sarum. This was of course defeated by 293 votes to 149. After the Portland government fell to the king's opposition to Fox's India Act, Pitt kissed hands on 19 December 1783 to become Britain's youngest First Minister, amid hearty laughter in the House of Commons led by his old mentor Fox. The chuckling stopped after Pitt called a general election in March 1784, in which 160 Foxites were unseated. Pitt now had a majority in the House of Commons and something akin to orderly government returned to British public affairs.

Before then Shelburne had negotiated a peace treaty with Franklin and by the manner in which it was done achieved the principal British objective, which was to drive a wedge between the Americans and the French. Vergennes could not formally protest until officially informed that the negotiations had concluded, and that a draft treaty was about to sail to America for ratification by Congress. His letter of 15 December 1782 to Franklin was icy:

> I am at a loss, sir, to explain your conduct and that of your colleagues on this occasion. You have concluded your preliminary articles without any communication between us, although the instructions from Congress prescribe that nothing shall be done without the participation of the King. You are about to hold out a certain hope of peace without even informing yourself on the state of the negotiation on our part.

The chutzpah of the old reprobate's reply of the 17th is representative, and probably forfeited the possibility of spending (*sic*) the rest of his life in the fleshpots of Paris:

> Nothing has been agreed in the preliminaries contrary to the interests of France [!]; and no peace is to take place between us and England till you have concluded yours. Your observation is,

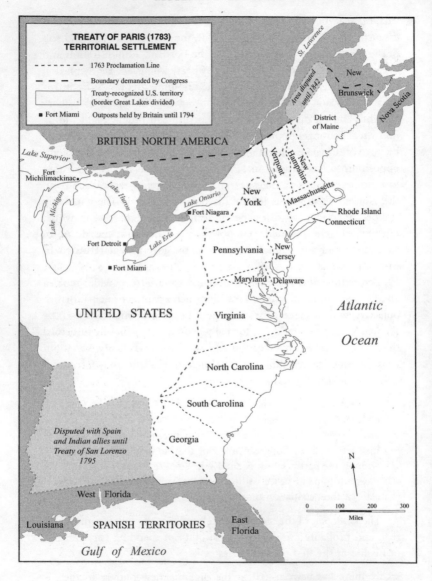

TREATY OF PARIS (1783) TERRITORIAL SETTLEMENT

- – – – – – – 1763 Proclamation Line
- – – – – – – Boundary demanded by Congress
- [ ] Treaty-recognized U.S. territory (border Great Lakes divided)
- ■ Fort Miami Outposts held by Britain until 1794

BRITISH NORTH AMERICA

St. Lawrence

New Brunswick

Nova Scotia

Area disputed until 1842

District of Maine

Lake Superior

Fort Michilimackinac ■

Vermont

New Hampshire

Lake Huron

Lake Michigan

Lake Ontario

Fort Niagara ■

New York

Massachussetts

Rhode Island
Connecticut

Fort Detroit ■

Lake Erie

■ Fort Miami

Pennsylvania

New Jersey

Maryland Delaware

UNITED STATES

Virginia

Atlantic

Ocean

North Carolina

South Carolina

Disputed with Spain and Indian allies until Treaty of San Lorenzo 1795

Georgia

N

West Florida

0   100   200   300

Miles

Louisiana

SPANISH TERRITORIES

East Florida

Gulf of Mexico

MAP 35

however, apparently just, that in not consulting you before they were signed, we have been guilty of neglecting a point of <u>biensé-ance</u> [propriety] . . . we hope it will be excused and, . . . certainly the whole edifice sinks to the ground immediately if you refuse on that account to give us any further assistance . . . <u>The English, I just now learn, flatter themselves they have already divided us.</u> I hope this little misunderstanding will therefore be kept a secret, and that they will find themselves totally mistaken.

The worldly-wise Vergennes knew all about leopards and their spots, and cannot have been either surprised or genuinely offended by Franklin's treachery. What stunned him was the apparent generosity of the terms agreed by Shelburne, including the frankly dishonourable betrayal of Britain's Indian and Loyalist allies. 'Their concessions exceeded all that I would have thought possible', he wrote. 'What could be the motive that would result in clauses such that they could be interpreted as a form of capitulation?' The answer, of course, was the unpicking of the web woven by Choiseul and Vergennes to ensure that Britain would be weakened by endemic conflict with her ex-colonies in the years to come. If there had been no containing the colonies before, how much less possible was it to contemplate doing so now that their population was soaring towards four million inhabitants and likely to overtake that of the British Isles within a generation?

Once it became apparent that trade with the ex-colonies was not affected by the loss of sovereignty, the power-brokers of Britain realized the precedent established by the offer of legislative autonomy made to the Americans by the Carlisle Commission in 1778 was the surest way to prevent further colonial rebellions. In due course this led to the Canada Act of 1791 and a generally decentralized administration of the new empire to which Britain muddled its way during the next century. Alas, strategically crucial Ireland remained an issue doomed to be handled neither humanely nor even intelligently, and the 1800 Act of Union came without the respect for the customs and rights of Roman Catholics that guided British policy in Québec, and which ensured Canada was never tempted to join the raucous union to the South. It has been suggested the British nobles recast themselves as a service elite following the shock of the American war, but as we have seen this was already a defining characteristic of a class defended by

Edmund Burke as a true natural aristocracy, not a separate interest within the state or separable from it. After centuries in which the House of Lords, on occasion alone, resisted relentless centralization, the British are now to find out whether it will be an improvement to have an upper house packed with government placepersons possessing all the attributes of petty criminals save the minimum courage required to rob the helpless openly.

The only heroes of our story went home to public indifference and official neglect. Ewald's Jägers were disbanded on return to Hesse with no thanks from the Landgrave for the money they had earned for him in eight years of service. 'All services performed were forgotten and we poor "Americans" who had flattered ourselves with the best reception, were deceived in our expectations in the most undeserved way . . . We became agitated, muttered in our beards, cursed our fate, and bent our proud backs under everything, because it could not be otherwise'. Across the Atlantic Joseph Martin and his colleagues met with the same reception, consoling themselves as soldiers always have with their memories of hardships shared and the mutual esteem of the only people whose opinion mattered. 'We had shared with each other the hardships, dangers and sufferings incident to a soldier's life [and] were as strict a band of brotherhood as masons and, I believe, as faithful to each other'. The British troops fared better than most, and it is particularly pleasant to record the generous appreciation shown to Roger Lamb, who resisted blandishments to stay and left the army to become a school teacher.

The true end of the war came in 1794, when to avoid a renewal of hostilities Chief Justice John Jay negotiated a treaty with Britain that buried the French alliance of 1778. More than that, it also validated the Navigation Acts of 1696 by recognizing the fact of British naval and commercial supremacy, and Britain's right to impose unilateral tariffs on American exports. Finally, it committed the government of the United States to pay prerevolutionary debts to British creditors, mainly owed by the Virginia and Maryland planters. 'It would give you a fever were I to name to you the apostates who have gone over to these heresies', Jefferson commented in a letter to a friend he naively thought would remain confidential, 'men who were Samsons in the field and Solomons in the council, but who have had their heads shorn by the harlot of England'. After this was made public, Washington never spoke or wrote to him again.

At the end of Washington's second term as president, Tom 'Rights of Man' Paine completed his return to despised obscurity by praying in print for the great man's early demise, wondering 'whether you have abandoned good principles, or whether you ever had any'. This in a publication that also printed documents purporting to show that Washington had been in secret correspondence with the British to betray the revolution, only to have his plans aborted by Arnold's defection. Biters were being bit all over the American political landscape, as the Founding Fathers turned upon each other the techniques of press and mob manipulation once employed to destroy British authority. It is impossible to believe that the forgers and agents of influence employed by the British secret service did not feed this frenzy, at one level to ensure that America would not make common cause with the French revolutionaries, at another to muddy the waters so thoroughly that its own American assets could swim undisturbed.

Both John Adams and Thomas Jefferson died on 4 July 1826, exactly fifty years after the date on the Declaration of Independence. It was no coincidence, for the document had long ago transcended its tactical, propagandistic origins to become the totem it remains today, and the two old men, competitors to the end, hung on grimly to reach the anniversary. In the words of Joseph Ellis' Pulitzer Prize-winning *Founding Brothers*, it was 'one final act of fate that everyone, then and now, regarded as the unmistakable voice of God'. One wonders whose voice was heard when Charles Carroll, among the largest slave-owners in America and last surviving signatory, and the separatist Thomas Sumter, the longest-lived general officer of the revolutionary period, both died six years later. Jefferson and Adams spent their last years putting the finishing touches to their own versions of the historical record, the former as always inhabiting a world of soaring rhetoric that impinged upon reality only in places, the latter disinclined to gild the lily. When Jefferson wrote about the reunion they would all have in the hereafter, Adams replied that he would not speak to Franklin before his old Paris colleague had *finished* doing penance for his sins, delicately indicating a hope that he had spent the last thirty-six years in hell.

The central principle of the revolution was that government was a parasite, to be kept in check by severely limiting its intake, and for that reason the American people progressively withheld their support for the struggle after 1777. It continued only because their self-appointed leaders had the administration of the French subsidy, in turn paid to them because they served the geopolitical interests of the Bourbon dynastic alliance. The new nation gained little in the treaty of 1782 that it could not have obtained in 1776 by granting the North administration the political cover of purely notional sovereignty, and probably less than it would have obtained after Saratoga, when the British were frantic to disengage. Accordingly, the watershed was not the French alliance, but the means it provided to a small group of men, wedded to conspiracy, to exploit the situation for their own advantage. That some went on to falsify the record may indicate a vestigial sense of shame, but more likely reflects a sober awareness of what their fellow citizens would do if the truth emerged. Even so, like the wretchedly treated soldiers of the Continental Army but with far more reason, the members of the wartime Congress were generally regarded with contempt by their contemporaries.

In mid 1780, with the Gordon riots around the corner, and the war going against Britain in the Mediterranean, the Caribbean and the Indian Ocean, George Washington wrote, 'we are at the end of our tether, and now or never [timely aid from France] must come'. At a time when the Loyalists were sustaining the British war effort in North America and the West Indies, the father of his country no longer looked to his own people for salvation. Fortescue observed 'we are tempted to ask, on meeting with this despairing lament, whether there was ever much real life at the heart of the American Revolution'. This was disingenuous, for he knew well that popular enthusiasm is no less sincere for being relatively short-lived. There was much real life, and a great deal of heart, in the war the colonists won in 1775–77. They nearly lost the continuation foisted on them by their greedy and conceited leaders because they did not like the new elite any more than the royal appointees they had overthrown.

In 1768 Hannah Griffits, a Pennsylvania Quaker lady, wrote scathingly about the abandonment of the highly effective nonimportation protest: 'Since the Men from a Party, on fear of a Frown, / Are kept by a Sugar-Plumb, quietly down'. In 1785 she drew the balance of a war during which she had witnessed 'the men from a party' posturing and profiteering, when not running away whenever the violence they preached seemed likely to visit them:

> The glorious fourth – again appears
> A day of days – and year of years,
> The sum of sad disasters,
> Where all the mighty gains we see
> With all their boasted liberty,
> Is only change of masters.

We have already touched upon the roots put down by Vermont, Kentucky and Tennessee during the war of independence, to which we should add the emblematic later history of the state of Maine. Although the British abandoned their plans for the territory, the frontier with Canada was not defined in this area until 1842, by which time Maine had become independent of Massachusetts. Among the 'White Indians' of this territory, as they were called by the authorities in Boston against whom they rebelled (under the banner of no taxation without representation) were Joseph Martin and nearly half the men who stood against the British at Concord in 1775, driven from their native states by the greed of the new elites. Despite wave after wave of culturally diverse immigrants, many of the thirteen original states retain the personalities established in 1775–82. Vermont is still a maverick state, while despite a political history of almost unparalleled corruption and judicial malfeasance, Massachusetts remains the preferred domicile of the tiresomely self-righteous. New York City and London remain more like each other than any other place on earth. Philadelphia treasures the cracked Liberty Bell, which perfectly symbolizes Pennsylvania's commitment to the cause of independence.

I am fond of the United States but much of it has succumbed to ambient blandness. The exception is the South; the only place in America where I have felt history is alive – and likely to inflict grievous bodily harm if you offend it. True Southerners do not regard Virginia as properly part of 'the South' at all, but had I the means I would live out my days on the haunted peninsula between the Potomac and James Rivers, pottering happily around the many battlefields where the destiny of the Anglo-Celtic peoples was played out. If not, somewhere along the mystic Shenandoah, in the shadow of the Blue Ridge Mountains where you have only to half-close your eyes to evoke the hard men in ragged buckskins and the ones in no less tattered grey who fought so heroically to live as they chose.

DRAMATIS PERSONAE

(with highest substantive or brevet rank attained 1775–83)

ADC	Aide de Camp	Md	Maryland
AG	Adjutant General	MP	Member of Parliament
BF	Benjamin Franklin	NC	North Carolina
Bt	Baronet	NH	New Hampshire
CA	Continental Army	NJ	New Jersey
CC	Continental Congress	NY	New York
DI	Declaration of Independence	Pa	Pennsylvania
Conn	Connecticut	QMG	Quartermaster General
Del	Delaware	RI	Rhode Island
Ga	Georgia	SC	South Carolina
GW	George Washington	Va	Virginia
i/c	in command	Vt	Vermont
KB	Knight, Order of the Bath	WI	West Indies
Mass	Massachusetts	*	the seven recipients of gold
Me	Maine;		medals from Congress.

Acland, Col John, MP (?-1778), i/c grenadiers with **Burgoyne**, crippled and POW at Bemis, wife Lady Harriet crossed enemy lines to nurse him and to become an iconic figure.

Adams, John (1735–1826), Mass lawyer, signed DI, with **BF** in Paris 1778–83, later ambassador to London, first vice president and second president of the United States. Wife Abigail's correspondence very illuminating.

Adams, Samuel (1722–1803), Mass revolutionary financed by **Hancock**, founder of the 'Sons of Liberty', signed DI, disruptive and widely distrusted, his influence declined once the war began.

Agnew, Brig-Gen James (1720?-77), Scots (44th), i/c brigade Brandywine, shot by a civilian at Germantown.

Alexander, CA Maj-Gen William 'Lord Stirling' (1726–83), wealthy NY, outstanding at Long Island (POW, exchanged), less so at Trenton, Brandywine, Germantown and Monmouth, died i/c Northern Department.

Allaire, Lt Anthony (1755–1838), NY Loyalist, adjutant to **Ferguson** in the Loyal American Volunteers, diarist.

Allen, Militia Col Ethan (1738–89), leader of Vt separatist guerrillas, seized Ticonderoga and was taken prisoner at Montréal 1775, negotiated for the defection of Vermont, exchanged for Archibald **Campbell** 1778.

Allen, Lt-Col Isaac (?-?), NJ Loyalist, i/c NJ Volunteers at Eutaw Springs.

André, Maj John (1751–80), Swiss-English, POW at Québec, exchanged 1776, in 1780 when AG to Clinton captured in civilian clothes liaising with **Arnold** for the betrayal of West Point and hanged.

Arbuthnot, Rear Adm Marriot (1711–94), grudgingly cooperated with **Clinton** at Charleston but not thereafter, bested by **Destouches** at Cape Henry but still managed to prevent the intended isolation of **Arnold**.

Armand: see **Rouerie**

Armstrong, Militia Maj-Gen John (1717–95), i/c Pa Militia Brandywine and Germantown, resigned 1779.

Arnold, CA Maj-Gen Benedict (1741–1801), Conn merchant, led invasion of Québec, leading role at Freeman's and Bemis, defected 1780, i/c Loyalist legion in Virginia as British brig-gen.

Ashe, CA Maj-Gen John (1720?-1791), NC, i/c detachment defeated at Briar Creek by Archibald **Campbell**.

Balcarres, Col Alexander, Earl of (1752–1825), Scots i/c light infantry at Hubbardton (wounded), Freeman's and Bemis, held for two years after Saratoga.

Balfour, Col Nisbet (1743–1832), Scots (23rd), wounded Breed's Hill, i/c Ninety-Six until ordered to Charleston by **Cornwallis** before he marched north to become nominally i/c South Carolina for the duration.

Bancroft, Dr Edward (1744–1820), friend of **Benjamin Franklin**, well-paid agent of **Eden** within the American delegation in Paris 1776–83 (truth emerged 150 years later), later Fellow of the Royal Society and the Royal College of Physicians.

Barras, Vice Adm Jacques-Melchior, Comte de (?-1800), i/c French fleet at Newport after **Destouches**, carried troops, siege artillery to join **Grasse** at Yorktown, captured Monserrat 1782.

Barré, Isaac, MP (1726–1802), coined term 'sons of liberty' in 1764, second only to **Wilkes** in using the American rebellion to castigate the North administration. Wilkes-Barre, Pa, named for them.

Baum, Lt-Col Friedrich (?-1777), Brunswick dragoon, led mixed column to destruction at Bennington.

Baylor, CA Col George (1752–84), wealthy Va, first ADC to **GW**, i/c dragoons surprised by **Grey** at Tappan where crippled by bayonet through lungs, regiment taken over by William **Washington**.

Beaumarchais, Augustin Caron de (1732–99), dramatist who wrote *Barber of Seville* (1773) *and Marriage of Figaro* (1781) employed by **Vergennes** to front a company to supply the Rebels with arms.

Boyd, Col James (1740–80?), leader of Ga Loyalists crushed by **Pickens** and **Clarke** at Kettle Creek, allegedly killed but a Georgia man of the same name and claiming the same rank died aged 105 in 1845.

Brant, Col Joseph (1742–1807), Mohawk Thayendanegea, British Army officer, adopted son of William **Johnson** who had eight children by his sister, with Guy and John **Johnson** in rivalry with the **Butlers** for leadership of Loyalist-Iroquois alliance throughout the war, afterwards won generous treatment for his people in Canada.

Bratton, Militia Col William (?-?), SC, destroyed **Huck**'s command at Williamson's Plantation.

Breymann, Lt-Col Heinrich (?-1777), Brunswick grenadier ambushed at Bennington, killed Bemis.

Browne, Brig-Gen Montfort (?-?), governor of the Bahamas, POW in 1776 raid, exchanged for **Alexander**, raised Prince of Wales Loyal American Volunteers.

Brown, Col Thomas (1750–1825), Yorkshireman whose King's Rangers held Georgia for the crown until the end.

Bouillé du Chariol, François-Claude-Amour, Marquis de (1739–1800), governor-general French Antilles.

Buford, CA Col Abraham (1749–1833), Va, i/c column destroyed by **Tarleton** at Waxhaws.

Burgoyne, Lt-Gen John, MP (1722–1792), dramatist, politician and enlightened officer who believed soldiers should be treated with humanity, but who wilfully led his army to defeat and capitulation at Saratoga.

Burke, Edmund, MP (1729–97), eloquent Irishman and **Rockingham** Whig who defended the colonists in the name of an Englishness long forgotten by those born in England.

Burr, CA Col Aaron (1756–1836), NJ merchant with **Arnold** to Québec, ADC to **Putnam** at Long Island, supported Charles **Lee** against **GW**, resigned 1779. Defeated **Schuyler** for Senate 1791, vice president 1800, killed **Hamilton** in a duel 1804, later with **Wilkinson** plotted to create a new nation in the southwest.

Bute, John Stuart, Earl of (1723–92), Scots, tutor, confidant and First Minister of **George III**.

Butler, Lt-Col John (1728–96), NY frontier Loyalist and friend of the Iroquois, raised Butler's Rangers, raided Wyoming Valley 1778, defeated by **Sullivan** at Newtown 1779, father of Walter who led the Cherry Valley raid.

Butler, CA Col Zebulon (1731–95), leader of Conn forces that drove 'Pennamites' out of the Wyoming Valley 1769–71, routed by **John Butler** at Wyalusing 1778, brother of William who took part in the Sullivan expedition.

Byron, Adm the Hon John (1723–86), aka 'Foul Weather Jack', missed **Estaing** off New York in 1778, fought inconclusive battle with him off Grenada June 1779, grandfather of the poet Lord Byron.

Cadwalader, Militia Brig-Gen John (1742–86), wealthy Pa, i/c division at Trenton, Brandywine and Germantown, provoked **Conway** to a duel and nearly killed him.

Campbell of Inverneill, Col Archibald (1739–91), Scots (71st), POW Boston 1776, exchanged for **Allen** and sent to recover Georgia late 1778, governor of Jamaica 1782–85, buried in Poet's Corner, Westminster Abbey.

Campbell, Lt-Gen John (?-1806), Scots (37th), to NY 1776, captured Fort Montgomery 1777, i/c West Florida late 1778, surrendered Pensacola 1781.

Campbell, Militia Brig-Gen William (1745–81), Va, elected i/c King's Mountain, i/c Va Militia Eutaw Springs.

Carden, Lt-Col John – NJ Loyalist defeated by **Sumter** at Hanging Rock.

Carleton, Gen Sir Guy, KB (1724–1808), Irish governor of Canada to 1778, failed to exploit 1776 defeat of Rebel invasion, replaced **Clinton** March 1782, tried to protect Loyalist, Black and Indian allies from betrayal by London.

Carlisle, Frederick Howard, Earl of (1748–1825), **Fox** Whig, friend of **Eden**, led 1778 peace commission.

Carroll of Carrolton, Charles (1737–1832), largest Md plantation owner and last surviving DI signatory.

Caswell, Militia Maj-Gen Richard (1729–89) NC, took credit for defeat of Highlanders at Moore's Creek to become governor and promote himself 1776–80, commanded NC Militia disastrously at Camden.

Cathcart, Lt-Col Sir William, Baron (1755–1843), 17th Light Dragoons, raised Caledonian Volunteers in Philadelphia, completed as British Legion in NY, led to Charleston 1780, invalided back to NY.

Chatham, William Pitt, Earl of (1708–1778), British premier during the War for Empire, passionately opposed the war until the French came in, when he made a no less passionate dying speech against a negotiated peace.

Choiseul, Etienne-François, Comte de Stainville (1719–85), foreign minister before **Vergennes**, initiated policy of covert encouragement and subsidies to American Rebels.

Church, Dr Benjamin (1734–80), RI, member inner circle of Mass plotters, first surgeon general of CA, well paid informer to **Gage** uncovered mid 1775, imprisoned, lost at sea while on the way to exile.

Clark, Militia Brig-Gen George Rogers (1752–1818), Va, led a raid to the Mississippi in 1778–79 that discredited British authority among the local Native Americans.

Clarke, Militia Col Elijah (?-1799), Ga, with **Pickens** defeated **Boyd**'s Loyalists at Kettle Creek, defeated by **Brown** at Augusta Sept. 1780, with **Sumter** at Blackstock, took Augusta with **Lee** and **Pickens** May 1781.

Cleveland, Militia Col Benjamin (1738–1806), NC, terror of the Yadkin, led a band to King's Mountain.

Clinton, CA Maj-Gen George (1739–1812), prominent NY Rebel landowner and governor, ejected by namesake Sir Henry from Fort Montgomery October 1777, present at Yorktown, vice president 1804–12, brother of James.

Clinton, Gen Sir Henry, KB, MP (1730–95), replaced **Howe** as C-in-C March 1778, replaced by **Carleton**.

Collier, Comm George (1738–95), led highly successful Connecticut, Virginia and Penobscot expeditions in 1779.

Conway, CA Maj-Gen Thomas (1735–1800), Irish émigré in the service of France, appointed inspector general by Congress against wishes of **GW**, discredited by the 'Conway Cabal'. See **Cadwalader**.

Cornstalk (1720?-77), Shawnee leader whose murder by Pa Rebels under flag of truce sparked vicious war.

Cornwallis, Lt-Gen Charles, Earl of, (1738–1805), Charleston 1776, i/c vanguard NY, NJ, Pa campaigns, **Carlisle** commission 1778, returned America 1779 with 'dormant' appointment as C-in-C to replace **Clinton**, i/c Southern campaign 1780–81, POW Yorktown, exchanged for **Laurens** 1782.

Craig, Lt-Col James (1748–1812), Scots (82nd), distinguished service at Penobscot and Wilmington.

Cristophe, Henri (1767–1820), future king of Haiti, wounded with French forces at the siege of Savannah.

Cromwell, Pvt. Oliver (1753–1853), NJ black freeman, with CA in every major battle of the war.

Cruger, Lt-Col John (1738–1807), NY Loyalist, son-in-law of **DeLancey**, i/c New York Volunteers south with Archibald Campbell in 1778, held Fort Ninety-Six until relieved by **Rawdon** 1780, fought at Eutaw Springs.

Cunningham, Brig-Gen Robert (1739?-1813), Loyalist Ga leader POW 1775, raised Loyal American Regiment.

Deane, Silas (1737–89), Conn, representative of CC to France with **Bancroft** 1775, recalled because of feud with Arthur **Lee** 1778, became an agent of **Eden** 1781 if not before.

Dearborn, CA Col. Henry (1751–1829), NH, with **Stark** at Breed's Hill, **Morgan** at Freeman's, Iroquois war.

DeLancey, Brig-Gen Oliver, Sr (1718–85), leading NY Loyalist, mortal enemy of the **Livingstons**, organized New York Volunteers brigade, received largest single compensation from the British after the war, father of Oliver.

DeLancey, Lt-Col Oliver Jr (1749–1822), Regular (17th Dragoons), AG to **Clinton** after **André**.

Destouches, Rear Adm Charles-René (?-?), commanded French fleet at Newport between the death of **Ternay** and the arrival of **Barras**, turned away from the Chesapeake by **Arbuthnot**.

Donop, Col Carl, Count von (1740–77), Hessian Jäger commander, killed attempting to storm Fort Mercer, Pa.

Dunmore, John Murray, Earl of (1732–1809), Va governor until expelled 1775, Emancipation Proclamation for slaves who joined H.M. forces, later sold the 'Ethiopian Regiment' back into slavery in WI.

Duportail, CA Maj-Gen Louis Le Begue de Presle (1743–1802), volunteer 1777, became Chief Engineer, scathing early report captured by the British, one of the few foreign officers respected by **GW**.

Eden, William (1744–1814), later 1st Baron Auckland, ran secret service for **North**, member of **Carlisle** mission. Great-great-grandfather of disastrous British Premier Sir Anthony Eden.

Estaing, Vice Adm Charles-Henri, Comte d' (1729–94), failed at Newport, took St Vincent and Grenada in July 1779, fought **Byron**, failed and wounded at Savannah, guillotined for defending Queen Marie Antoinette.

DRAMATIS PERSONAE

Ewald, Capt Johann (1744–1814), Hessian Jäger officer and perceptive diarist who served for the duration.

Ewing, Militia Brig-Gen James (1736–1805), i/c Pa Militia with **Cadwalader** at Trenton and Princeton.

Fanning, Col David (1755–1825), NC Loyalist guerrilla leader, raided from Wilmington to capture entire NC Rebel government at Hillsboro September 1781.

Ferguson, Lt-Col Patrick (1744–80), Scots officer (71st), inventor of a breech loading rifle 1776, formed and led American Volunteers legion destroyed at King's Mountain, killed and mutilated.

Fox, Charles James, MP (1749–1806), Earl of Holland's younger son and hence **Rockingham** Whig, member of the Hell Fire Club, strong opponent of **North**'s American policies.

Franklin, Benjamin (1706–90), polymath Philadelphian, only internationally-known American in 1775, member of the Hell Fire Club, hugely popular in France where he represented Congress 1778–82, negotiator and signatory of the Peace of Versailles with **Adams** and **Jay**.

Fraser, Brig-Gen Simon (1729–1777), Scots (24th), i/c **Burgoyne**'s light infantry, killed at Bemis.

Gage, Lt-Gen Thomas (1720–87), C-in-C 1763–75 (military governor Mass 1774–75), replaced by **Howe**.

Galloway, Joseph (1731–1803), Pa lawyer and close friend of **BF**, proponent of colonial autonomy within the empire, worked for **Eden**, civil administrator of Philadelphia under **Howe**, whose most severe critic he became.

Gálvez, Bernardo de (1746–86), Spanish governor of Louisiana, funnelled aid to the Rebels 1774–78, took Baton Rouge and Natchez 1779, Mobile 1780, Pensacola 1781, Bahamas 1782. Galveston, Texas, named for him.

Gambier, Rear Adm James (1723–89), briefly i/c North American fleet 1778–79, much the worst of all the admirals involved in the war, his departure was the cause of 'universal joy'.

Gansevoort, Militia Col Peter (1749–1812), NY, with Montgomery to Québec, defended Fort Stanwix 1777.

*Gates, CA Maj-Gen Horatio (1727–1806), retired British officer, **GW**'s first AG, replaced **Schuyler** and took credit for the defeat of **Burgoyne**, only serious rival to **GW** as C-in-C until defeated at Camden August 1780.

George III (1738–1820), active constitutional monarch cursed with recurrent bouts of mental illness and by a political oligarchy that belonged in the Augean stables.

Germain, Lord George (1716–85), reverted to his birth name as Viscount Sackville in 1782 when he resigned the office of Colonial Secretary, held since 1775, during which time he had handled the war as well as anyone realistically could, given the institutions and men he had to work with.

Girty, Simon (1741–1818), one of four brothers captured by the Seneca in 1756, played a prominent part in the savage struggle against American expansion along the Ohio River 1778–94.

Grant, Lt-Gen James, MP (1720–1806), Scots (55th), vehemently anti-American, i/c brigade Breed's Hill, Long Island, Brandywine, Germantown, Monmouth, to WI late 1778 where he captured St Lucia.

Grasse, Vice Adm François-Joseph, Comte de (1722–88), i/c French fleet that drove off **Graves** at the Chesapeake and doomed **Cornwallis** in 1781, later defeated and captured by **Rodney** at the Saintes in April 1783.

Graves, Rear Adm Samuel (1713–87), incompetent i/c North American fleet 1774 until replaced by Richard **Howe**.

Graves, Rear Adm Thomas (1725–1802), unfortunate i/c North American fleet 1780–82, arrived days too late to stop **Ternay** at Newport, let down by **Hood** v. **Grasse** at Virginia Capes, blamed by everyone.

Greene, CA Maj-Gen Nathanael (1742–1786), RI lapsed Quaker, youngest general 1775 and only one other than **GW** to serve for the duration, QMG 1778–80, much-defeated commander Southern Department 1780–83.

Grey, Maj-Gen Sir Charles, KB (1729–1807), led night bayonet assaults at Paoli and Tappan (hence his nickname 'No Flint'), to England late 1778, designated to replace **Clinton** in 1782 but peace intervened.

Guichen, Vice Adm Luc-Urbain, Comte de (1712–90), avoided defeat by **Rodney** off Martinique in April 1780 but lost a vital WI convoy off Ushant in December 1781.

Haldimand, Lt-Gen Sir Frederick, KB (1718–91), Swiss in British service, commander in Florida before becoming ruthless C-in-C and governor of Canada in succession to **Carleton** (June 1778-November 1784).

Hamilton, CA Col Alexander (1757–1804), born WI educated NY, son-in-law of **Schuyler**, ADC and chief intelligence officer to **GW**, led the last significant combat by the CA in the assault on Outpost Ten at Yorktown.

Hamilton, Lt-Col Henry (?-1796), Scots 2-in-C to **Carleton**, based at Fort

Detroit, dubbed 'hair-buyer', captured by **Clark** at Vincennes, foully treated by **Jefferson** in captivity until **GW** intervened.

Hamilton, Brig-Gen John (?-1817), NC, son-in-law of **Schuyler**, raised NC Loyalist Volunteers, unusually honourable behaviour permitted him to remain in NC after the war.

Hampton, Militia Col Wade (1751–1835), swore allegiance 1780, reneged and joined **Sumter**, i/c mixed Legion at Eutaw Springs, became richest man in America, namesake grandson prominent cavalry leader for the CSA 1861–65.

Hancock, John (1737–93) Mass, wealthiest man in New England, puppet of Samuel **Adams**, signed DI, president of second CC, of decreasing prominence thereafter.

Hand, CA Brig-Gen Edward (1744–1802), to Pa with Royal Irish 1767, resigned 1774, conducted brilliant delaying action in Trenton/Princeton campaign, enabled **Clark**'s expedition, Iroquois war, AG to **GW** 1781.

Hazen, CA Brig-Gen Moses (1733–1803), Mass, **Rogers** Ranger, land grant in Québec, recruited 200 Canadians, report of Howe's flank march at Brandywine ignored by **GW**, commanded brigade under **La Fayette**.

Heath, CA Maj-Gen William (1737–1814), Mass, Lexington and Concord, 2-in-C to **Putnam** Long Island 1776, blackguarded by **GW** after failure at Fort Independence in early 1777, later i/c Hudson Highlands.

Heister, Maj-Gen Leopold Philip de (1707–77), led Hessians at Long Island and White Plains, ill health and disagreements with **Howe** led him to hand over to **Knyphausen** and return home.

Herkimer, Militia Brig-Gen Nicolas (1728–77), NY frontier, killed at Oriskany.

*****Howard, CA Col John** (1752–1827), Md, very wealthy landowner and exceptional regimental commander, fought at White Plains, Germantown, Monmouth, Cowpens, Guilford, Hobkirk's Hill and Eutaw Springs.

Howe, Vice Adm Richard, Viscount (1726–99), i/c North American fleet 1776–78, refused to serve again under **Sandwich**, conducted third relief of Gibraltar 1783, First Lord of the Admiralty 1783–88.

Howe, CA Maj-Gen Robert (1732–96), NC 'Rice King', commander Southern Department 1777–78, lost Savannah, acquitted by court martial, spent remainder of the war in the North.

Howe, Gen Sir William, Bt, MP (1729–1814), replaced **Gage** as C-in-C October 1775, resigned 1778.

Hood, Rear Adm Sir Samuel, Bt, MP (1724–1816), able but disloyal 2-in-C to **Rodney** and Thomas **Graves**.

Huck, Capt Christian (?-1780), SC, attached **Tarleton**'s legion, killed at Williamson's Plantation

Huger, CA Brig-Gen Isaac (1743–97), Va, defeated at Savannah, Monck's Corner, Guilford, Hobkirk's Hill.

Hutchinson, Thomas (1711–1780), Mass, last royal governor of the colony whose authority was undermined by mob action and British appeasement, died in exile.

Innes, Col Alexander (?-?), Scots regular, appointed Inspector General of Provincial Forces by **Howe** and colonel of the South Carolina Royalists by **Clinton**, crippled at Musgrove's Mill.

Jay, John (1745–1829), NY lawyer opposed independence until 1776, president of CC 1779, minister to Spain 1779–82, with **BF** and John **Adams** negotiated peace with Britain 1782 and again in 1794.

Johnson, Guy (1740–1788), Irish, nephew (?) and son-in-law of William, whom he succeeded as Indian Sup't in Niagara until 1782 when succeeded by John (below).

Johnson, Col Sir John, Bt (1742–1830), NY frontier, illegitimate son of William, formed Loyalist Johnson's Greens, with St Leger to Fort Stanwix/Oriskany, directed 1780 raids along the Mohawk Valley, succeeded Guy.

Johnson, Sir William, Bt (1715–74), Irish, Indian Sup't and key figure in Iroquois-British alliance, post taken over when he died by nephew Guy, illegitimate son John led Johnson's Greens, adopted son **Brant** led the Mohawk.

Johnston, Commodore George (1730–87), wildly indiscreet , fought duel with **Germain** in 1770, member of **Carlisle** commission whose clumsy attempts to suborn members of Congress got him sent home.

Jones: see **Paul**.

Kalb, CA Maj-Gen Johann, 'Baron de' (1721–1780), Bavarian in French service sent by **Choiseul** to the colonies in 1764–5, volunteered his services to Congress 1777, mentor of **La Fayette**, killed at Camden 1780.

Keppel, Vice Adm Augustus, MP (1725–86), dispute with **Palliser** and courts martial over his handling of the battle of Ushant in 1779 resulting in division of the navy into 'Montagus (**Sandwich**) and Keppelites'.

Knyphausen, Maj-Gen Wilhelm, Baron von (1716–1800), i/c Hessians after **Heister** for duration.

Kosciuszko [Bonawentura], CA Col Tadeusz (1746–1817), Polish engineer officer in French service volunteered to North America 1776, designed fortifications of Bemis Heights, West Point, failed at Fort Ninety-Six.

Knowlton, CA Col Thomas (1740–76), Conn, hero of Breed's Hill, killed Harlem Heights.

Knox, CA Maj-Gen Henry (1750–1806), Me-born bookseller with only theoretical military knowledge who brought artillery to Boston from Fort Ticonderoga 1776, decisive at Trenton, i/c artillery for the duration.

La Fayette, CA Brig-Gen Marie-Joseph, Marquis de (1757–1834), with mentor **Kalb** volunteered 1777, ADC and virtual son to **GW**, wounded Brandywine, returned France to encourage alliance 1778, appointed i/c brigade sent to combat **Arnold** in Va 1781, helped corner **Cornwallis** at Yorktown.

Lamb, Sgt Roger (1756–1830), Irish memoirist (23rd), POW at Saratoga and Yorktown, escaped both times.

Laurens, Henry (1724–1792), wealthy SC president of first and second CC, captured at sea 1780, held in the Tower, exchanged for **Cornwallis**, joined Paris peace negotiations. Father of John, who led the failed assault on Savannah, captured at Charleston, exchanged, to Paris 1781, on return killed in one of the last battles of the war.

Lawson, Militia Brig-Gen Robert (?-1805), i/c Va Militia at Guilford.

Learned, Militia Brig-Gen Ebenezer (1728–1801), Mass, i/c brigade Long Island, Freeman's, Bemis.

Lee, Dr. Arthur (1740–92), Va, educated in Britain, doctor, barrister and Fellow of the Royal Society, with **BF** to France, feud with **Deane**, brother of **Richard** who was instrumental in moving the Va oligarchy to resistance.

Lee, CA Maj-Gen Charles (1731–82), widely read and experienced, if repulsive, half-pay English officer, 3-in-C to **GW** 1775; i/c Charleston 1776, disenchanted with **GW** after White Plains, captured by **Tarleton**, maybe turned in captivity, exchanged for **Prescott** 1778, i/c vanguard at **Monmouth**, cashiered for insubordination.

*Lee, CA Col 'Light Horse Harry' (1756–1818), Va, led raid on Paulus Hook, i/c cavalry Guilford and Eutaw Springs, profligate and finally disgraced father of Robert E. Lee.

Leslie, Maj-Gen the Hon Alexander (1731–94), Scots (64th), i/c Light Infantry brigade 1776–78, permitted **GW** to march around him to Princeton, i/c right wing Guilford, ended war in Charleston, killed in a Glasgow riot.

Lincoln, CA Maj-Gen Benjamin (1733–1810), Mass, wounded Saratoga, surrendered Charleston 1780.

Livingston, prominent Rebel NY/NJ land-owning family, mortal enemies of the **DeLancys**.

Locke, Militia Col Francis (?-?), NC back-country Militia, defeated **Moore** at Ramsauer's Mill.

MacDonald, Flora (1722–90), Scots patriot who smuggled Bonny Prince Charlie to Skye 1746, put in the Tower, to NC with husband Donald who led Loyalists defeated at Moore's Creek, returned to Britain.

McDougall, CA Maj-Gen John (1732–86), Scots, NY privateer, i/c brigade White Plains, Germantown.

McDowell, Militia Brig-Gen Charles (?-?), NC, leader of back-country guerrilla band.

McDowell, Militia Brig-Gen James (1742?-1801), as above, brother of Charles

McGillivray, Alexander (1759–93), mixed-blood associate of **Brown**, who helped the Creek to preserve their autonomy allied to Spain until his death.

MacLean, Brig-Gen Allan (1725–97), Jacobite who raised the Royal Highland Emigrants (84th) in Canada, instrumental in preventing the capture of Québec by **Montgomery** and **Arnold** in 1775.

Maitland, Lt-Col the Hon. John, MP (1732–79), Scots (71st), victor at Stono Ferry, i/c Beaufort, his prompt march through swamps to Savannah saved it from **Estaing** and **Lincoln** but he died soon afterwards of malaria.

Malmédy, CA Col François, Marquis de (?-?), volunteer 1775, i/c North Carolina Militia at Eutaw Springs.

Marion, Militia Brig-Gen Francis 'Swamp Fox' (1732–95), effective SC partisan leader who conducted successful joint operations with William **Washington** and **Greene**, fought at Eutaw Springs.

Marjoribanks, Maj John (?-1781), saved the day at Eutaw Springs when i/c flank companies, died 45 days later.

Martin, Pvt Joseph Plumb (1760?-1830), Conn CA and memoirist who served for the duration.

Mawhood, Col Charles (?-1780), 17th Foot, i/c Cornwallis's rearguard at Princeton.

Maxwell, CA Brig-Gen William (1733–96), Scotch-Irish, i/c riflemen before Chad's Ford, resigned 1780.

Mercer, CA Brig-Gen Hugh (1725–77), Scots, surgeon's mate with British at Culloden, emigrated to Pa, led brigade at Trenton, killed at Princeton.

Middleton, Henry (1742–84), 'Rice King' and largest plantation owner in SC, president of the first CC.

Mills, Col Ambrose (?-?), SC Loyalist, victor at **McDowell**'s Camp.

Moncrieff, Lt-Col James (1744–83), Engineer officer i/c Savannah defence works 1779, siege works Charleston 1780, took over 1,000 of his black Pioneers with him to the Bahamas at the end of the war.

Montgomery, CA Brig-Gen Richard (1738–75), Irish officer who served with the British Army in the Americas, emigrated NY 1772 married a **Livingston**, took over invasion of Canada from **Schuyler**, killed Québec.

Moore, Lt-Col John (?-1780), leader of NC Loyalists defeated and scattered by **Locke** at Ramsauer's Mill, from which Loyalist cause in NC did not recover, hanged after King's Mountain.

*Morgan, Maj-Gen Daniel (1735–1802), Va, wagoneer in Braddock's expedition 1755, POW Québec 1775, exchanged, i/c riflemen Freemans's, Bemis, resigned (gout), rejoined 1780, victor at Cowpens, resigned again.

Morris, Gouverneur (1752–1816), from a Loyalist New York family, appointed assistant to Robert **Morris** after a leg amputation in 1781, competent but widely distrusted and disliked.

Morris, Robert (1734–1806), Pa, English-born, chief financier of the rebellion and key **GW** ally.

Moultrie, CA Maj-Gen William (1730–1805), SC, hero of Sullivan Island and Beaufort, captured at Charleston.

Musgrave, Brig-Gen Thomas (1737–1812), hero of Germantown (40th), WI 1779, ADC to the king 1782.

North, Lord Frederick (1732–92), heir to the earldom of Guilford and premier 1770–82, urbane parliamentary manager but ineffectual war leader who failed to coordinate policies of **Sandwich** and **Germain**.

Odell, Lt-Col William (?-1783), i/c Loyal American Rangers to Jamaica 1780.

O'Hara, Maj-Gen Charles (1740–1802), Irish, i/c Guards battalion Germantown, hero of Guilford, surrendered Yorktown for **Cornwallis**, exchanged 1782. In 1795 captured at Toulon and exchanged for **Rochambeau**.

Orvilliers, Admiral Louis Guillouet, Comte d' (1708–92), commander of failed 1779 invasion of Britain.

Paine, CA Capt Thomas (1737–1809), failed English stay-maker and tax collector, author of pamphlets about low pay for tax collectors, American independence, the *Rights of Man* and desiring the unpleasant death of **GW**.

Palliser, Vice Adm Sir Hugh, KB, MP (1723–96), **Sandwich** protégé, see **Keppel**.

Parker, Vice Adm Sir Hyde (1714–82), Irish, i/c fleet that transported Campbell to Georgia 1779, prevented **Guichen** from taking St Lucia in 1780.

Parker, Vice Adm Sir Peter, KB (1721–1811), Irish, de-bagged at Charleston 1776, C-in-C Jamaica 1779–81.

Paul, Capt John alias Jones (1747–1792), Scots adventurer who won a celebrated battle with HMS *Serapis* off the coast of Yorkshire in 1779, later admiral in the Russian navy.

Peebles, Capt John (1739–1823), Scots (42nd) and detailed diarist of events 1776–82.

Percy, Lt-Gen Hugh, Lord (1742–1817), salvaged Lexington and Concord column, took and held Newport 1776, returned home 1777 after disputes with **Howe**.

Phillips, Maj-Gen William (1731?-81), pioneer of horse artillery tactics, POW at Saratoga, exchanged for **Lincoln**, led raid on Virginia, died of typhoid.

Pickens, Militia Brig-Gen Andrew (1739–1817), SC guerrilla leader, i/c Kettle Creek, POW at Ninety-Six, paroled 1779, returned to war when farm burned by Loyalists, fought alongside CA at Cowpens, Eutaw Springs.

Pigot, Sir Maj-Gen Robert (1720–96), i/c brigade Breed's Hill, Long Island, Newport garrison.

Pitt: see **Chatham**

Pitt, William MP (1759–1806), son of **Chatham**, First Minister 1783–1801, 1804–06.

Poor, CA Maj-Gen Enoch (1736–80), NH, at Québec, Freeman's and Bemis, Iroquois war.

Prescott, Maj-Gen Richard (1725–88), captured Montréal Nov 1775 exchanged for **Sullivan** Sept 1776, kidnapped Newport July 1777 exchanged for **Lee** March 1778, i/c Newport when evacuated October 1779.

Prescott, CA Col William (1726–95), Mass, hero of Breed's Hill, served NY, Saratoga, resigned 1777.

Prevost, Maj-Gen Augustine (1723–86), Swiss-born colonel of the Royal Americans (60th), invaded Ga and SC from East Florida and defended Savannah 1779, returned to England 1780 after 22 years' service in America.

Pulaski, CA Brig-Gen Kazimierz (1747–1779), Polish adventurer, recruited destructive (to friend and foe) cavalry unit of British deserters and prisoners, killed stupidly charging Savannah fortifications.

Putnam, CA Maj-Gen Israel (1718–90), Conn, **Rogers** Ranger, i/c Long Island and Hudson, stroke 1779.

Rall, Col Johann (1720?-76), Hessian grenadier, White Plains, Fort Washington, killed Trenton.

Rawdon, Lt-Col Francis, Lord (1754–1826), Irish heir to Earl of Moira, raised Volunteers of Ireland, i/c Hobkirk's Hill, relief of Ninety-Six, returned Britain because of ill health.

Reed, CA Col Joseph (1741–85), Pa, friend of **GW** and AG in 1776, represented him in a meeting with the **Howe** brothers, wrote disloyally to Lee but masterminded Trenton, resigned 1777, accused of treason by Arthur Lee.

Revere, Militia Lt-Col Paul (1735–1818), Boston silversmith, 'Son of Liberty' and one of the couriers who alerted the countryside before Lexington and Concord, later court-martialed and acquitted for his role at Penobscot.

Riedesel, Lt-Gen Friedrich von, Baron Eisenbach (1738–1800), i/c Brunswickers in Saratoga campaign with wife Frederika who wrote a telling memoir. Exchanged, he remained until 1783.

Robinson, Col Beverley (1721–92), wealthy NY Loyalist, forced to abandon his Hudson Highlands mansion by **Jay** 1777, organized the Loyal American Regiment and ran effective intelligence operation in upper NY.

Rochambeau, Lt-Gen Jean-Baptiste, Comte de (1725–1807), Newport 1780, liaised respectfully with **GW** leading to joint success at Yorktown.

Rockingham, Charles Wentworth-Watson, Marquis of (1730–82), vast Irish landowner and parliamentary patron of **Fox, Burke** and other prominent opponents of **North**'s American policies, premier 1765–66 and 1782.

Rodney, Adm George, Baron (1718–92), i/c WI fleet fought battles Finisterre, St Vincent and Martinique 1780, took St Eustatius 1781, defeated Grasse at the Saintes 1782.

Rogers, Col Robert (1731–95), organized and led his eponymous Rangers during the War for Empire, after **GW** refused his services in 1776 he organized first the Queen's then the King's Rangers for **Howe**.

Rouerie, CA Brig-Gen Charles, Marquis de (1750–93), aka Armand, volunteer arrived 1777, joined **Pulaski** Legion, took over at his death, shattered at Camden, later served under Deux-Ponts at Yorktown.

Rumford: see **Thompson.**

Rush, Dr. Benjamin (1746–1813), Pa, medical pioneer, signed DI, involved in the **Conway** cabal.

Rutherford, Militia Brig-Gen Griffith (1731–1800), NC, defeated **Moore** at Ramsauer's Mill, POW at Camden.

Rutledge, Gov John (1739–1800), Rice King, key figure in the SC rebellion, governor-in-exile 1780–81.

St Clair, CA Maj-Gen Arthur (1737–1818), Scots, i/c brigade Trenton and Princeton, censured for abandoning Fort Ticonderoga, resigned, served as volunteer at Brandywine and against the Iroquois.

St Leger, Col Barry (1737–89), i/c column stopped at Fort Stanwix 1777, liaison with Ethan **Allen** 1781.

Salstonstall, Capt Dudley (1738–96), Conn privateer, senior officer Rebel navy, made scapegoat for Penobscot.

Sandwich, John Montagu, Earl of (1718–92), First Lord of the Admiralty 1771–82, member Hell Fire Club.

Schuyler, CA Maj-Gen Philip (1733–1804), NY, father-in-law of Alexander **Hamilton**, wealthy landowner hated by humbler New Yorkers and the New England radicals, i/c Northern Department, claiming ill health handed over Canada invasion to **Montgomery**, Congress replaced him with **Gates** before Saratoga, resigned 1777.

Scott, CA Brig-Gen Charles (1739–1813), Va, took over **Stephen**'s brigade, Monmouth, POW Charleston.

Sevier, Militia Col John (1745–1815), NC frontier, led band at King's Mountain, first governor of Tennessee.

Shelburne, William Petty, Earl of (1737–1805), patron of a parliamentary faction that opposed **North**'s American policies, although as a large East India Company shareholder responsible for the Tea Acts, premier 1782–83.

Shelby, Militia Col Isaac (1750–1826), NC frontier, led band at King's Mountain, first governor of Kentucky.

Simcoe, Col John (1752–1806), 40th, severely wounded at Brandywine, i/c Queen's Rangers, POW and exchanged 1779, with **Arnold** to Va, POW Yorktown.

Skinner, Brig-Gen Cortlandt (1728–99), NJ Loyalist, POW 1776 exchanged for **Alexander**, organized NJ Volunteers and Skinner's Horse aka 'Cowboys', reputedly the best cattle rustlers on either side.

Smallwood, CA Maj-Gen William (1732–92), Md, wounded White Plains, i/c reserve Camden, replaced **Kalb**.

Stark, CA Maj-Gen John (1728–1822), NH member of **Rogers'** Rangers, i/c left wing at Breed's Hill, commanded at Bennington, last surviving CA general.

Stephen, CA Maj-Gen Adam (1730?-1791), Va, nearly ruined **GW**'s plan at

Trenton by premature crossing, cashiered for drunkenness and firing into **Wayne**'s division at Germantown.

Steuben, Maj-Gen Friedrich von (1730–1794), spurious Prussian baron, volunteered 1777, i/c training at Valley Forge winter 1777–78, appointed Inspector General, i/c support services for **Greene** in the South.

Stevens, Militia Maj-Gen Edward (1745–1820), Va, i/c brigade at Camden, Guilford.

Stewart, Col Alexander (1741–1794), Scots (3rd), took over field command from **Rawdon**, i/c Eutaw Springs.

*Stewart, CA Col Walter (1756–96), Pa, outstanding regimental commander at Germantown, Monmouth and Stony Point, instrumental in defusing Philadelphia Line mutinies 1780–81, leader of Newburgh protests 1783.

Stirling: see **Alexander**

Sullivan, CA Maj-Gen John (1740–1795), NH lawyer, captured Long Island and exchanged for **Prescott** 1776, liked by **GW** but associated with many defeats, resigned commission in 1779 after leading the Iroquois expedition.

Sumner, CA Col Jethro (1733–85), very wealthy NC, mainly recruiting but i/c brigade at Eutaw Springs.

Sumter, Militia Brig-Gen Thomas 'Gamecock' (1734–1832), psychopathic SC guerrilla leader who duelled mercilessly with his spiritual twin **Tarleton** for control of the hinterland, refused to cooperate with CA, retired after defeat at Quinby Bridge April 1781, oldest surviving Militia general.

Tarleton, Lt-Col Banastre (1754–1833), as Ensign in 17th Light Dragoons captured Charles **Lee**, i/c British Legion in the South, most brutal and effective British light cavalry leader of the war.

Ternay, Rear Adm Charles-Henri de, Chevalier (1722–80), took **Rochambeau** to Newport, died of typhoid.

Thompson, Maj Benjamin (1753–1814), Mass-born spy for **Gage**, favourite and possibly lover of **Germain**, returned as an officer in the King's American Dragoons 1780–81, behaving despicably. Also the father of thermodynamics, British knight, Bavarian general and count (Rumford), who married the widow of Lavoisier.

Tryon, Maj-Gen William (1729–88), NY, Loyalist governor and C-in-C Provincial Forces, led raid on Danbury.

Turnbull, Lt. Col. George (?-?), NY Loyalist, DeLancey's Volunteers, defeated **Sumter** at Hanging Rock.

Vaughn, Maj-Gen John, MP (1728–95), wounded White Plains, to WI 1780, took St Eustatius with **Rodney**.

Vergennes, Charles Gravier, Comte de (1719–87), Foreign Minister from 1770, architect of the war.

Vernier, CA Maj Pierre-François (1737–1780), volunteer, **Pulaski** Legion cavalry, killed at Monck's Corner.

Warner, Militia Brig-Gen Seth (1743–84), Vt 'Green Mountain Boy', redeemed Hubbardton defeat at Bennington.

*****Washington, CA Lt-Gen George** (1732–99), wealthy Va plantation owner, sole C-in-C, sole outstanding figure of the war, and sole legitimate 'father' of the United States.

Washington, CA Lt-Col William (1752–1810), Va cousin of **GW**, took over dragoons from **Baylor**, in all the major battles of the Carolinas (personal duel with **Tarleton** at Cowpens), wounded and POW at Eutaw Springs.

Ward, CA Maj-Gen Artemas (1727–1800), i/c Mass army 1775, 2-in-C to **GW**, resigned 1776.

*****Wayne, CA Maj-Gen 'Mad' Anthony** (1745–96), wealthy Pa tanner, French and Indian War wagoneer, i/c division at Brandywine, Paoli, Germantown, Monmouth, Stony Point and Yorktown, ended war besieging Savannah.

Webster, Brig-Gen James (1743–81), Scots, i/c **Cornwallis**'s right wing at Camden, killed at Guilford.

Wemyss, Maj James (?-1789), 40th, with **Simcoe** and Queen's Rangers at Brandywine, led punitive expedition through **Marion**'s heartland 1780, wounded and left in the care of **Sumter** at Fishdam's Ford.

Wentworth, Paul (?-1793), NH-born chief of Loyalist secret agents in London, cut out for contact with **Deane**.

Wilkes, John, MP (1727–97), founded scurrilous *The North Briton* 1763, provoked and won confrontations with the establishment, expelled and re-elected from Parliament, elected Mayor of London and disbarred twice, member of the Hell Fire Club, with **Barré** fiercely defended American rebellion. Wilkes-Barre, Pa, named for them.

Wilkinson, CA Brig-Gen James (1757–1825), Md, with **Arnold** and **Burr** at Québec, **Gates** at Saratoga, betrayed the '**Conway** Cabal', clothier-general to the army 1779–81, embezzled, resigned, after war secretly agent for Spain, betrayed **Burr** plan for a separate southwestern nation, C-in-C of US Army in 1796 and 1812, finally sacked.

Williams, CA Brig-Gen Otho (1749–94), Md memoirist, POW Fort

Washington, exchanged 1778, commanded division at Camden, Guilford, Hobkirk's Hill and Eutaw Springs.

Winston, Militia Col Joseph (1746–1815), NC, Yadkin (with **Cleveland**), led band to King's Mountain.

BRITISH REGIMENTS SERVING IN THE THIRTEEN COLONIES

*(see **Appendix D** for regiments from the American Establishment)*

* = Irish establishment [ ] = colonel or notable officer in text

CAVALRY

16th (Queen's Own)	NY 1776, to England December 1778 [Burgoyne].
*17th Light Dragoons	Boston 1775, one troop South 1780 to Yorktown [Preston, Gage].

FOOT

Marines	Boston 1774, Québec 1776, recalled to Home Fleet March 1778.
Composite Guards Batt.	NY 1776, Charleston December 1780 to Yorktown [O'Hara].
3rd (The Buffs)	Charleston March 1781, Jamaica December 1782.
4th (King's Own)	Boston 1774, with Grant to Florida/WI October 1778.
5th (Northumberland)	Boston 1774, to fleet as Marines October 1778 [Percy].
*6th (1st Warwicks)	WI to NY October 1776, dispersed.
7th (Royal Fusiliers)	POW Canada 1775 exchanged NY 1776, Charleston December 1779.
8th (King's)	Canada 1768, fort duties, St Leger's expedition.
*9th (East Norfolk)	Québec 1776 to Saratoga.

10th (North Lincolns)	Boston 1774, dispersed NY 1779.
14th (Bedfordshire)	Virginia 1775, dispersed NY December 1776.
*15th (East Yorks)	Charleston 1776, with Grant to Florida/WI October 1778.
16th (Bucks)	Southern posts 1776–82.
*17th (Leicester)	Boston 1775, Virginia April 1781 to Yorktown.
18th (Royal Irish)	Boston 1774, dispersed 1775. Used v. Gordon Riots.
19th (North Yorks)	Charleston June 1781, WI December 1782.
*20th (East Devon)	Québec 1776 to Saratoga.
21st (Royal North British)	Québec 1776 to Saratoga.
*22nd (Cheshire)	Boston 1775, Newport 1776, NY 1779, duration [Gage, O'Hara].
23rd (Royal Welch)	Boston 1775, Charleston December 1779 to Yorktown [Howe].
*24th (2nd Warwick)	Québec 1776 to Saratoga [Fraser].
26th (Cameronian)	Captured Canada 1775, exchanged NY 1776, dispersed 1779.
*27th (Enniskilling)	Boston 1775, with Grant to Florida/WI October 1778.
*28th (Gloucester)	Charleston 1776, with Grant to Florida/WI October 1778 [Grey].
29th (Worcester)	Boston 1774, Québec 1776 to Saratoga.
30th (Cambridgeshire)	Charleston June 1781, WI December 1782.
31st (East Surrey)	Québec 1776, flank companies to Saratoga [Holmes].
*33rd (1st West Yorks)	WI to Charleston 1776, again December 1779 to Yorktown [Cornwallis].
*34th (Cumberland)	Québec 1776, flank companies to Saratoga.
*35th (Dorset)	Boston 1775, with Grant to Florida/WI October 1778.
*37th (North Hants)	Charleston 1776, Nova Scotia/East Florida September 1779.
38th (1st Stafford)	Boston 1774, Newport 1776, NY 1779, duration [Pigot].
*40th (2nd Somerset)	Boston 1775, with Grant to Florida/WI October 1778 [Grant].
*42nd (Royal Highland) aka 'Black Watch'	2 batts. NY 1776, E. Florida Nov 1778, Charleston December 1779, Virginia 1780, NY 1781, duration.

43rd (Monmouth)	Boston 1774, Newport 1776, Virginia April 1781 to Yorktown.
*44th (East Essex)	Boston 1775, to Canada September 1779.
*45th (Nottingham)	Boston 1775, dispersed NY 1777.
*46th (Cornwall)	Charleston 1776, to fleet October 1778 [Howe, Vaughn].
47th (Lancashire)	Boston 1774, Québec 1776 to Saratoga [Carleton].
49th (Hertfordshire)	Boston 1775, with Grant to Florida/WI October 1778.
50th (West Kents)	WI to NY 1776, dispersed.
52nd (Oxfordshire)	Boston 1774, dispersed NY Aug 1778. Used v. Gordon Riots.
*53rd (Shropshire)	Québec 1776 to Saratoga.
*54th (West Norfolks)	Charleston 1776, Newport 1776, NY 1779, Halifax 1782.
*55th (Westmoreland)	Boston 1775, with Grant to Florida/WI October 1778.
*57th (West Middlesex)	Charleston 1776, NY to Halifax 1782.
59th (2nd Nottingham)	Boston 1774, dispersed Halifax 1776.
60th (Royal American)	1st & 2nd batts, WI duration.
3rd & 4th batts	(raised 1775), Florida [Prevost].
*62nd (Wiltshire)	Québec 1776 to Saratoga.
*63rd (West Suffolk)	Boston 1775, Charleston December 1779, part WI 1782 [Grant, Leslie].
64th (2nd Staffords)	NY 1776, Charleston December 1779, WI 1782.
65th (2nd North Yorks)	Boston 1769, dispersed Halifax 1776.
70th (Surrey)	Halifax 1778, flank companies south [Tryon].

NEW FORMATIONS

71st (Fraser's Highlanders)	1775. 3 batts. NY 1776, everywhere thereafter [Campbell].
74th (Argyle Highlanders)	1777. Canada 1778, Penobscot 1779, [MacLean].
76th (M'Donnell's)	1777. NY 1779, Virginia April 1781 to Yorktown.
80th (Edinburgh)	1778. NY 1779, Virginia April 1781 to Yorktown.

| 82nd (Lanarkshire) | 1778. Canada 1779, part Penobscot 1779, Charleston December 1780, Wilmington 1781 [Craig] |
| 84th, 105th, 110th | See **Appendix D**. |

GERMAN CONTINGENTS

	29,875 hired at a cost of over £4.5 million, of whom approx. 7500 died and 5000 deserted
Anhalt-Zerbst	One regiment, 1160 men. Mainly garrison duties.
Anspach-Beyreuth	Three regiments, 2353 men of which 1077 surrender at Yorktown.
Brunswick	Seven regiments [Baum, Breymann, Riedesel], 5723 men to Canada of which 3130 lost during Saratoga campaign.
Hesse Cassel	Twenty-two regiments [Donop, Knyphausen, Lossberg, Rall], 16,992 men. Mainly NY/NJ, four regiments to Newport 1776–9, Bose and Prince Hereditary regiments surrender at Yorktown.
Hesse Hanau	Two regiments, 2422 men. Mainly garrison duties.
Waldeck	One regiment, 1225 men with Grant to Florida/WI October 1778.

Sources:

Curtis, Edward, *The Organization of the British Army . . .* (New Haven 1926).
Fortescue, Sir John, *The War of Independence* (London 1911, 2001).
Katcher, Philip, *King George's Army 1775–83* (Reading 1973).

AMERICAN TROOPS 1775–83[1]

(66% of gross figures to allow for multiple enlistments)

[ ] = authorized battalions in 1776 and 1781

Massachusetts + Maine[2]

Population 1770/1780	Free: 266,565/317,760	Slave: 0/0
Continentals [15–11]	44,800	
Militia	13,200	
Total enlisted	58,000	

Virginia + Kentucky

Population 1770/1780	Free: 462,716/538,004	Slave: 190,105/227,782
Continentals [5–11]	17,600	
Militia	19,800	
Total enlisted	37,400	

Connecticut[2]

Population 1770/1780	Free: 183,881/206,701	Slave: 5,698/5,885
Continentals [8–6]	21,100	
Militia	5,950	
Total enlisted	27,050	

Pennsylvania

Population 1770/1780	Free: 240,057/327,305	Slave: 5,761/7,855
Continentals [12–9]	16,950	
Militia	6,600	
Total enlisted	23,550	

New York

Population 1770/1780	Free: 162,290/210,541	Slave: 19,112/21,054
Continentals [4–3]	11,750	
Militia	6,600	
Total enlisted	18,350	

South Carolina

Population 1770/1780	Free: 124,244/180,000	Slave: 75,178/97,000
Continentals [6–2]	4,250	
Militia	13,200	
Total enlisted	16,450	

Maryland

Population 1770/1780	Free: 202,599/245,474	Slave: 63,818/80,515
Continentals [8–5]	9,200	
Militia	5,950	
Total enlisted	15,150	

North Carolina + Tennessee

Population 1770/1780	Free: 198,200/280,133	Slave: 69,800/92,500
Continentals [9–4]	4,800	
Militia	8,600	
Total enlisted	13,400	

New Jersey

Population 1770/1780	Free: 117,431/139,627	Slave: 8,220/10,460
Continentals [4–2]	7,100	
Militia	4,600	
Total enlisted	11,700	

New Hampshire + Vermont[2]

Population 1770/1780	Free: 72,396/135,422	Slave: 654/541
Continentals [3–2]	8,250	
Militia	2,650	
Total enlisted	10,900	

Georgia

Population 1770/1780	Free: 23,375/56,081	Slave: 10,625/20,831
Continentals [1–1]	1,750	
Militia	5,300	
Total enlisted	7,050	

Rhode Island

Population 1770/1780	Free: 58,196/52,945	Slave: 3,761/2,671
Continentals [1–1]	3,900	
Militia	2,650	
Total enlisted	6,550	

Delaware

Population 1770/1780	Free: 35,496/45,385	Slave: 1,836//2,996
Continentals [1–1]	1,575	
Militia	660	
Total enlisted	2,235	

TOTAL

Population 1770/1780	**Free: 2,148,076/2,780,369**	**Slave: 459,822/575,420**
Continentals [77–58]	**152,025**	
Militia	**95,760**	
Total	**247,785**	

1. Boatner III, Col. Mark, *Encyclopedia of the American Revolution* (Mechanicsburg 1994).
2. High proportion of Continentals reflects the wholesale adoption by Congress of the New England Militia around Boston in 1775 – and the fact that the Yankees subsequently missed no opportunity to charge local costs to the collective purse.

APPENDIX D

MAJOR LOYALIST REGIMENTS

Militia and Local units not included

[ ] = Colonel or notable officer in text

Royal Artillery, 17th Light Dragoons, 9th, 38th, 42nd, 43rd, 60th, 71st, and 79th of Foot.

AMERICAN TO REGULAR ESTABLISHMENT

1779	84th (Royal Highland Emigrants)	Raised Canada 1775 [MacLean].
	2nd battalion	Raised Canada 1776.
1782	105th (Volunteers of Ireland)	See below.
1782	110th (King's American)	See below.
1782	Royal Garrison Battalion	Raised Canada 1778.
1782	Royal Newfoundland	Raised Canada 1780.
1782	King's American Dragoons	As a favour to Thompson see **Appendix A**.
1782	Queen's Rangers (cavalry)	See below.
1782	British Legion (cavalry only)	See below.

AMERICAN ESTABLISHMENT

1779	1st (Queen's American Rangers)	Raised New York 1776 [Rogers/Simcoe].
1779	2nd (Volunteers of Ireland)	Raised Philadelphia 1777 [Rawdon].

287

1779	3rd (New York Volunteers)	Raised Halifax 1776 [Duncan Campbell]
	1st Battalion	[DeLancey].
	2nd Battalion	[Cruger].
	3rd Battalion	[Turnbull].
1781	4th (King's American)	Raised New York 1776 [Rogers/Fanning].
1781	5th (British Legion)	Raised New York 1778 [Cathcart, Tarleton].
1781	King's American Dragoons	Raised New York 1781 (See above).

MAJOR PROVINCIAL UNITS

American Legion	Long Island 1780, Virginia 1781 [Arnold].
(Loyal) American Volunteers	New York to South Carolina 1779–80 [Ferguson].
Black Pioneers	1776–83 [Moncrieff].
Butler's Rangers	New York/Canada border 1777–83.
Duke of Cumberland's	From Charleston deserters, to Jamaica 1781 [Montagu].
Guides and Pioneers	1776–83
King's Loyal Americans	Canada 1775, Saratoga campaign [Jessup].
King's Orange Rangers	New York 1776, to South Carolina 1780 [Coffin].
King's Rangers	Georgia/Florida 1779–83 [Brown].
King's Royal Regiment (2 batts)	New York/Canada border 1776–83 [Johnson].
Loyal American Rangers	From New York deserters 1779, to Jamaica 1781 [Odell].
Loyal Americans	New York 1776–83 [Robinson].
Maryland/Pennsylvania Loyalists	From Philadelphia deserters 1777, to Jamaica 1778.
New Jersey Volunteers (6 batts)	1776, 2 batts to Georgia 1779 [Skinner, Allen].
Pennsylvania Loyalists	1777–83
Prince of Wales (2 batts)	Connecticut 1777, to South Carolina 1780 [Brown].

Queen's Loyal Rangers	Canada 1776, Saratoga campaign [Peters].
Royal North Carolina (2 batts)	Charleston 1780, Florida 1782–3 [Hamilton].
Royal Nova Scotia Volunteers	1775–83
South Carolina Royalists (2 batts)	Florida 1778–83 [Prevost, Innes].

BIBLIOGRAPHY

FUNDAMENTAL

Boatner III, Col. Mark, *Encyclopedia of the American Revolution* [An awe-inspiring and indispensable guide for any student of the conflict] (1966, 1974, Mechanicsburg 1994).

Buchanan, John, *The Road to Guilford Courthouse* (New York 1997).

Dwyer, William, *The Day is Ours!* [Trenton & Princeton] (New York 1983).

Higginbotham, Don (ed.), *Reconsiderations of the Revolutionary War* (Westport 1978).

Mackesy, Piers, *The War for America* (1964, Lincoln 1993).

Shy, John, *A People Numerous and Armed* (1976, Ann Arbor 1990).

Tourtellot, Arthur, *Lexington and Concord* (1959, London 1963).

EYEWITNESS ACCOUNTS

Anecdotes – etext.lib.virginia.edu/toc/modeng/public/HarCamp.html

Camden – www.battleof camden.org/ohw-narrative.htm [Otho Williams].

Commager, Henry & Richard Morris (eds.), *The Spirit of Seventy-Six* (New York 1975).

Ewald, Johann von (ed. & trans. Joseph Tustin), *Diary of the American War* (New Haven 1979).

King's Mountain – www.tngenweb.org/revwar [Allaire diary, *et al.*].

Lamb, Roger, *An Original and Authentic Journal* . . . (Dublin 1809).

Lee, Henry, *Memoirs of the War* . . . (1812, ed. 1869 by Robert E. Lee, New York 1969).

Loyalist site – www.royalprovincial.com

Martin, Joseph, *A Narrative of a Revolutionary Soldier* (1830, New York 2001).

Peckham, Howard (ed.), *Sources of American Independence*, 2 vols. (Chicago 1978).

Peebles, John (ed. Ira Gruber), *John Peebles' American War* (Midsomer Norton 1998).

Raphael, Ray, *A People's History of the American Revolution* (New York 2001).

Scheer, George & Hugh Rankin, *Rebels & Redcoats* (Cleveland 1957).

Simcoe, John, *Military Journal* (1784, Toronto 1962).

Tarleton, Lt. Col. Banastre, *A History of the Campaign of 1780 and 1781 . . .* (London 1787).

ILLUMINATING

Alden, John, *A History of the American Revolution* (New York 1969).

Babits, Lawrence, *A Devil of a Whipping* [Cowpens] (Chapel Hill 1998).

Bailyn, Bernard, *The Ideological Origins of the American Revolution* (Harvard 1967).

Bakeless, John, *Turncoats, Traitors and Heroes* (New York 1959).

Bass, Robert, *The Green Dragoon* [Tarleton] (London 1958).

—— *Swamp Fox* [Marion] (London 1960).

—— *Ninety-Six* (London 1978).

Bemis, Samuel, 'The British Secret Service and the French-American Alliance,' *American Historical Review* 29 (1923–24).

Billias, George (ed.), *George Washington's Generals and Opponents* (New York 1994).

Boatner, Col. Mark III, *Landmarks of the American Revolution* (Harrisburg 1975).

Bolton, Charles, *The Private Soldier under Washington* (Williamstown 1976).

Bowler, R. Arthur, *Logistics and the Failure of the British Army in America* (Princeton 1975).

Bowman, Allen, *The Morale of the Revolutionary Army* (Port Washington 1943).

Brown, Gerald, *Jemmy Twitcher* [Sandwich] (London 1962).

Brown, Sanborn, *Benjamin Thompson, Count Rumford* (MIT 1981)

Brown, Weldon, *Empire or Independence* [reconciliation policy] (Baton Rouge 1941).

Buker, George, *The Penobscot Expedition* (Annapolis 2002).

Burke, Edmund, *Reflections on the Revolution in France* (1790, London 1969).

Calhoon, Richard, *Loyalists in Revolutionary America* (New York 1973).

Callahan, North, *Flight from the Republic* (New York 1967).

Carp, E. Wayne, *To Starve the Army at Pleasure* [Continentals] (Chapel Hill 1984).

Cashin, Edward, *The King's Ranger* [Thomas Brown] (Athens 1999).

Chandler, David, *The Art of Warfare in the Age of Marlborough* (London 1976).

Colley, Linda, *Britons* (Yale 1992).

Currey, Cecil, *Code Number 72: Ben Franklin Patriot or Spy?* (Englewood 1972).

Curtis, Edward, *The Organization of the British Army . . .* (New Haven 1926).

Dixon, Norman, *On the Psychology of Military Incompetence* (London 1976).

Duffy, Christopher, *Military Experience in the Age of Reason* (London 1987).

Dull, Jonathan, *A Diplomatic History of the American Revolution* (New Haven 1985).

Ellis, Joseph, *Founding Brothers* (New York 2000).

Ferling, John, *Setting the World Ablaze* (New York 2000).

—— (ed.), *The World Turned Upside Down* (Westport 1988).

Freeman, Douglas, *George Washington*, 7 vols (New York 1948–57).

French, Allen, *General Gage's Informers* (Ann Arbor 1932).

Frey, Silvia, *The British Soldier in America* (Austin 1981).

Fortescue, Sir John, *The War of Independence* (1911, London 2001).

Fuller, J.F.C., *British Light Infantry in the Eighteenth Century* (London 1925).

Gallagher, John, *The Battle of Brooklyn* (New York 1995).

Gore, Al, *Earth in the Balance* (Boston 1992).

Gravil, Richard, *Romantic Dialogues* (New York 2000).

Greene, J. & J. Pole (eds.), *A Companion to the American Revolution* (Oxford 2000).

Gruber, Ira, *The Howe Brothers and the American Revolution* (New York 1972).

Harvey, Robert, *"A Few Bloody Noses"* (New York 2002).

Hatch, Charles Jr., *The Battle of Guilford Courthouse* (Washington 1971).

Hayter, Tony, *The Army and the Crowd in mid-Georgian England* (London 1978).

Higginbotham, Don, *Daniel Morgan, Revolutionary Rifleman* (Chapel Hill 1961).

—— *The War of American Independence* (New York 1971).

Hoffman, Ronald & Peter Albert (eds.), *Arms and Independence* (Charlottesville 1984).

Hofstadter, Richard, *The Paranoid Style in American Politics* (London 1966).

Holmes, Richard, *Redcoat* (London 2001).

Jackson, John, *With the British Army in Philadelphia* (San Rafael 1979).

Jenkins, E.H., *A History of the French Navy* (London 1973).

Kammen, Michael, *A Season of Youth* [creative interpretations](New York 1978).

Ketchum, Richard, *Decisive Day* [Breed's Hill] (New York 1974).

—— *Saratoga* (New York 1997).

Larrabee, Harold, *Decision at the Chesapeake* (London 1965).

Lopez, Claude-Anne, *Mon Cher Papa: Franklin and the Ladies of Paris* (New Haven 1966).

Macfarlane, Alan, *The Origins of English Individualism* (Cambridge 1978).

McGuire, Thomas, *Battle of Paoli* (Mechanicsburg 2000).

Morris, Richard (ed.), *The American Revolution Reconsidered* (London 1967).

Olasky, Marvin, *Fighting for Liberty and Virtue* (Washington 1995).

Pancake, John, *This Destructive War* [the Carolinas] (Tuscaloosa 1985).

Pearson, Michael, *Those Damned Rebels* (Mechanicsburg 2000).

Peckham, Howard, *The Toll of Independence* (Chicago 1974).

Quarles, Benjamin, *The Negro in the American Revolution* (Chapel Hill 1961).

Roberts, Michael, *Splendid Isolation 1763–80* (Reading 1970).

Rodríguez, Mario, *La revolución americana de 1776 y el mundo hispánico* (Madrid 1976).

Seymour, William, *The Price of Folly* (London 1995).

Smith, Paul, *Loyalists and Redcoats* [British policy] (Chapel Hill 1964).

Sowell, Thomas, *Race and Culture* (New York 1994).

—— *Migrations and Culture* (New York 1996).

—— *Conquests and Culture* (New York 1998).

Symonds, C. & W. Clipson, *Battlefield Atlas of the American Revolution* (Mount Pleasant 1986).

Thomas, Peter, *Lord North* (London 1976).

Tillyard, Stella, *Citizen Lord* [Edward Fitzgerald] (London 1997).

Treese, Lorett, *Valley Forge* (Pennsylvania State University 1995).

Tucker, D. & D. Hendrickson, *The Fall of the First British Empire* (Baltimore 1982).

Van Doren, Carl, *Benjamin Franklin* (New York 1938).

——, *Secret History of the American Revolution* (New York 1941).

Weigley, Russell, *The Partisan War* (Columbia 1970).

Wilkinson, James, *Memories of My Own Times*, 4 vols (Philadelphia 1816). [He was a thorough-going scoundrel and not a word should be believed unless independently verified.]

Willcox, William, *Portrait of a General* [Clinton], (New York 1964).

Wilson, James, *The Moral Sense* (New York 1993).

Wood, Col. W. J., *Battles of the Revolutionary War* (Chapel Hill 1990).

REFERENCE TOOLS ADDITIONAL TO BOATNER

Dictionary of American Biography (New York 1943).
Dictionary of American History (New York 1942).
Dictionary of National Biography (London 1901).
British and allied generals www.revwar75.com/crown/bio.htm
Virtual library www.ku.edu/~ibetext/rev

INDEX

Page numbers in *italics* refer to maps.